Words
Were
Originally
Magic

Words
Were
Originally
Magic

STEVE de SHAZER

W. W. Norton & Company, Inc.
New York • London

The text of this book is set in Elante, with display set in Optima.
Composition by Bytheway Typesetting Services, Inc.
Manufacturing by Haddon Craftsmen, Inc.

Book design by Justine Burkat Trubey

Library of Congress Cataloging-in-Publication Data

De Shazer, Steve.
    Words were originally magic / Steve de Shazer.
      p. cm.
    "A Norton professional book."
    Includes bibliographical references.
    ISBN 0-393-70171-9
    1. Solution-focused therapy.   2. Brief psychotherapy.
    3. Psychotherapists—Language.   4. Psychotherapy patients—Language.
    I. Title.
    RC489.S65D4   1994
    616.89'14—dc20   94-2713
                                                     CIP

W. W. Norton & Company, Inc., 500 Fifth Avenue, New York, NY 10110
W. W. Norton & Company, Ltd., 10 Coptic Street, London WC1A 1 PU

2 3 4 5 6 7 8 9 0

To

Insoo Kim Berg
Dar (Charles Darwin) de Shazer
John H. Weakland

Three of my favorite people

CONTENTS

ACKNOWLEDGMENTS

FIRST OF ALL, I wish to thank Insoo Kim Berg for her continued support. Without her this book would not have been possible. In fact, without her the approach to therapy described in my books would not have been possible.

I also want to thank John H. Weakland for many hours of conversation over the years about things that are of mutual interest. In ways too numerous to mention, John has influenced all of my work ever since we first came into contact.

Next, I wish to thank Gale Miller and Ray Gurney for their careful reading of earlier versions of the manuscript and continuing discussions about many of the topics I deal with here.

I also wish to thank all of the people who have worked with me in the many workshops and seminars I have been part of in recent years. Without their questions and comments to point the way, I would never have been able to figure out what this book should have been about.

Unfortunately, there are just simply too many people to thank. Certainly Susan B. Munro of W. W. Norton needs to be thanked for her highly skillful editorial work and for her faith in what I write.

Of course the many, many clients I've talked to and observed through the see-through mirror must be thanked for all they have taught me over the years.

INTRODUCTION

He impaired his vision by holding the object too close. He might
see, perhaps, one or two points with unusual clearness, but in so
doing he, necessarily, lost sight of the matter as a whole. Thus
there is such a thing as being too profound. Truth is
not always in a well.
— C. Auguste Dupin
(*The Murders in the Rue Morgue*)

ONCE UPON A TIME there was a certain Sigmund Freud who lived in
Vienna, the City of Dreams, the capital of a magic empire; where, at
the turn of the century, it was clear that nothing was what it seemed
to be (Janik & Toulmin, 1973). Freud spent his time listening to troubled people talking about their troubled and troubling lives. He found
these stories rather strange, sometimes enigmatic, often inexplicable.
So, he would hypnotize the troubled people, and again listen to their
troubled talk about their lives. But the stories they told while in a
trance were even more inscrutable and mysterious. He wondered,
which of these is true? Which expresses the reality of their lives? These
people would also tell Freud about their dreams, stories that seemed
rather disorganized and meaningless. However, living in a magic king-
dom, he knew that the bizarre and outlandish were not grotesque and
exotic just for the hell of it; they were masks hiding reality.

Thus Freud had three types of tales he listened to: (a) stories people
told him when they were wide awake, (b) stories told when in a trance,
and (c) stories told about dreams, or stories told about stories that
happened while the teller was actually asleep.

And he wondered, what was really real?

So, he organized what he heard and, since he had not been able to tell which of the three stories was the truth, impelled by an intuition as to the laws of nature underlying the disparate phenomena he was studying, he looked behind and beneath to find the truth. Being modern, scientific, and objective, he decided that the only way to explain why someone did what he did was to postulate something inside the person, such as drives or instincts.

Once he did his analysis, once he found the truth, Freud was able to categorize and explain these stories people told him. Then he started to tell other people his stories about the underlying truth of the stories he had been told. Being a physician, Freud built his stories built upon the scientific, positivistic model of his day with diseases, categories, causes, mechanisms, forces, displacements, repressions, and resistances—all to explain "why" the troubling troubles happened. As Don Jackson pointed out, there is a certain scientific/metaphoric similarity between Freud's superego and Clerk-Maxwell's demon (Jackson, 1967).

And the world was spellbound; after all, these were Viennese tales, magical stories in which nothing was quite what it seemed to be.

Fortunately, these ways of storytelling sometimes helped some people tell new stories that were less troublesome. And, therefore, it came to pass that, being modern and objective, other physicians found that they could retell the stories of the troubled people they worked with using the plots developed by Sigmund Freud. Thus a scientific, analytical paradigm—a storytelling industry—was born.

Being modern, everybody believed in science, believed in the truth of these stories. There was little or no doubt that these troubling stories were the products of troubled minds, troubled souls, troubled psyches, and involved faulty reality-testing.

In the due course of time, many other therapists, scientists or not, found the plots of these Viennese tales worth retelling. The storytelling industry spread throughout Europe and across the seas.

*   *   *

In Palo Alto, a city far away and long distant in every way from magical Vienna, there was Don D. Jackson, both a physician and a scientist, who developed some new plots in order to tell the stories he retold. Living in the age of togetherness, the troubled people who told their troubling stories to Don Jackson told him about their families; they told stories that were beyond analysis, stories that fell outside of the Freudian repertoire of available characters and plots. Being a physician who hung around with a research group (Gregory Bateson, John Weakland, and Jay Haley), Jackson retold stories that were built upon the scientific model of his day with systems, homeostasis, redundancy, runaways, categories, communication, relationships, symmetry and asymmetry, circular causes, mechanisms, class and members, double-binds, and resistances.

As we all know, believing is seeing; therefore, as researchers and scientists, Jackson, Bateson, Weakland, and Haley not only used the inquisitive, scientific model of their day as a prototype for the plots of the stories they retold, but also used the most up-to-date technology available. They knocked holes in walls and put in see-through mirrors, they tape recorded and made movies of troubled families telling their distressing stories. Now they no longer had to hang on every word of the therapist's retelling of the story; they could hear it and witness its being told and they could retell the story, each in his own scientific way.

And it came to pass that, also being modern and scientific, other therapists found that they could retell the stories of the troubled people they worked with using the new plots developed in Palo Alto. Thus a new scientific paradigm was born—a new, competing storytelling industry. The form of these new stories reminds the listener of Einstein's story of relativity: Event "x" is seen differently by the various observers, i.e., father sees it one way, mother a different way, and daughter yet a third way.

Being unabashedly scientific and modern, another hole was made in another wall in another city by another physician, a brother scientist, a certain Salvador Minuchin. Like Jackson, he heard stories he did not understand, distressing and disquieting stories told to him by families, stories that were not Viennese stories. He invented another series of highly or even overly involved plots, ones that were so different in structure from those favored in California that Jay Haley fled across country to join this rival storytelling industry, where he better fit the hierarchy, leaving Palo Alto to the short stories of Weakland & Co. (The difference between Jackson's stories and Minuchin's stories is similar to the difference between the "wave theory" and the "particle theory," different plots that divided the stories of physics for a long time.)

Other scientists retold these familial stories, carrying the plots across the seas. They were heard in Italy where Mara Selvini-Palazzoli, a physician both modern and objective, retold Machiavellian stories, no matter how dirty, told to her by Italian families.

Of course, so that the old science might not be lost, Nathan Ackerman and some other inexorably modern scientists retold these familial stories using Freudian characters and plot lines. Murray Bowen and some other story retellers, of course, found the truths of the old science compelling, found the old stories and plots so revealing and powerful that they retold the familial stories the troubled families told them using the Viennese genre, giving the stories marvelous and eerie twists and turns; the undifferentiated family ego mass, jitterbugs pretending to waltz.

From another faraway land, out of the desert came another voice, another physician telling stories about the stories troubled people told him. These plots were so different from the orthodox plots that scientists said they were the stories of a wizard, a shaman — and thus unscientific. Like Jackson's and Minuchin's stories, Milton H. Erickson's stories were beyond analysis, since they too formed a different genre. These stories were profoundly nonscientific: Not only were types, categories, causes, mechanisms, forces, displacements, repressions, and resistances gone — or redefined out of existence — but systems, homeostasis, redundancy, runaways, categories, communication, relationships, symmetry and asymmetry, circular causes, mechanisms, class and members, double-binds, and resistances — the new scientific language — were also absent. Erickson's plots took different shapes, reminding us of a story told by Heisenberg, i.e., the observer and his tools determine whether he tells stories about "waves" or "particles." Another rival storytelling industry was born.

* * *

The majority of the stories therapists retold tend to fall into the Sherlock Holmes style of story. In the Sherlock Holmes style, the therapist — whether Freud or Ackerman or Jackson or Erickson — needs specialized knowledge of similar events or patterns, logic, observation skills, the ability to single-mindedly pursue the truth, and the ability to tell the difference between clues and red-herrings. Holmes was in many ways the prototypical modern scientist. He would gather all the evidence, the clues, and then he would interpret these logically, inferentially arriving at "the truth," which no one else arrived at. The Sherlock Holmes style is only effective when the therapist has ignored the great many red-herrings and focused on the clues that he and the client have discovered. This is not always a simple process: Acting like Inspector Lestrade and chasing after red-herrings is always possible.

Recently, there has been a shocking shift in style. Sherlock Holmes has disappeared from the retold tales and has been replaced by Doctor Who. In the Doctor Who style, therapy works because of systemic magic. Doctor Who, as he travels through time and across galaxies, works with several partners, including a robot-dog known as K-9. The good doctor frequently comes upon both problems and solutions by accident. Often his time machine malfunctions and he arrives at the wrong place at the wrong time, accidentally and serendipitously creating a situation in which a solution will become necessary. Thus Doctor Who and his team create misunderstanding and misunderstand as much as they are misunderstood. Doctor Who solves these problems using logic and luck, plan and accident, and the most advanced technology available. Friends, enemies, machines, and his team may be involved; but whatever they do seems to be essentially random and to have essentially random effects. His team is usually after Doctor Who not to do something because when he does intervene it can go either way; intervention makes things worse as frequently as it makes things better.

In the Doctor Who style, the therapist needs to have a good team with lots of specialized knowledge about the way systems react to the random or unplanned events that are always happening. Client, therapist, and team, like Doctor Who and his team, need to take advantage of this mutual misunderstanding and the random happenings of day-to-day life, helping the client to turn chance events into good fortune.

As Buddhists might say, we need to remember that Objectivity is an Illusion. Being modern, being new scientists, being objective and positivistic, these story retellers saw but they did not observe (as Sherlock Holmes once said of Doctor Watson). All they saw was a troubled family telling their troubling story to a therapist. They looked too closely, saw too much and failed to see something while looking through the looking glass. Their science and their objectivity put and kept the therapist in their blindspot, kept the therapist and the observers independent from the troubled storytellers, kept the knower separate from the known.

* * *

In a not too distant time, in a place far away and different in many ways from Vienna and Palo Alto and Philadelphia, we looked through the looking glass and were shocked by what we saw. At first it was incredible, unbelievable. We were amazed that we had made so surprising a discovery, or better, we were amazed that we had invented something so astonishing. What we observed was so simple and obvious and so easy to see, since it was right on the surface and had long been readily available to any observer; yet it had remained hidden away by the objectivity of modern science. We saw a therapist who was talking with the client.

It quickly became clear that the therapist, the reteller of the story, was not just a reporter. In fact, we saw that the reteller of the story is part of the story he retells. The shape of the reteller's story is always already shaped in the telling of it by the teller. And it came to pass that one day a client asked, "What do they (the therapists behind the looking glass) think?" We saw that the unseen members of the team were also part of the story being told. We were not detached and detachable observers. We too were reflected in the looking glass. And yet another rival storytelling industry was born.

* * *

It soon became clear that questions stemming from a Freudian plot lead to stories that fit the Freudian genre; questions coming from a Jacksonian plot lead to stories about families; yet other questions lead to a wizard's plot.

That is, if I pretend to be Sherlock Holmes, then I will retell a story in a scientific way. If I pretend to be Doctor Who, I will retell the same story in a systemic way. You can never know which story is true; you can never know what is really real. Doctor Who style stories are beyond analysis, beyond understanding, like a single story simultaneously about waves and particles retold by Heisenberg.

The stories these retellers tell are no longer modern, no longer scientific. They are stories about the telling of stories, the shaping and reshaping of stories so that the troubled people change their story. Gone from these stories are such things as types, categories, causes, mechanisms, forces, displacements, repressions, homeostasis, redundancy, runaways, categories, communication, relationships, symmetry and nonsymmetry, circular causes, mechanisms, class and members, double-binds, and resistances.

These stories are not just the product of the troubled individual or a crazy-making family; they are simultaneously the product of the troubled people and the therapist and the observers. Stories of therapy do not come only from something that happens "inside" the troubled or even between them, not even something inside and between, but rather they come from all this plus something else that happens between them and the therapist.

As Freud knew all too well, understanding is not as easy as it looks.

PART I

Calvin and Hobbes

by Bill Watterson

Chapter One

"NOTHING . . . BUT AN INTERCHANGE OF WORDS"

Words are the physicians of a mind diseased.
— *Aeschylus*

WHEN I FIRST STARTED to talk and write about therapy as a "conversation" (de Shazer, 1988) and as "nothing but a bunch of talk" (de Shazer, 1989), I had forgotten or perhaps did not know that in Sigmund Freud's introductory lecture on psychoanalysis in 1915 he said:

Nothing takes place in a psycho-analytic treatment but an interchange of words . . . the patient talks . . . the doctor listens. . . . Words were originally magic and to this day words have retained much of their ancient magical power. By words one person can make another blissfully happy or drive him to despair. . . . Words provoke affects and are in general the means of mutual influence among men. Thus we shall not depreciate the use of words in psychotherapy and we shall be pleased if we can listen to the words that pass *between* the analyst and his patient. (Freud, 1915–1917, Vol. 15, p. 17, emphasis added)

Words are, of course, part of language. So are silences, gestures, facial expressions, etc. To look at the magic of words, we need to look at language, the context within which words work their magic.

Therapy happens within language and language is what therapists and client use to do therapy; thus, as Freud says, therapy can be seen as "an interchange of words," a conversation. However, this is a somewhat dangerous way to put it, since conversation is a normal and

3

natural activity for two or more people in the same place at the same to do together; we automatically make the assumption that we know what we are talking about when we use the word "conversation." It seems so simple and obvious that we do not even need to know anything about conversations to participate in them. Assuming we know what such a general term means leads us to use it "too freely — that is, not as [one of our] tools of thinking, but instead of thinking" (Weakland, 1993a, p. 139).

All this use leads to a probably inescapable vowel shift from "a" to "i"[1] and what might have become a useful concept switches into a metaphor with two undefined terms. An earlier example involved the switch from viewing the family as a system to saying the family *is* a system.[2] In this way a pronouncement develops, "therapy *is* conversation" and we reasonably start to think that "therapy equals conversation." (The equation: If therapy *is* conversation, then conversation *is* therapy. This is a real metaphor, substituting one noun for another with a transport of meaning.)

Through the grammatical form built around the "is," we mistakenly and inadvertently lead ourselves into thinking that we know all there is to know about doing therapy: primarily the skills involved in maintaining a conversation or continuing a dialogue. We thus mistakenly seduce ourselves into thinking that it is the conversation itself which is the therapy, i.e., talking together is the "curative factor." Like the "therapeutic relationship" before it, "therapy is conversation" is a comparison that seems to explain what therapy is all about and yet is so vague and nonspecific that it actually tells us nothing because we do not stop to think when we believe we know what we are talking about. The idea that doing therapy can be seen as a conversation points to and reminds us of the interactional aspects of the endeavor — something that is quite easy to neglect.

Additionally, the notions developed from viewing therapy as a conversation, as an activity involving two or more people, serve to counterbalance the traditional, dictionary meanings of the word "therapy"

---

[1]Which is already happening at least in workshops and training sessions.
[2]The "is" has two distinct uses: (1) the rose is red, and (2) twice two is four. Only the latter allows us to substitute "equals" for "is." Obviously, in the phrases "the family is a system" and "therapy is conversation," the "is" is being used in the second sense of equality or sameness.

(from the Greek, meaning *to nurse, to cure*), which certainly can mislead us into thinking of the therapist as operating upon the patient or client. For instance,

> **therapeutic,** serving to cure or heal; curative; concerned in discovering and applying remedies for diseases. That part of medical science which relates to the treatment and cure of diseases.

That is, seeing therapy as a conversation seems to be a useful contradiction-in-terms, in that it leads us into seeing the *doing of therapy* and the *using* of the term "therapy" in ways that undermine and contaminate the usual dictionary definitions of "therapy" (that the term, unfortunately, automatically carries with it).

Throughout the writing of this book and the previous one (de Shazer, 1991), it has been with the greatest reluctance, hesitation that I have continued to use the word "therapy." I have used the word, even though it is not quite the right word, since it is the only word available to even begin to say what it is that I am talking about, what it is that my clients and I do. Unfortunately, "therapy" says both more and less than what I want to say when I use that term, but I have not yet thought of or heard any other word that could take its place.[3] Throughout both books I should have written it this way: ~~Therapy~~. (This sort of strikethrough indicates a word used but not really meant. Since the word is inadequate, it is crossed out; since the word is necessary, it remains legible.) ~~Therapy~~ says it better, but the constant repetitive use of the strikethrough would have been both irksome and distracting to both me (as author and reader) and you (as readers). But "~~therapy~~"? How do I say it?

*   *   *

> Do you want to learn the sciences with ease?
> Begin by learning your own language.
> —*Etienne Condillac*[4] *(1947, pp. 216–217)*

---

[3]See Chapter Seven.
[4]The scope of Etienne Condillac's definition of "science" in the eighteenth century was, of course, much broader than that used in the late twentieth century.

Any conversation is full of magical words, and words, silences, gestures, etc., are parts of language. The idea that therapy can be seen as conversation points to Condillac's idea that we need to learn our own language in order to learn about therapy. In fact, we need to learn our own language to learn about conversations, narratives, stories, or any other human endeavor. After all, conversations, narratives, and stories all use language both as tool and context.

Certainly Condillac's readers as well as mine believe that they know their own language(s). Certainly I, as an author, want to believe the same. After all, we use it all the time, particularly when talking, listening, reading, and writing. Using one's own language seems a simple, uncomplicated thing.

As Part One of an experiment, imagine that you are reading a 1914 vintage book written by Sigmund Freud. On page 4 you come across the word "depression" for the first time in that book. (Actually, Freud would probably have written "melancholia.") Can you have any confidence whatsoever that you know exactly what Freud meant by that term? Although we want to say "yes," the answer is really "probably not." Freud brought to his writing down of that word all of his experiences with that word, including years of practice and hours of discussion with various colleagues. You and I bring to our reading of the word all of our experiences, including the vast amount of literature and research on the topic of depression that has been done since Freud's time. Each of us probably has read some of this work, which Freud could not have known anything about. Certainly there is some minimal overlap that we share with Freud but that is probably no more than a standard dictionary entry. As a result, we cannot know exactly what Freud meant.

As Part Two of the experiment, imagine that you and I are flies on the wall watching Freud writing this book. At noon on Monday he stops, just having written the word "depression." He spends the rest of the day doing various other, unrelated things.

When he returns to his writing at noon on Tuesday, he reads where he left off—the word "depression." At this point, noon on Tuesday, can Freud himself have any confidence that he means the same thing by the term "depression" that he meant at noon on Monday? Although it may seem counter-intuitive, the answer is again "probably not." After all, something might have happened during that interval that he suppressed or repressed or simply did not think had any influence on his view of depression—but it did.

Furthermore, can Freud at noon on Tuesday predict with any confidence that he will mean the same thing by the word "depression" at noon on Wednesday that he means at noon on Tuesday? Again, the answer is "probably not," since he cannot know what might happen in the next 24 hours to shift his thinking, either directly or indirectly.

Although this experiment may involve some oversimplifications, nonetheless, this instability of meaning is part of the way language works. (It is one of the primary reasons authors revise what they write.)

LEARNING YOUR OWN LANGUAGE

> There cannot be language without sense and nonsense.
> —*Raimond Gaita (1991, p. 105)*

In subsequent chapters "language" will be looked at much more closely. The sketches of four major views of language that follow are only meant to set the stage, to give you, the reader, some background hints about where the following chapters are going.

1. On the one hand, the common-sense assumption is that language is a transparent medium expressing already existing facts, i.e., when we use the term "tree," or "river," or "marital problem," or "sexual problem," or "depression," what the term means is known, is set ahead of time and for all time. The meaning of words is clear and unambiguous: a word refers directly to the thing itself. This means that, or least implies that, change does not come about in language. Language is assumed always to only reflect changes which occur prior to the changes in language. The author or speaker is seen as able to perceive the truth of reality and to express this experience through language. And thus the reader and listener can know exactly what the author or speaker meant. Obviously, then, using the common-sense view, a marital problem is a marital problem, a depression is a depression. Plain and simple; everybody knows exactly what we mean when we use those words. Clearly, then, individual problems are obviously distinct from marital problems.

(As a counter-example, we learned something interesting about our work from a recent six-month follow-up: We are more successful at reaching the client's "marital goals" when we see only one of the partners (86%) than we are when we see both (81%).)

At times, and for many purposes, the common-sense view is "good enough." However, as the above experiments and the counter-example suggest, it is not so simple. There are at least three other distinct ways to think about how language works.

2. On other hand, in traditional Western thought, language is usually viewed as somehow representing reality. This is based on the notion that there is a reality out there to be represented, i.e., there are specific somethings that are called "marital problems" or "depressions." Therefore, language can be studied by looking at how well it represents that reality. This, of course, leads to the idea that language can represent "the truth," which, in turn, inevitably leads to the traditional ideas behind Western science. Specifically, this leads to the idea that a science of language and a science of meaning can be developed by looking behind and beneath the words — an approach usually called "structuralism" (Chomsky, 1968, 1980; De Saussure, 1966), which was explicitly used by Bandler and Grinder (1975a, b) to look at hypnotherapy and psychotherapy. Thus, although their meanings might be arbitrary, we can know what the terms "marital problem" or "sexual problem" or "depression" mean because their meanings are fixed by tradition.

In both the common-sense and structural views individual and marital problems are seen to exist out there in the so-called real world and we can know the difference between these two classes of problems because the differences exist in the so-called "real world." Obviously, then, given the further assumption that solutions are dependent on problems, i.e., that solutions to marital problems lie within the marital relationship and solutions to individual problems lie within the individual, these views limit and constrain options. Within this framework, there is no sense at all in a therapist working with a wife by herself to improve the marriage. Likewise, there would be no sense whatsoever in working with a couple to resolve the husband's depression. That is, both the common-sense view and the structuralist view tell you where to look and where *not* to look for a solution.

At times, and for many purposes, like the common-sense view, the structuralist perspective works and is "good enough." However, it is not always so simple. There are at least two other distinct ways to think about how language works when these views run into difficulties.

3. On the third hand, and from another point of view, the Buddhists would say that language blocks our access to reality (Coward, 1990). That is, they too think there is a reality out there. So, naturally enough, this point of view leads Buddhists to the idea of meditation, which is used to turn off thinking and language, thus putting one in touch with reality. The ideas behind Western science (a structuralist view) naturally appear illogical in this context.

From this point of view, the words/concepts "individual problems" or "marital problems" or "depression" are seen as illusions getting in our way, preventing us from knowing "reality." Thus all we can do is shut up and let the patterns flow, because once you interfere you can never stop interfering. At times, and for many purposes, like the common-sense and the structuralist views, the Buddhist view works and is "good enough."

There is at least one more distinct way to think about how language works when these three views run into difficulties.

4. On the fourth hand, there is another view, which is usually labeled "post-structuralism"[5] (de Shazer, 1991; de Shazer & Berg, 1992; Harland, 1987), a view that suggests, simply, that *language is reality*. "Depression," "marital problems," and "individual problems" are simply constructions of the users of those terms. What these terms mean is both arbitrary and unstable, i.e., meaning varies depending on who is using the term and to whom it is being addressed within a specific context.

This way of thinking suggests that we need to look at how we have ordered the world in our language and how our language (which comes before us) has ordered our world. This has led me to believe that we need to study language in order to study anything at all. That is, rather than looking behind and beneath the language that clients and therapists use, I think that the language they use is all that we have to go on. As the above experiments point out, neither author or speaker

---

[5]A term such as "astructural" would probably be more exact, but we are stuck with the term "post-structural" which signals that this view was developed after structuralism.

nor reader or listener can be certain that they can get at what the other *really* meant with any certainty, because each brings to the encounter all of their previous, unique experience. Meaning is arrived at through negotiation *within* a specific context. That is, messages are not sent, but only received; this goes as well for the author as it does for the reader and, therefore, the author (like Freud in the above experiments) is only one of many readers. Contrary to the common-sense view, change is seen to happen *within* language: What we talk about and how we talk about it makes a difference, and it is such differences that can be used to make a difference (to the client). Thus reframing a "marital problem" into an "individual problem" or an "individual problem" into a "marital problem" makes a difference both in how we talk about things and in where we look for solutions.

Chapter Two

LANGUAGE & STRUCTURE, STRUCTURE & LANGUAGE

I never guess. It is a shocking habit—destructive to the logical faculty.
—*Sherlock Holmes (The Sign of Four)*

The world is in all its parts a cryptogram to be constituted
or reconstituted through . . . deciphering.
—*Jacques Derrida (1978, p. 76)*

THE MOST OBVIOUS and yet most frequently ignored fact is that therapy sessions involve two or more people talking together. This may seem a simple observation, but it is not, since language makes talking together possible, and language itself is far from simple. For thousands of years philosophers, theologians, linguists, grammarians, etc., have tried to answer the question, "How does language work?" In the twentieth century, the predominant view has been what is called "structuralism." As a result of this dominance, structuralism seems reasonable, obvious, and almost natural.

The whole notion of structure has a very seductive appeal. Umberto Eco (1992) describes this structural urge or compulsion as part of the second century Gnostics' reading of scripture; their search for truth was based on the idea that:

Each and every word must be an allusion, an allegory. They [the words] are saying something other than what they appear to be saying. Each one of them contains a message that none of them will ever be able to reveal alone . . . Secret knowledge is deep knowledge (because only what

11

is lying under the surface can remain unknown for long). Thus truth becomes identified with what is not said or what is said obscurely and must be understood beyond or beneath the surface of a text. The gods speak . . . through hieroglyphic and enigmatic messages. (p. 30)

Eco goes on to say that "truth is secret and any questioning of the symbols and enigmas will never reveal ultimate truth but simply displace the secret elsewhere" (1992, p. 35); that is, further behind or deeper beneath the surface.

Mystery of any kind shares in this kind of allure for many of the same reasons. As any reader of murder mysteries will admit, trying to follow clues, digging behind and beneath, and thus figuring out what is "really going on" is indeed a pleasure quite unlike others. Trying to out-guess the author and beat the author's detective to the solution is an integral part of reading murder mysteries.

While reading, I find it quite fascinating to watch Sherlock Holmes draw large inferences from small facts. It can be equally fascinating to see how Sigmund Freud or Jacques Lacan or Ferdinand de Saussure do much the same thing: digging behind and beneath what is happening because (in a structural frame) what is happening is not all that is happening. Freud and Lacan share many things with Sherlock Holmes, despite the fact that Holmes was a fictional character. (Arthur Conan Doyle's prototype was Joseph Bell, a renowned Edinburgh physician and diagnostician.) Freud read the Sherlock Holmes stories and at least once compared himself with Holmes: "I made it appear as though the most tenuous of clues had enabled me, Sherlock Holmes-like, to guess the situation" (Freud, 1974, p. 234).

Jonathan Culler (1976) sees some of the similarities between Saussure and Freud (and Holmes): "In each case, then, despite pretentions to causal analysis, one might say that what is being offered is a structural rather than a causal explanation: one attempts to show why a particular action has significance by relating it to the system of underlying functions, norms, and categories which makes it possible" (pp. 73–74), i.e, confounding reasons and causes. Freud, Lacan, Holmes, and Saussure's drive to dig deeper and deeper, looking for an explanation, is very appealing and seductive. As I continue to read each of them, sometimes long after I decided to quit, I wonder over and over whether they will ever get to the bottom of things. Part of the appeal is the notion of structure itself, i.e., that there is a bottom to get to and that whatever is happening can be explained. But that is not the whole of the allure.

Freud and Lacan are also writers of great style and charm. This latter attribute is shared by Jacques Derrida (who is certainly not a structuralist). Interestingly, reading Freud, Lacan, and Derrida can become fascinating in the same way as reading a poet such as Dylan Thomas simply because of their way with words (which shows through when a good translator is involved). Within this context, reading Ludwig Wittgenstein ("late" Wittgenstein is not a structuralist) is rather unlike reading a poet such as Dylan Thomas and is more similar to reading Japanese Haiku, the *I Ching*, or even the enigmatic and cryptic messages in fortune cookies.

A LANGUAGE CONSTITUTES A SYSTEM

> A language constitutes a system. In this one respect language is not completely arbitrary but is ruled to some extent by logic; it is here also, however, that the inability of the masses to transform it becomes apparent. The system is a complex mechanism that can be grasped only through reflection; the very ones who use it daily are ignorant of it. We can conceive of a change only through the intervention of specialists, grammarians, logicians, etc.; but experience shows us that all such meddlings have failed.
> —*Ferdinand de Saussure 1911 (1966, p. 73)*[1]

According to Saussure,[2] (who is generally seen as the founder of "structural linguistics" and frequently of "structuralism" as a way of developing explanations), "the linguistic sign is a two-sided psychological entity" (1966, p. 66) that can be represented by the drawings:

$$\text{concept} \quad = \quad \text{signified}$$
$$\updownarrow \qquad\qquad \updownarrow$$
$$\text{sound-image} \quad = \quad \text{signifier}$$

---

[1]The *Cours de linguistique général* was originally published in 1922 by Payot of Paris.
[2]Saussure started out studying Sanskrit and then moved to the comparison of languages and dialects prior to developing this general view.

The combination of concept and sound-image, or word such as "tree," is called a *sign* "because it carries the concept 'tree,' with the result that the idea of the sensory part implies the idea of the whole" (p. 67). His terms "signifier" and "signified" have, according to Saussure, "the advantage of indicating the opposition that separates them from each other and from the whole of which they are parts" (p. 67), while also simultaneously indicating their relationship to each other and the term "sign." Traditionally, the relationship between the sound-image and the concept was seen as *fixed* and *determined* both ahead of time and for all time, perhaps by some divine law-giver. However, (interestingly and importantly), Saussure points out that "the bond between the signifier and the signified is *arbitrary* . . . [that is,] the idea of 'sister' is not linked by any inner relationship to the succession of sounds s-ö-r which serves as its signifier in French; that it could be represented equally by just any other sequence is proved by differences among languages and by the very existence of different languages" (pp. 67–68, emphasis added). The signified "sister" has as its signifier "soeur" in France and "sister" in England. There is no reason for preferring *sister* to *soeur*, *Ochs* to *boeuf* to *beef*.

Although the relationship between signifier and signified is arbitrary and unmotivated, Saussure sees that "the signifier, though to all appearances freely chosen with respect to the idea that it represents [the signified], is *fixed*, not free, with respect to the linguistic community that uses it" (p. 71, emphasis added). "Because the sign is arbitrary, it follows no law other than that of tradition, and because it is based on tradition, it is arbitrary" (p. 74); importantly, "language never exists apart from this social fact" (p. 77).

$$\begin{array}{ccc} & \rightarrow \text{signified} \leftarrow & \\ \text{arbitrary} & & \text{fixed} \\ & \rightarrow \text{signifier} \leftarrow & \end{array}$$

That is, each word (signifier) is arbitrarily related to its meaning (signified) but its meaning is fixed by tradition. Furthermore, since for Saussure "in language there are only differences *without positive terms*" (1966, p. 120), it is a system in which each word (signifier) is distinct from every other word and each concept or meaning (signified) is distinct from every other one.

> Better to interpret the dream than to dream it
> — *Old Korean proverb*

It is easy to see the relationship between Saussure's structuralism and the work of his contemporary Sigmund Freud,[3] which might be drawn in this way:

$$\text{signified} \; = \; \text{unconscious}$$
$$\updownarrow \qquad\qquad \updownarrow$$
$$\text{signifier} \; = \; \text{conscious}$$

That is, for both Saussure and Freud, meaning is not necessarily transparent or obvious and therefore one needs to look at the underlying structure (the concept, the signified, the unconscious).

According to Freud (1912):

> Unconsciousness is a regular and inevitable phase in the processes constituting our mental activity; every mental act begins as an unconscious one, and it may either remain so or go on developing into consciousness, according as it meets with resistance or not. . . . A rough but not inadequate analogy to this *supposed*[4] relation of conscious to unconscious activity might be drawn from the field of ordinary photography. The first stage of the photograph is the 'negative'; every photographic picture has to pass through the 'negative process,' and some of these negatives which have held good in examination are admitted to the 'positive process' ending in the picture. (p. 264, emphasis added.)

The psychoanalytic enterprise is based on (1) "the interpretation of dreams [which] is the most complete piece of work the young science [psycho-analysis] has done up to the present" (Freud, 1912, p. 265), or rather more precisely, the interpretation of conscious reports of dreams designed to get at their unconscious meanings, and (2) the

---

[3]There is no reason to assume that Saussure was aware of Freud's work or that Freud was aware of Saussure's work. "Even if . . . Saussure's son Raymond became a psychoanalyst under Freud, and Freud was aware of Saussure's work, still, Saussurian semiology is at best a *post hoc* knowledge that Freud did not use at the time of his formulations" (Grosz, 1990, p. 93).

[4]This is an interesting choice of words here. Why did the translator pick it? What in Freud's text led to that weak term?

interpretation of various conscious productions, including symptoms, to get at their unconscious meanings.

> **interpret,** 1. to explain the meaning of; to make understandable, as by translating; to elucidate. 2. to have or show one's own understanding of the meaning of; to construe; as, he interpreted the silence as contempt. 3. to bring out the meaning of, especially to give one's own conception of, in performing, criticizing, or producing a work of art.

Consciousness, as Freud (1938) puts it:

> cannot be the essence of what is mental. It is only a *quality* of what is mental, and an unstable quality at that—one that is far oftener absent than present. The mental, whatever its nature may be, is in itself unconscious and probably similar in kind to all the other natural processes of which we have obtained knowledge. (p. 283)

Thus, for Freud (1938), "our scientific work in psychology will consist in translating unconscious processes into conscious ones, and thus filling in the gaps in conscious perception" (p. 286). This means that the relationship between unconscious and conscious is seen as fixed enough that one can be translated to the other much as German can be translated into French or at least that the unconscious can be deciphered like a code.

The philosopher Ludwig Wittgenstein (1972), Freud's younger contemporary (who was also from Vienna), in his 1943 "Conversations on Freud," makes these remarks about dreams and interpretation:

> There seems to be something in dream images that has a certain resemblance to the signs of a language. As a series of marks on paper or on sand might have. There might be no mark which we recognized as a conventional sign in any alphabet we knew, and yet we might have a strong feeling that they must be a language of some sort: that they mean something. There is a cathedral in Moscow with five spires. On each of these there is a different sort of curving configuration. One gets the strong impression that these different shapes and arrangements must mean something.
>
> When a dream is interpreted we might say that it is fitted into a context in which it ceases to be puzzling. (p. 45)

The dominance of interpretation in Freud's psychoanalysis led Wittgenstein to believe that Freud, influenced by the 19th century idea of dynamics,

> wanted to find some one explanation which would show what dreaming is. He wanted to find the *essence* of dreaming. And he would have rejected any suggestion that he might be partly right but not altogether so. If he was partly wrong, that would have meant for him that he was wrong altogether — that he had not really found the essence of dreaming. (Wittgenstein, 1972, p. 48)

Furthermore, the French philosopher Jacques Derrida (1988) sees this emphasis on interpretation as a compulsion — as did Freud himself — which leads to a rather unsettling but profound difficulty:

> He [Freud] will only go so far as admitting that the only thing he has in common with the superstitious man is the tendency, the "compulsion" (*Zwang*) to interpret: "not to let chance count as chance but to interpret it." The hermeneutic compulsion — that is what superstition and "normal" psychoanalysis have in common. Freud says it explicitly. He does not believe in chance any more than the superstitious do. What this means is that they both believe in chance if to believe in chance means that one believes that all chance means something and therefore that there is no chance. Thus we have the identity of non-chance and chance and of misfortune (*mé-chance*) and fortune (*la chance*). (p. 22)

Joseph Jastrow points to a feature of Freud's work (in a book originally published in 1932) which says a lot about the simultaneous problems and allures of any structural approach: "It is human to err; it seems to be Freudian to divine cryptic causes for the self-evident" (1948, p. 154).

A MAGIC ACT

Within contemporary therapeutic discourse, Bandler and Grinder (1975a, 1975b) are clearly heirs to this whole structural tradition that has evolved through various intermediate steps from Saussure and Freud, a relationship which might be drawn in this way:

signified = unconscious =   deep structure

$\updownarrow$ $\updownarrow$ $\updownarrow$

signifier =   conscious   = surface structure

According to Bandler and Grinder (in a series of classic books that should be required reading for therapists), what the client actually says (called the "Surface Structure") is not necessarily what he meant, or at least it is not all that he meant, since, "in the case of a Surface Structure, its source and fullest representation is the Deep Structure" (Bandler & Grinder, 1975a, p. 44). That is, to get at what the client really meant, i.e., the pieces missing in the Surface Structure, the therapist may "choose to *interpret* or *guess*" (p. 42, emphasis added). For them,

> the effectiveness of a particular form of therapy is associated with its ability to recover "suppressed" or missing pieces of the client's model . . . to identify the fact that linguistic deletion has occurred. The pieces that are missing in the Surface Structure are the material that has been removed. (p. 43)

Such interpretation can be seen as the search for the truth that is missing in the Surface Structure and is hidden in the Deep Structure and, therefore, being kept a secret. The meaning of what the client says can be determined with certainty by looking at the Deep Structure. Thus Bandler and Grinder describe a closed structural system very much akin to both Saussure's and Freud's.

However, according to Bandler and Grinder (1975b), there are times when, "in order to find a relevant meaning in the Surface Structure . . . information must be obtained from *outside* the Deep Structure meaning that is derived from the Surface Structure actually said" (p. 152, emphasis added). This might be drawn in this way:

Deep Structure [inside] $\leftrightarrow$ [? outside ?]

$\updownarrow$

Surface Structure

They give the following example:

Surface Structure   ↔   "Something was given"

    ↕

Deep Structure   ↔   "Someone gave something to someone"

"The words *someone* and *something* have no referential index. The meaning of just who gave what to whom is not available even in the Deep Structure. How, then, is the meaning made clear?" (p. 153). Their answer is some "new Deep Structures which contain referential indices (noun phrases) [which] must, of course, come from somewhere . . . " (p. 155), but where? This whole idea of a "new Deep Structure" runs counter to their own structuralist logic that meaning is fixed and determinable.

If the Deep Structure, which is the Surface Structure's source, is full, how can anything be missing? Where is this "outside" that one needs to go to in order to fill in the missing pieces of something that is already full? To stay within the original Surface Structure/Deep Structure logic, the only place to go that is "outside" the Deep Structure's "inside" is the original Surface Structure itself.

[outside?] Deeper Structure

    ↕

[inside] Deep Structure ↔ [outside?] Deep Structure

    ↕

Surface Structure [outside?]

Such an opposition of two concepts, "inside"/"outside" is never a simple "face-to-face of two terms, but a hierarchy and an order of subordination" (Derrida, 1982, p. 329). What exactly is the structural relationship between the full Deep Structure and this other "outside" new Deep Structure used to fill in what is missing is this fullness? Or, what exactly is the structural relationship between the full Deep Structure and some "outside" new Deeper Structure used to fill in whatever was lacking inside the originally full Deep Structure?

To stay within strict structural, closed system logic, the only place there is to go that is "outside" to look for what is lacking inside the full, original Deep Structure is back to the original Surface Structure.

However, this original Surface Structure is, within structural logic, already deficient or lacking as such. After all, the holes in the Surface Structure are what led to the concept of the Deep Structure in the first place. Simply inverting the "inside"/"outside" hierarchy to "outside"/ "inside" is a way to begin to deal with this conundrum.

> The hierarchical opposition can be turned on its head and the sup-
> posedly present term exposed as a lack against which the other
> term is defined. This is not to establish a new hierarchy but to un-
> balance and subvert the old, showing that what is in question is
> not dominance, but a two-way relation between terms.
> —*Andrea Nye (1988, p. 187)*

Clearly, if one is going to determine meaning structurally, one needs to do something when the Deep Structure is lacking so that "a set of derivations which are formally equivalent to the Deep Structure will be generated" (Bandler & Grinder, 1975b, p. 155). But there is no equivalent Surface Structure from which one can generate this for- mally equivalent "outside" Deep Structure: The only option open is to guess (Bandler & Grinder, 1975b, p. 155). This clarifies the equation they draw (above) between "interpretation" and "guess"[5]:

> **guess,** to conjecture; to form an opinion or estimate of (something) with-
> out means of knowledge; to judge of at random.

(Sherlock Holmes, at least, would draw distinctions between each of the following: a "guess," an "interpretation," a "deduction," and "drawing an inference" based on data.)

Once the Deep Structure is discovered to have some missing pieces, how can the relationship between this "inside" and "outside" be seen as anything but arbitrary, indeterminable, undecidable, and thus *unfixed*?

$$\begin{array}{c} \rightarrow \textbf{Deep Structure} \leftarrow \\ \text{arbitrary} \qquad\qquad \text{unfixed} \\ \rightarrow \textbf{Surface Structure} \leftarrow \end{array}$$

---

[5]Jastrow puts it this way: "Unraveling the dream-work, guessing the process from the product, tracing the primitive paternity and genealogy of the dream-relations, is part of the art that Freud inaugurated" (1948, p. 47).

Text-focused Reading[6]

This sort of approach to reading Bandler and Grinder, focused on the text itself, is meant to describe a project that "entails the rigorous analysis of the hierarchy of . . . values, and then the elaboration of 'concepts' that do not practice the logic programmed by these values" (Bass, 1988, p. 75), simultaneously following a text-focused imperative, which is "to take nothing on trust and attend always to the letter of the text" (Norris, 1989, p. 165). The resulting undermining of the concepts of Deep and Surface Structure quickly leads to blurring the distinction between "interpreting" and "guessing." One can never be sure that any one particular interpretation (or guess) is the final one; there might yet be another secret hidden behind this interpretation (or guess). The urge to look behind and beneath, to understand and explain, to find the hidden secret meaning, leads to endless iteration because we can never be certain that digging yet another level deeper (guessing) might not be both necessary and possible.

One result of this way of looking at structuralism is that the certainty built into the relationship between the Deep Structure and the Surface Structure simultaneously includes uncertainty, because the Deep Structure, which is the full representation of the meaning of the Surface Structure, may turn out not to be full enough.

To reiterate, within structural logic, the unit of analysis is (a) the Deep Structure, (b) the Surface Structure, and (c) the relationship between them. The Surface Structure has missing pieces; these missing pieces are to be found in the Deep Structure which is the full representation of the Surface Structure. It turns out, however, that the Deep Structure can have missing pieces! Since the Deep Structure can have missing pieces, this makes it into sort of a Surface Structure, because the missing pieces of the Deep Structure are to be found in something formally equivalent to the Deep Structure.

We can have no certainty whatsoever, no matter where we look,

---

[6]"Text-focused reading" is usually called by the term "deconstruction," which was coined by French philosopher Jacques Derrida. However, the term "deconstruction" has received too much abuse and therefore is more confusing than it is useful. The term's use in this context is further confused by the use of the term "constructivism" within the therapeutic discourse. "Deconstruction" and "constructivism" are terms from two different discourses and their use together can only confound things — as I have learned from my previous uses (de Shazer, 1988, 1991).

that we can find the missing pieces: There is a hole at the center of the structure: It is open, not closed. Thus, like an echo from Derrida on Freud (above), we have the identity of uncertainty/certainty, guessing/interpretation, chance/non-chance within the very structure of the structural enterprise.

The structural hierarchy is lost. It simply flattens out as one Signifier or Surface Structure just leads to another Signifier, even though it may have to beat around the bush by first going through a Deep Structure or a Signified which is really just another Signifier.

> This signals a constitutive lack at the core of language, a lack which marks the absence of a fixed anchoring point, the absence of a solid core of meaning for any term—its necessarily open, ambiguous potential. The sliding of the signifier over the signified is only momentarily arrested in specific contexts . . . all terms can only be understood relative to language as a whole. (Grosz, 1990, p. 96)

This hole at the bottom of Structuralism was pointed to by French psychoanalyst Jacques Lacan (1981) in 1953, although he was probably not the first to do so.

*   *   *

For damn good reasons, magicians are taught not to explain their tricks because, if they were to do so, the magic would disappear. Bandler and Grinder's structural magic or magical structure actually works too well; the structure disappears and all we are left with is Freud's magical words.

Chapter Three

LACAN'S [W]HOLE

It is this implied circularity and autonomy of language that leads
Lacan into postulating a sort of fault in the system, a hole, a funda-
mental lack in which, one might say, meaning is poured.
—Anthony Wilden (1981, p. 217)

What consequences derive from the fact that something
possible—a possible risk—is always possible, is somehow a
necessary possibility [?] And if such a possibility being granted,
[does] it still constitute an accident [?]
—Jacques Derrida (1982, p. 324)

AT BEST, FINDING A HOLE at the bottom is unsettling for the entire
structuralist enterprise, since it involves a logically closed system.
Structuralists need to reject any suggestion that they might be partly
right but not altogether so, because if they were partly wrong, their
own logic would dictate that they were wrong altogether, that they
had not really found the essence of language. But where does this
meaning come from that Wilden says is poured into the hole within
structuralism; a hole that Derrida sees as an *necessary* possibility rather
than an accident? Once the meaning is poured into this hole, where
does it go? On one hand, if the meaning can be contained within the
hole, that would, in effect, become sort of a bottom, which would save
the structuralist enterprise. On the other hand, if meaning is poured
into the hole and somehow dissipates or vanishes, then the hole turns
out to be a bottomless pit.

Since Lacan works very hard to plug this hole, I write the name for
what Derrida sees as an "essential" hole with the "w" in brackets, "La-

can's [w]hole." This is an attempt to indicate graphically that the hole is, in many respects, simultaneously a fundamental *lack* at the bottom of structuralism and yet also the *whole* story of meaning. Meanwhile, the use of [w]hole plays on the fact that in English the two words (hole and whole), in some ways sort of opposites, actually sound the same.

Since the Deep Structure or the Signified is never enough to guarantee meaning of the Signifier or Surface Structure because of Lacan's [w]hole, how is meaning fixed? How do we go about "filling in the gaps" Freud saw? Or, how can we ever have any confidence that we know what something means when meaning is both *arbitrary* and *unfixed* or *unstable*? "This procedure of free association and so on is queer, because Freud never shows how we know where to stop — where is the right solution" (Wittgenstein, 1972, p. 42). Is repeated guessing or endless interpretation the only option available to us?

THE WORD IS THE MURDER OF THE THING[1]

The meaning of a word, any word, is dependent on language. Each word is different from every other word, each concept distinct from every other one. One word is always dependent on other words.

Merleau-Ponty wondered about this (in 1951): "If eventually the language means or says something, it is not because each sign carries a signification belonging to it, but because they all allude to a signification forever in suspense, when they are considered one by one" (cited in Wilden, 1981, p. 217): He points to Lacan's [w]hole.

When you try to define a sign (signifier + signified), you only have *one* to define, e.g., the signified defines the signifier; the Deep Structure defines the Surface Structure. However, the Deep Structure or the signified has proved to be lacking, insufficient; it is not up to the job by itself.

Since the signifier cannot depend on the signified to give it meaning, and the signifier does not function as the signified's representative, and, as Jacques-Alain Miller (1991) put it:

> you can never define just one signifier. You always define two. So the minimum of the sign is one, but the minimum of the signifier is two.

---

[1]"Le mot est la meurtre de la chose" according to Jacques Lacan (Miller, 1991, p. 30).

You can understand the difference between sign and signifier in this sense. A sign is supposed to take its meaning from the reference. A signifier is supposed to take its meaning from another signifier. So it takes two, [which is] ... the minimum of signifiers ... which you find as such in Lacan, as simple as that. (p. 31)

If one word takes its meaning from another word, that second word takes its meaning from both the first word and yet another third word, etc.; this leads us to an endless string or chain of signifiers. How can we know we have gone far enough (or too far) along this chain? Where does it stop? According to Elizabeth Grosz (1990), it is Lacan's view that "this 'indefinite sliding of meaning' constitutive of signification is, however, halted in the operations of the symptom, dream, or unconscious manifestation" (pp. 95–96).

* * *

For Lacan, "in the play of symbolism, mostly unconscious, in the metaphors and metonymies that make up the signifying chain, there must be a master signifier, one signifier which symbolizes representation or presence itself and which allows the subject [the patient in analysis] to have a place. Thus the Phallus, the master signifier, becomes the symbol of desire" (Nye, 1988, p. 139). And thus the desire to fill the [w]hole at the bottom of language is what Lacan sees as preventing this [w]hole from becoming a bottomless pit. "For Lacan, there can be ... no question of the replacement of the phallus ... because without these symbolisations [sic] there would be no language and therefore no human life at all" (Nye, 1988, p. 140). That is, according to Henry Sullivan (1991), "no account of human language and mind can make sense without reference to Lacan's theories on desire as the sign of a lack out of which representation and meaning are created" (p. 37).

Lacan wants to plug this [w]hole with a "universal or transcendental signifier," the "phallic signifier." For Lacan

the phallic signifier has no signified, that this signifier only symbolizes the learning of difference as an effect which posits a materiality in language which differentiates the word *qua* meaning from the word *as* the sense of its meaning(s). That is, meanings always point to other meanings, to missing pieces. (Ragland-Sullivan, 1991a, p. 55)

However, according to Derrida (1978), the structural view of language

> no longer has any meaning . . . because the nature of the field—that is,
> language and a finite language—excludes totalization. This field is in
> effect that of *play*, that is to say, a field of infinite substitutions only
> because . . . there is something missing from it: a center which arrests
> and grounds the play of substitutions. (p. 289)

From a structuralist perspective, Derrida's ideas are intolerable at best,
utter nonsense at worst.

*   *   *

Grosz (1990) sees that "three key areas in Lacan's work—the inter-
locking domains of subjectivity, sexuality, and language—define broad
interests shared by many French feminists. [Lacan's work has] helped
to free feminist theory of the constraints of a largely metaphysical
and implicitly masculine, notion of subjectivity—humanism. He thus
raised the possibility of understanding subjectivity in terms other than
those dictated by patriarchal common sense" (pp. 148–149).

Yet it remains curious that French feminists, and some other feminists, have found Lacan's notions attractive since,

> [f]or Lacan meaning and the symbolic order as a whole, is fixed in rela-
> tion to a primary, transcendental signifier Lacan call the *phallus*, the
> signifier of sexual difference, which guarantees the patriarchal structure
> of the symbolic order. The phallus signifies power and control in the
> symbolic order through control of the satisfaction of desire, the primary
> source of power within psychoanalytic theory. (Weedon, 1987, p. 53)

The result, for women, seems much as that diagnosed earlier by Freud
and thus women continue to be placed at a disadvantage. In fact, it
seems that "Lacan's reading of Freud fixed women's inferior situation
even more securely" (Nye, 1988, p. 140).

That is, Lacan sees Lacan's [w]hole only as a hole, a fault in the
structure. The [w]hole, plugged by the "phallus," is often treated like
an accident rather than a condition necessary for meaning and making
sense of something to somehow develop. However, "phallus" and "desire," like any other words or concepts, have language as their condition. "Once the simple presence/absence of phallic logic is abandoned,

the feminine can appear as a value in its own right, opening the way, Irigaray[2] argued, for a real, not sham, sexual difference in which both sexes are valorised" (Nye, 1988, p. 151). As Derrida (1982) puts it:

> Is this general possibility necessarily that of a failure or a trap into which language might *fall*, or in which language might lose itself, as if in an abyss situated outside or in front of it? ... Does [it] ... *surround* language like a kind of *ditch*, a place of external perdition ... that it might avoid ... ? Or indeed is this risk, on the contrary, its internal and positive condition of possibility? this outside its inside? the very force and law of its emergence? (p. 325)

After all, Lacan's [w]hole led us to reject the notion of the primacy of the signified—of meaning over word—but this should not lead us to attempt to satisfy our longing for certainty by giving primacy to the signifier—word over meaning. It is not that simple. However, Derrida "feels that Lacan might have perpetrated precisely this. The signifiers in Lacan are the symbols that relate the subject through the structure of desire to the unconscious" (Spivak, 1976, p. lxiv). For Derrida, "the signifier and signified are interchangeable; one is the difference of the other; the concept of the sign itself is no more than a legible yet effaced, unavoidable tool" (Spivak, 1976, p. lxv). That is, misunderstanding is not an accident that happens between users of a language. Rather, it is misunderstanding that allows meaning, allows making sense of something, no matter how unstable, to happen in the first place.

It seems that the components that form the semantic base of any language are oppositional:[3] male/female, living/non-living, animal/human, inside/outside. Therefore, phallus/non-phallus and desire/non-desire. "Truth/falsity, veiled/unveiled, hidden/revealed—all become part of a play of meaning in which the priority of any term can be uncentered to reveal the mastery of its opposite" (Nye, 1989, p. 189). Again, "an opposition of ... concepts ... is never the face-to-face of two terms, but a hierarchy and an order of subordination" (Derrida,

---

[2]Irigaray, Luce (1985). *Speculum of the other woman* (trans. G. Gill). Ithaca: Cornell University Press.
[3]See, for instance, C. Ferguson and E. Moravisk (Eds.) (1978). *Universals of human language.* Stanford: Stanford University Press.

1982, p. 329). We have seen the limits of this hierarchical opposition. The "inside" of the Deep Structure necessarily includes the "outside" which needs to be excluded, and thus the conceptual order, structuralism, lapses unintelligibly into nonsense: Lacan's [w]hole is not a fault to be avoided but it is rather the "force and law of its emergence" (Derrida, 1982, p. 325).

Chapter Four

GETTING TO THE SURFACE
OF THE PROBLEM

In the Chinese view, it is better to have too little than to have too
much, and better to leave things undone than to overdo them,
because although one may not get very far this way, one is certain
to go in the right direction.
— *Fritjof Capra (1977, p. 95)*

WHEN I BEGAN LOOKING at the doing of therapy, I was searching for
the *essence* of doing therapy, an essence that provides a fixed stable
center or foundation (that was perhaps determined ahead of time and
for all time); a "scientific," "structuralist" set of assumptions.[1] I began
my search by reading, over and over, the works of Milton H. Erickson
(Haley, 1967). From my structuralist perspective at that time (late '60s,
early '70s), the "essence" was seen to be in the clinical work itself and
then put into the written descriptions by Erickson himself. In this
situation, it is the reader's job to discover the "essence" and to pull it
out so that it can be properly interpreted. The quest, as I saw it, was
to look for an underlying, fundamental theory upon which Erickson
built his approach. Of course, once you start reading Erickson's many
papers, it becomes obvious that this is not a simple task.

In this sort of endeavor, the more complex the subject matter, the

---

[1]A previous version of some of the material in this chapter appeared in a paper presented at
the 1992 Fifth International Congress on Ericksonian Approaches to Hypnosis and Psychotherapy (de Shazer, 1992).

29

more puzzling the meanings involved. Simple structures combine into highly elaborate ones which, in turn, increase the depth of the interpretation, thus confirming the "fundamental" nature of the theory. Such a program, of course, privileges complexity over simplicity, although there is frequently a concomitant urge to reduce this complexity to simple fundamentals. Erickson's work was an obvious and classic case, a real gold mine, for such an approach (see also, in this regard, Bandler and Grinder's and Haley's work). Although I knew that these assumptions did not necessarily hold for literature, I nonetheless believed they held in the "scientific, objective" world. Viewed in this way, to borrow a term from literary criticism, Erickson's papers, read in the usual "scientific" fashion, became "verbal icons" or containers of truth, i.e., a fundamental theory.

When I first began learning how to do brief therapy with — or, better, from — my clients (in the late '60s and early '70s), I was fascinated with Milton Erickson's work, particularly with the ways Erickson and Jay Haley wrote about this unique approach to clinical practice. It was certainly not standard psychotherapy; that much was clear to me. Each case was apparently unique and there seemed to be no unifying theme or theory; that is to say, the essence was hidden away. These papers seemed to be reports about the work of a shaman or wizard. As Haley put it, "Part of the problem when examining Erickson's therapeutic technique is the fact that there *is* no adequate theoretical framework available for describing it. . . . When one examines what he actually does with a patient . . . traditional views do not seem appropriate" (Haley, 1967, p. 532, emphasis added). Perhaps mistakenly, I read Haley as at least implying that no theory was even possible.

While I agreed with Haley that, at that time, there was no adequate theory available, that did not convince me that Erickson did not have a theory, since Erickson said that "I know what I do, but to explain how I do it is much too difficult for me" (Erickson, 1975, p. viii). It is perfectly understandable that Erickson thought it was too difficult to explain what he did; that seems to be inherent in the nature of such expertise. But, if Erickson *knew* what to do, then he also knew what *not* to do. Therefore a theory, a set of rules, could be described by an observer even if Erickson himself could not do it.

Both by inclination and training, I thought that from Erickson's cases an essence could be abstracted and then a theory could be constructed that included rules — rules explicit enough so that at some point when working with a client a therapist could say "Now I can go on!" with some confidence that she[2] was following Erickson's rules. That is, she would "know" what to do and be able to do it.

Both in my practice and in Erickson's reports, there were always the odd-ball, miscellaneous cases that did not fit. No matter what approach to theory construction I tried, I continuously found myself in danger of violating Sherlock Holmes' advice and twisting the data (e.g., the facts reported) to fit the Theory rather than twisting the theory to fit the data. (Of course, what constitutes a "fact" or "data" or "fluke" are products of the theory; if the theory changes, what had been a fluke could be seen as "data.") I decided to set them aside as aberrations or flukes certain that someday a Theory could be invented that would include these weird cases. I was certain that a rule-based approach would eventually work. And certainly this approach has proved fruitful. Since then, my colleagues and I have been able to construct a rather elegant and strikingly simple yet rather comprehensive model using this approach to theory construction and model building (de Shazer, 1982, 1985, 1988).

About ten years ago, as part of our project, we learned that *exceptions* are at least as important as the rules, if not more so (de Shazer, 1985). Even if these exceptions are accidents (and of course accidents are always possible), then these exceptions need to be included within the theory. It was no longer possible to view the cases in the damn miscellaneous pile as flukes: These cases involving seemingly arbitrary therapist activity (activities outside the rules) *must* be included within the theory, within the rules, and not left outside as examples of Erickson's idiosyncratic genius. That is, this apparent arbitrariness must necessarily be covered by the rules of a theory for doing therapy that includes and is based, in part, on Erickson's approach. To me, this whole damn project now seemed hopeless.

I began to wonder if I had been missing the point all along. Perhaps the secret or conundrum was that there was nothing hidden away and that variety and diversity were the "essence" of Erickson's approach. If so, just accepting things as they are would be the only option available to me. This would mean that my theory of Erickson's approach had

---

[2]The pronouns "he," "she," "him," "her," etc. will be used randomly unless referring to a specific person.

many branches but no center whatsoever. Furthermore, this would mean that there was no Theory, no grand design, but instead, just local, rather idiosyncratic, activities that were primarily situationally dependent.

Faced with this situation, I decided that my only recourse was to follow Wittgenstein's advice (1958) and renounce all Theory: "To put all this indefiniteness, correctly and unfalsified, into words" (#227). And this is what I decided to do. This led me to abandon structuralism as an approach for looking at doing therapy. However, "the difficulty of renouncing all theory [is that] one has to regard what appears so obviously incomplete, as something complete" (Wittgenstein, 1980, #723)!

> When you have eliminated the impossible, whatever remains,
> however improbable, must be the truth.
> —Sherlock Holmes (The Sign of Four)

*   *   *

In order to re-read Erickson's case examples as though for the first time, I needed to adopt a reading strategy that would allow me to not drag along all of my previous (structural) readings, which involved the pursuit of a Theory. Somehow I had to take the words at face value, to keep my reading on the surface, to avoid any and all reading between the lines, and to somehow overcome the urge to look behind and beneath. This is not an easy job; the structural urge can be overwhelming.

To aid me in this re-reading, I decided to interpret these case examples as stories—not as exemplary lessons, but pure stories. That is, to read them as if they were fiction, which meant that I was no longer taking the distinction between "literature" and "science" very seriously at all. It was no longer feasible for me to search for the author's intention or what he really meant while ignoring my role as reader. That is, the unit of investigation switched from (1) Erickson and his papers to (2) Erickson, his papers, and me.

These are good stories with plots and subplots, beginnings, middles, and endings, strong characterizations, frequent unexpected twists and turns. Erickson-the-author has a very definite style and a command of the language. Everything a reader could want. As I read story after story, I came to see Erickson, the therapist in these stories, as the persona developed by Erickson-the-author; this persona I came to call "Erickson-the-clever."

As I continued to read using this strategy, I started to see myself and Haley and even Erickson-the-author in much the same relationship to these tales as the Baker Street Irregulars have to the Sherlock Holmes adventures.[3] That is, we were all seduced by Erickson-the-author into believing in the reality of Erickson-the-clever much as the Baker Street Irregulars were seduced into believing, or at least pretending to believe, that Sherlock Holmes was indeed a real human being who existed like you and I exist. Then I started to see Haley's writing about Erickson-the-clever as somewhat similar to Doctor Watson's role in the Sherlock Holmes stories. That is, I started to see Haley-the-author as an invention of Erickson-the-author that Erickson-the-author used to strengthen the reader's sense of Erickson-the-clever as clever. Importantly, like Watson, Haley's view helped to point the reader in a certain direction by always seeing things clearly from a direction that is "wrong"[4] but not as "wrong" as the official psychiatric view. Sherlock Holmes and Doctor Watson's view of Holmes and of his view of the various events depicted—in contrast to Holmes' view or the views of the official police—are part of what makes the Holmes stories something special. Viewed from this angle, these stories would be very boring indeed without the persona of Erickson-the-clever. All of which helps to make a story into a good story.

It then dawned on me that the Erickson-the-clever stories, like the Sherlock Holmes stories, actually under-develop or under-realize all the other characters that appear in the stories, particularly the clients. Sometimes these other characters, like Inspector Lestrade, no matter how important to the story itself, are just cardboard cutouts. We have little or no idea about their contributions to the therapeutic endeavor. However, as you and I know, and as Erickson and Haley also know, in order to have a therapeutic enterprise there needs to be both therapist and client.

As I re-read my own cases from this point of view I came to realize

---

[3] I have often wondered if Erickson read and re-read the Sherlock Holmes stories as avidly as I do. Long before I wanted to emulate Erickson's approach to problems I wanted to emulate Holmes' approach. Is there or is there not a strong similarity between the character "Sherlock Holmes" and the persona "Erickson-the-clever"?

[4] See Haley (1985) for many, many examples of this.

what clever clients I had. Most of the ideas for "unusual interventions" in the miscellaneous pile in fact came from the clients themselves! Fortunately we were cleverly listening when they told us what to do. (Compare Weakland's homework task [Chapter Seven] with Insoo Kim Berg's [Chapter Twelve] in which the client reinvents Weakland's task.)

To re-read my own case stories using the persona of clever-clients unfortunately forces the therapist-in-the-story to appear to be incredibly stupid. Undoubtedly we therapists could not learn as much from de Shazer-the-stupid[5] as we did from Erickson-the-clever. Maybe we all need to remember the dialogic or conversational nature of doing therapy and re-read all these stories with an interactional focus which would lead us to the idea that clever therapy depends on having clients and therapists cleverly working together in clever ways.

READING

> Recent literary theory suggests that the ability of a text to make
> sense in a coherent way depends less on the willed intentions of
> an originating author than on the creative ability of a reader.
> — *James Clifford (1988, p. 52)*

In some ways, at least, the situation one person listening to another finds himself or herself in is similar to the situation of a person reading a book. Likewise, writing and speaking are also similar, although we tend to be less formal when we talk. The most obvious difference is that when reading the author is absent and when writing the reader is absent. However, just because the other person in a conversation is there does not necessarily make things any easier. Of course you can ask the other person what he or she meant by what was said, but that alone may not resolve your question; the difficulties with language dealt with in the previous chapters remain.

Writing and reading are interwoven. It is clear that while somebody writes something he is simultaneously reading what he has written, which helps him continue on with or cease writing. The writing/read-

---

[5]Actually, I should have seen all this long ago, since the two major influences on my interviewing style have been John Weakland's persona "Weakland-the-dense" and Insoo Kim Berg's persona "Insoo-the-incredulous."

ing of the beginning of a professional book or article not only sets the stage for reading/writing subsequent parts but also limits and constrains both: The writing/reading of the ending not only serves to tie things together but also limits and constrains both the reading and the writing of what came before.

Of course neither "reading" nor "writing" is without enigmas uniquely its own, and each has its own specialized areas of study. It is beyond the scope of this book to deal extensively with either "writing" or "reading." However, reading and writing, using these terms more or less as we usually use them on a day-to-day basis, are too important to be completely ignored.

Part of the enigma of reading/writing is that what's in the author's mind has no priority over the meaning of his words. On the contrary, the writer only discovers the meaning of his words in the act of writing them. Each word on its own says both more and less than I meant it to say. It turns out that meanings cannot be sent reliably: What is received is not necessary what it sent. Thus, within family therapy discourse, or any other discourse, disciplined and clear reading is just as important as clear and disciplined writing.

TEXT-FOCUSED READING

The approach to reading Structuralism (Chapters Two and Three) is similar to an approach usually described by the term "deconstruction." The use of the term "deconstruction" is very problematic and perhaps dangerous, because its use (abuse or at least misuse) within philosophy, (British and American) literary criticism, and even family therapy[6] has been very loose and even contradictory. It was with great hesitation that I used the term before and therefore I have decided to use my own term "text-focused reading,"[7] since that adequately fits my own approach to both reading and doing therapy.

Although there is no unified definition of "text-focused reading" (or deconstruction), and one would be neither possible nor desirable, nonetheless there is a certain family resemblance among text-focused

---

[6]See, for instance, the various uses of the term "deconstruction" in *Therapeutic Conversations* (Gilligan & Price, 1993).
[7]One might think of "text-focused reading" as the name for a class of activities one member of which is called "deconstruction.

readings (Norris, 1982, 1983). For instance, Elizabeth Grosz in her feminist study of Jacques Lacan describes her reading as involving "a very careful, patient reading of the text," frequently involving looking at a text "from a point of view sympathetic to the text's concerns and its logic; and at the same time, reading it from the point of view of what is left out, foreclosed, or unarticulated by it but is necessary for its functioning." Thus, this mode of "reading a text from both inside and outside its terms, i.e., from its margins, must remain ambivalently an act of love and respect, and of self-assertion and critical distancing" (Grosz, 1990, p. 190). The unit of analysis here is author and reader together dealing with the text itself as a text. If we carry over the framework of this activity into the therapy world, the unit of analysis is client(s) and therapist and the conversation they have together about the client's concerns. These approaches use the internal logic, concerns, and structure of a construction (including what is left out, foreclosed, etc.) in order to open up the construction itself thus allowing space for new meanings to develop.[8] For example, a text-focused reading of a set of traditional Chinese recipes could be done from the point of view of a Chinese chef.

"Text-focused reading" will be contrasted with "reader-focused reading," which will be used to describe a reading of a text *from the outside* of the concerns of the text itself, frequently using a logic that is not part of the text under consideration.[9] A "reader-focused reading" is a perfectly useful, long accepted, and highly respected kind of activity. A reader-focused reading of this same set of traditional Chinese recipes could be done from the point of view of a nutritionist. This would produce a very different reading and a very different critique from the first, text-focused type.

Text-focused reading (and deconstruction) is not, as its opponents and as some of its proponents (i.e., various British and American literary critics) would have it, "a discourse with no further use for criteria of reference, validity, or truth," and its main practitioners "squarely repudiate the 'anything goes' school of hermeneutic thought" (Norris, 1992, p. 17). In fact, according to Jacques Derrida, it "is not a discursive

---

[8]As I see it, this is reflected in our use of the client's own language and logic (rather than ours) to put any difference that is noticed to work in such a way that difference opens up the possibility of new meanings, behaviors, feelings, etc. developing.

[9]Such as an Heideggerian "destrukion" (Gasché, p. 111).

or theoretical affair, but a practico-political one, and it is always produced *within* the structures (somewhat quickly and summarily) said to
be institutional" (1987, p. 508, emphasis added).

> In ethical terms likewise, it is a gross misunderstanding to suppose that
> [text-focused reading] ignores or suspends the question of interpretive
> responsibility, the requirement that texts should be read — or utterances
> construed — with a due respect for those other-regarding maxims (of
> good faith, fidelity, attentiveness to detail etc.) which prevent it from
> becoming just a super-subtle game, a license for all kinds of readerly
> extravagance. (Norris, 1992, p. 17)

Derrida, the inventor or at least the "central figure" of "deconstruction," while hesitant to offer any unified definition of his work, nonetheless thinks that deconstruction and text-focused reading involve, in
part, a kind of

> reading [that] must always aim at a certain relationship, [usually, fre-
> quently, perhaps always] unperceived by the writer, between what he
> commands of language and what he does not command of . . . the lan-
> guage he uses. This relationship is . . . a signifying structure that critical
> reading must produce. . . . [Without] all the instruments of traditional
> criticism, . . . critical production would risk developing in any direction
> and authorize itself to say almost anything. (Derrida, 1976, p. 158)

Paul de Man, an American literary critic who is, in his own way,
as rigorous as Derrida in his text-focused readings, describes Rueben
Brower's teaching of "practical criticism" (sometimes called "close reading"), which is also a partial description of de Man's methods. In fact,
this description is quite similar to the close reading technique used to
look at structuralism and, in later chapters, to look at doing therapy
through looking at transcripts of therapy sessions.

> Students, as they began to write on the writing of others, were not to
> say anything that was not derived from the text they were considering.
> They were not to make any statements that they could not support by a
> specific use of language that actually occurred in the text. They were
> asked, in other words, to begin by reading texts closely as texts and not
> to move at once into the general context of human experience or history.
> Much more humbly or modestly, they were to start out from the baffle-

ment that such singular turns of tone, phrase, and figure were bound to produce in readers attentive enough to notice them and honest enough not to hide their non-understanding behind the screen of received ideas that often passes, in literary instruction, for humanistic knowledge. (de Man, 1986, p. 23)[10]

Regardless of label (and this is not at all a naive question of terminology), a critique—whether based on text-focused reading, reader-focused reading, or critical social theory, etc.—involves rigorous reading/writing, i.e., scholarship and care.

Misreading

As we read a sentence, its meaning is always delayed. We are always waiting for the next word to help us make sense of the previous word(s); a later sentence changes the sense made of earlier ones and subsequent ones. There is always this moratorium on making sense, on meaning, because of the context in which the words are working. As we read, we bring along with us all of our previous experiences, all of our previous uses of the words and concepts. This delay and deferral of meaning contaminate everything we read. There is no way to be sure we can figure out exactly what the author *really* meant: This some deconstructivists call "misreading." Because of Lacan's [w]hole, one cannot read, one can only misread. All texts allow for a host of potential misreadings involving supplemental meanings.

There is, of course, another possibility, which is reading in bad faith (an all too common event). This might be called "dys-reading" or "mal-reading." (This actually not reading at all.) Simply, this happens if the reader refuses to take the author's words seriously, and/or refuses to pay attention to details, and/or refuses to read with at least of modicum of charity.

Grammar, which "describes the use of words in the language" (Wittgenstein, 1974, p. 60), and logic are the primary constraints against bizarre misreadings (but not against mal-readings), although these "rules" of language and usage can turn out to be disjunctive. That

---

[10]De Man (1986) continues that, as a result of this training, "the profession is littered with the books that the students of Reuben Brower failed to write" (p. 24).

is, grammar "has somewhat the same relation to the language as the description of a game, the rules of a game, have to the game" (Wittgenstein, 1974, p. 60); the difference between use and either logic or grammar is, at times, similar to the difference between the playing of a game and the rules of the game. (In poker, through bluffing, a player with five miscellaneous cards might win over a player with a pair of jacks, even though the "rules" would call for the player with the pair to win since he has the "best" cards.)

Chapter Five

BATESON'S "EPISTEMOLOGY": A BLACK [W]HOLE?

But ways have changed, and most ways lead
To different places than were said
By those who planned the obvious routes
And now, mistaking the direction,
On miles of milestones,
Perplexed beyond perplexion,
Catch their poor guts.
—*Dylan Thomas*[1]

AS A NEXT STEP in examining in detail some of the difficulties of developing meaning, reading the "abstract" section of "The cybernetics of self: A theory of alcoholism" (Bateson, 1972) will prove useful. Bateson's work is an important part of therapeutic discourse—at least, of family therapy discourse; furthermore, this particular paper has been influenced how "alcohol addiction" has been viewed by many therapists.

Bateson's abstract:

The "logic" of alcoholic addiction has puzzled psychiatrists no less than the "logic" of the strenuous spiritual regime whereby the organization Alcohol-

---

[1]"With windmills turning wrong directions," third stanza (Thomas, 1971).

ics Anonymous is able to conteract the addiction. In the present essay it is suggested: (1) that an entirely new epistemology must come out of cybernetics and systems theory, involving a new understanding of mind, self, human relationship, and power; (2) that the addicted alcoholic is operating, when sober, in terms of an epistemology which is conventional in Occidental culture but which is not acceptable to systems theory; (3) that surrender to alcoholic intoxication provides a partial and subjective short cut to a more correct state of mind; and (4) that the theology of Alcoholics Anonymous coincides closely with an epistemology of cybernetics. (Bateson, 1972, p. 309)

Using the dictionary can help us in our attempt to read this paragraph with its juxtaposition of terms and concepts from various fields of endeavor.

epistemology, n. [Gr. *episteme,* knowledge, and *logos,* discourse.] the theory or science that investigates the origin, nature, methods, and limits of knowledge.

cybernetics, n. pl. [construed as sing.] [from Gr. *kybernetes,* helmsman, and *-ics.*] the comparative study of the human nervous system and of complex electronic calculating machines, aimed at increasing the understanding of how the human brain functions.

As a reading tactic, we can substitute the definitions (using them as a sort of a feature of a Deep Structure) for the words used,[2] and thus read Bateson as saying that he is going to suggest *an entirely new* theory or science that investigates the origin, nature, methods, and limits of knowledge *that must come out of* the comparative study of the human nervous system and of complex electronic calculating machines, aimed at increasing the understanding of how the human brain functions *and systems theory.*[3] This is a rather difficult reading. It seems that Bateson is promising an expansive or grand Theory with a scope explicitly covering alcoholism, addiction, self, human relationship, and power.

---

[2]We could, of course, look up the various "difficult" words used in the dictionary definitions but this effort might well lead to reprinting the whole dictionary!

[3]In 1971 when I first read this paper, I thought I knew what "systems theory" meant and what Bateson meant by the term, although it is not at all clear to me now what it might mean (see de Shazer, 1991).

According to Bateson, the alcoholic, when sober, is operating in terms of an epistemology, e.g., which is (according to the dictionary) the theory or science that investigates the origin, nature, methods, and limits of knowledge, which is "*not acceptable*" to systems theory. Furthermore, he is saying that there is an "epistemology" that *is* more correct and therefore is acceptable to systems theory. Systems theory is thus, in Bateson's eyes, the sort of something that can determine whether an epistemology[4] is correct or not. Systems theory is thus a unified something, here essentially personified and given the ability to judge theory and science.

Is Bateson equating "state of mind" with "epistemology"? This is certainly suggested by reading points 2 and 3: "*(2) that the addicted alcoholic is operating, when sober, in terms of an epistemology which is conventional in Occidental culture but which is not acceptable to systems theory; (3) that surrender to alcoholic intoxication provides a partial and subjective short cut to a more correct state of mind.*" Does this also mean that we need to re-read point 1? In this case, then, Bateson is saying, in point 1, (a) *that an entirely new* state of mind *must come out of cybernetics and systems theory, involving a new understanding of mind, self, human relationship, and power* — which is altogether different from the first reading — (b) *that an entirely new* theory or science that investigates the origin, nature, methods, and limits of knowledge *must come out of cybernetics and systems theory. . . .*

These readings of points 1, 2, and 3 have produced two very different sets of meanings. Perhaps point 4 will help clarify things. We need to return to the dictionary to help us read point 4, since Bateson introduces significant new terms: "*that the theology of Alcoholics Anonymous coincides closely with an epistemology of cybernetics*":

theology, n, [Gr. *theologia; theos*, god, and *logos*.] 1. the study of God and the relations between God and the universe; study of religious doctrines and matters of divinity. 2. a specific form or system of this study, as expounded by a particular religion or denomination.

coincides, 1. to take up the same place in space; to be exactly alike in shape, position, and area. . . . 3. to concur; to be identical; to agree; as, the judges did not *coincide* in opinion.

---

[4]Philosophically, epistemology is usually defined as a theory of knowledge.

Substituting the dictionary definitions for the words in point 4 suggests a way to begin to see what Bateson is getting at: The specific form or system of this study of God and his relationship with the universe, as expounded by Alcoholics Anonymous, is identical with one of the following:

(a)   a theory or science that investigates the origin, nature, methods, and limits of knowledge
[or] (b) a state of mind
[or] (c) rules by which an individual construes his experience.

Which reading are we to choose?

1. Theology = Epistemology = Theory of knowledge?
2. Theology = Epistemology = State of mind?
3. Theology = Epistemology = Rules . . . ?

There seem to be some pieces missing, pieces that should have helped us figure out what Bateson intended to say, or at least what Bateson wanted the readers to get out of reading this abstract. Moving back and forth between the text and the dictionary has not helped to fill in the missing pieces; rather, it has led us to conclude that there are even more missing pieces. Where can we look for these missing pieces? Obviously, the next place to look is the context in which this abstract was put to work, the article itself.

On page 314, Bateson explains/defines his idiosyncratic, non-philosophical use of the word epistemology:

> I shall therefore use the single term "epistemology" in this essay to cover both aspects of the net of premises which govern adaptation (or maladaptation) to the human and physical environment. In George Kelly's vocabulary, these are the rules by which an individual 'construes' his experience. (p. 314)

However, he had already brought "philosophers who have thought about the implications of cybernetics and systems theory" (p. 309) into the context:

> Philosophers have recognized and separated two sort of problems. There are first the problems of how things are, what is a person, and what sort

of world this is. These are the problems of ontology. Second, there are the problems of how we know anything, or more specifically, how we know what sort of world it is and what sort of creatures we are that can know something (or perhaps nothing) of this matter. These are the problems of epistemology. (p. 313)

Up until page 314 Bateson induced the first reading, equating theology with theory of knowledge and then on page 314 he switched to the second and then to the third. The third reading is infected by the second reading and both are, separately and together, automatically contaminated by the first, etc.

Of course, there is nothing unusual in importing a technical term from another field and giving it a different signification from what it had in its old field. But, up until page 314 there is no indication that Bateson is using the term "epistemology" in a non-philosophical way; in fact, given the authority Bateson invests in philosophers (who, according to Bateson, have already thought about the things Bateson is writing about [p. 309]), everything indicates a traditional philosophical usage. (Of course, since "epistemology" is a part of a larger system and not an independent atom, Bateson accidentally brings along the whole of philosophy when he borrows the term—as any reader of the family therapy journals can attest.) By introducing his non-philosophical meaning on page 314 he inadvertently reframes the entire essay up to that point, leaving readers to simultaneously handle three rather different readings. It seems that there are still pieces missing: What does Bateson mean by the term "epistemology"? For help in this, we might look to either other works by Bateson (enlarging the context) or other works within family therapy discourse (an even larger context) to see if we can find these missing pieces.

*   *   *

Paul Dell (1985) has done some of this work for us. He points out that, to further complicate matters, at various times Bateson used the term "epistemology" with at least five different signifieds. Dell came to the conclusion that "for Bateson, almost everything is epistemology" (p. 4), which is at least part of the reason he thought that Bateson's writing has a "difficult-to-grasp quality" (p. 4).

The whole matter perhaps could have been easily resolved if Bateson had simply used Kelly's vocabulary from the start. As it is, with

Kelly's "rules by which an individual construes his experience" as an alternative term (to be substituted for "epistemology"), we now have a third reading, since "rules by which an individual construes his experience" are certainly different from either a "state of mind" or a theory of knowledge or a theology. There are still pieces missing.

* * *

Stepping outside of Bateson's text (i.e., a reader-focused reading), outside of his logic, we see that there was a perfectly good term/concept available to Bateson that covers the "rules" and the "state of mind" aspects of how he uses "epistemology" and which also suggests a direct link to "theology" rather than to philosophy. The term/concept "ideology," used in a descriptive sense by the Frankfurt school of social criticism (Geuss, 1981) (but not in the sense of false consciousness), fits quite well:

(a) various beliefs are widely shared by the agents [i.e., alcoholics] in the group
(b) various beliefs are systematically interconnected
(c) these beliefs are central to the agents' [alcoholics'] conceptual scheme, i.e., the agents [alcoholics] will not easily give them up
(d) these beliefs have a wide and deep influence on the agents' [alcoholics'] behavior and/or on some important or central sphere of action
(e) the beliefs are "central" in that they deal with central issues of life, i.e., death, work, sexuality, etc.

Using the term "ideology" would have made for a far less difficult reading and, furthermore, would have clarified the relationship Bateson points to between "epistemology" and the "theology" of AA.

* * *

Trying to figure out what meaning Bateson had for the term "epistemology" in this abstract illustrates how the delay and deferral of signification lead us to more and more attempts at interpretation. Of course the meaning of a piece of writing cannot depend on the reader's being able to ask the author, since writing needs to be independent of the author's presence in order to function as writing; his absence or even death cannot prevent what he has written from functioning in the usual way. In fact, the author's absence is a given; otherwise, why write? After all he cannot know to whom he writes — or, for that matter, he cannot know if anyone, at any time, will ever read what he has written. The author, when writing, needs to depend on the reader's absence in order for writing to make any sense whatsoever.

The dictionary, as well as the first few pages of Bateson's article itself, both expand our efforts at reading "epistemology" and constrain these same efforts. For instance, Bateson's mentioning philosophers-as-authorities at the very beginning of the article (p. 309) and explaining their use of the term (p. 313) naturally lead readers to become rather certain about a philosophical reading of the term. The abstract and the early part of the article makes for difficulty in reading the rest of the article (after page 314). Unfortunately for us as readers, it seems that Bateson's mentioning of philosophers turned out to be a red-herring rather than a clue.

As we have just seen, the fixing of meaning is always temporary and precarious. Meaning is the product of the differences between words and the deferral and delay that results from Lacan's [w]hole.

According to Derrida (1973), "the elements of signification function not by virtue of the compact force of their cores but by the network of oppositions that distinguish them and relate them to one another" (p. 139). That is, we can only conclude that the meaning of the term "epistemology" (for Bateson at least in this particular context) is multiple, contradictory, variable, and thus, ultimately undecidable. Perhaps all of the available meanings should be used simultaneously rather than differentially; this would certainly enrich the meaning of the term "epistemology." However, it would then be rather difficult to figure out how "epistemology" is different from other words, other concepts. It leaves us wondering, along with Dell, about just what exactly epistemology *is not* within the context of Bateson's work.

*   *   *

The muddle that developed through attempting to read "epistemology" could be just a simple result of a "mistake," which can always be put down to careless thinking or slipshod writing or poor editing. Or, more interestingly, it could be the result of a determinate "error," which cannot be so easily dismissed, since this sort of "error" results from a conflict of aims and/or a disparity of meaning and intent.[5] Perhaps because of Bateson's status, the latter seems more likely than the former.[6] This calls to mind Paul de Man's idea that authors' "moments of greatest blindness are also the moments at which they achieve their greatest insight" (de Man, 1983, p. 109).

Indeed, Bateson's epistemology is similar to a theology: There are right ways and wrong ways of looking at what it is that is going on. Bateson's equating epistemology, theology, rules, etc. strongly suggests an "error" that is determined by Bateson's primary concern with the structural unity of mind and nature (a romantic point of view which is rather pantheistic and mystic). Bateson had found an ally in AA (i.e., a group whose position he could construct as similar to his own while remaining within their logic), and together they could sell psychiatry on this marginal point of view called "systems theory." In the early 1970s, when the article was written, both "systems theory" and Alcoholics Anonymous were *outside* with regard to psychiatry. They certainly were much further outside than they are today. And, as Bateson said, alcoholism and AA were mysteries to psychiatry. Systems theory was also an unknown, a mystery. What better ploy or strategy than to link philosophers (high status associates) and George Kelly (another relatively high status associate) to these two mysteries in an effort to open psychiatry to these different views? Was the ploy successful? Did the strategy work? Well, at least the paper was published.

---

[5] This distinction between "mistake" and "error" is taken from Paul de Man (1983).
[6] This could be wishful thinking on my part.

Chapter Six

FREUD WAS WRONG: WORDS HAVE LOST NONE OF THEIR MAGIC

How can I say what I know with words whose signification is multiple?
—*Edmond Jabès (1959, p. 41)*

WE STARTED OFF following Condillac's advice, "by learning [about our] own language" (1947, p. 217) and ended up by discovering Lacan's [w]hole. This [w]hole turns out to be a rather queer place, a black hole or bottomless pit that sucks up the various attempts to plug it. As Ragland-Sullivan (1991b) put it, "language gives rise to a void, as a lack of all things *qua* immediately graspable or knowable. We cannot be whole. Nor can anything else" (p. 4).

What really makes this [w]hole queer is that in spite of or perhaps because of it, language somehow works: We are able to do things we call "reading" and "communicating" and "having conversations." In some ways at least, this is analogous to some situations in mathematics. For instance, Gödel's proof demonstrates that arithmetic, number theory, and perhaps all of mathematics is inconsistent and incomplete (Nagel & Newman, 1958); there is sort of a [w]hole at the bottom. And yet arithmetic, number theory, and mathematics still work. Even imaginary numbers do practical work (Spencer-Brown, 1969)!

This discovery of a queer [w]hole seems rather unsettling and unsatisfactory. We are tempted to think that something is missing or hidden away, "that language consists of two parts: an inorganic part, the handling of signs, and an organic part, which we may call understanding these signs, meaning them, interpreting them, thinking" (Wittgenstein, 1965, p. 3), i.e., sort of another language behind language, either structuralism or some sort of metalanguage. Perhaps we have been expecting or even demanding that language behave in certain precise ways, following hard and fast rules, when, it turns out, we do not really use it that way and we did not learn it according to the rules. Instead, we simply learned to use it. Perhaps we have been asking the wrong question or asking our question in a wrong way. As Derrida suggests, we frequently "find . . . that the question can be inscribed only in the form dictated by the answer which awaits it" (Derrida, 1973, p. 126). Since the answer is so queer, perhaps the question we have been asking is also queer in some way(s).

As Wittgenstein (1965) puts it in "The Blue Book" of 1933/34:

> Our craving for generality has a[nother] main source: our preoccupation with the method of science. I mean the method of reducing the explanation of natural phenomena to the smallest number of primitive natural laws. . . . Philosophers constantly see the method of science before their eyes, and are irresistibly tempted to ask and answer questions in the way science does. This tendency is the real source of metaphysics, and leads the philosopher into complete darkness. (p. 18)

Thus the complete darkness of Lacan's black [w]hole.

Therapists and their clients use language within their conversation or dialogue, and it is this use of language rather than language itself that we are trying to learn about. Like Freud, Saussure, Bandler and Grinder, and Lacan, we have so far taken an entirely monologic approach focusing on the individual and static aspects of language and mind, a point of view that suggests that mind and language are connected but separate, mind leading to language. However, as George Herbert Mead (1934) suggests, "Mind" can also be seen to arise "through communication by a conversation of gestures in a social process or context of experience — not communication through mind" (p. 50). Bahktin's and Wittgenstein's points of view (see below) suggest that mind can be seen as a condition of language/conversation. As Wittgenstein's student Rush Rhees (1970) puts it, "not all speech is conversation . . . but I do not think there would be speech or language without it" (p. 81).

We have been looking only at *words* and meaning instead of looking at their use in *dialogue* or conversation and in making sense of something. We need to look at what happens between therapists and clients, how language works in conversation in spite of, or rather, because of Lacan's [w]hole. Although Freud thought that words had lost some of their magic, the discovery of Lacan's [w]hole and the fact that language works because of this [w]hole means that words are even more magical than Freud thought they were originally: Words have lost none of their magic.

BAKHTIN'S BRIDGE

> [A] *word is a two-sided act*. It is determined equally by *whose* word
> it is and for whom it is meant. As a word, it is precisely *the product
> of the reciprocal relationship between speaker and listener, addresser
> and addressee*. Each word expresses the "one" in relation to the
> "other." I give myself verbal shape from another's point of view.
> — *Mikhail Bakhtin (Volosonow/Bakhtin, 1986, p. 86)*[1]

> For a *large* class of cases — though not for all — in which we employ
> the word "meaning" it can be defined thus: the meaning
> of a word is its use. . . .
> — *Ludwig Wittgenstein (1958, #42)*

One way out of our difficulty is to begin again, to start with a different answer in mind. This new answer (and thus, the new question) has actually been around a long time. Wittgenstein, as a philosopher of language, was not alone in seeing the "scientific" method of the usual approach as leading into total darkness. For instance, Mikhail Bakhtin, a Russian literary critic and theorist (Todorov, 1984), drew a distinction between language and dialogue along these lines: "the object of linguistics" and the philosophy of language in general are "constituted by *language*" but what we are interested in is the pragmatics of conversations or "discourse, which is represented . . . by individual utterances" (Todorov, 1984, p. 25) and the relationship between one utterance and another. For Bakhtin (as early as 1929): "Understanding is opposed to utterance like one reply is opposed to another within a dialogue.

---

[1]For various Soviet reasons, Bakhtin published under various names.

Understanding is in search of a counter-discourse to the discourse of the utterer" (quoted in Todorov, 1984, p. 22). For instance, the meaning that Bandler and Grinder find difficult to explain in structural terms (1975b, pp. 152–153), that they and we puzzled over above:

Surface Structure   ↔   "Something was given"

   ↕

Deep Structure   ↔ "Someone gave something to someone"

might well be perfectly obvious within the context of a dialogue or conversation. "The word in living conversation is directly, blatantly, oriented toward a future answer word," Bakhtin says. "It provokes an answer, anticipates it and structures itself in the answer's direction" (Bakhtin, 1981, p. 280). A social or dialogic view suggests that language and speech originate and develop through use, through social interaction and communication. From this perspective, mind can be seen as a condition of language.

For instance, a therapist's utterance during a particular session is related to all of his previous utterances (during that session), all of his future utterances (during that session), and all of the client's utterances on a particular subject during that session as well—a situation Bakhtin called "intertextuality" and Wittgenstein called a "language-game" (1965). Thus, for Bakhtin, reading is also a dialogue, with the reader creatively providing a counter-discourse in interaction with the text and the author.

A quick look at Bakhtin's 1927 critique of Freud will illustrate the differences between Bakhtin's approach, focused on dialogue, and the "scientific" one, focused on language.

> The motifs of the unconscious revealed during psychoanalytic sessions by means of the method of "free association" are *verbal reactions* of the patient, as are all the other habitual motifs of consciousness. They are different one from the other, so to speak, not by any generic distinction of their being, but only by their content, that is *ideologically*. In this sense, the unconscious according to Freud can be defined as an "unauthorized consciousness" in distinction to the habitual "official" consciousness.... What is reflected in these verbal utterances is not the dynamics of the individual soul, but the *social dynamics* of the interrelations of doctor and patient. (quoted in Todorov, 1984, p. 31)

That is, "for Bakhtin, 'at the bottom of man' we find not Id but the other" (Todorov, p. 33). Lacan's work—within the context of psycho-analysis—points to a [w]hole at the bottom of language, which indicates that in Lacan's view psychoanalysis is not interactional; it is not a conversation—it is just talking. However, in a different context:

> When you give a child a smack, well! it's understandable that he cries—without anybody's reflecting that it's not at all obligatory that he should cry. I remember a small boy who whenever he got a smack used to ask—*Was that a pat or a slap*? If he was told it was a slap he cried, that belonged to the conventions, to the rules of the moment, and if it was a pat he was delighted. But this isn't the end of the matter. When one gets a smack there are many other ways of responding than by crying. One can return it in kind, or else turn the other cheek, or one can say—*Hit me, but listen*! A great variety of possibilities offer themselves.... (Lacan, 1993, p. 6)

(As an experiment, next time you are in a conversation, pretend that you are not a part of that conversation. What happens to you? What happens to the other person? Since while you are pretending whatever the other person says has no connection with you, do you not have to imagine that whatever the other is saying must necessarily be related to something going on inside the other person? Is this not similar to eavesdropping on a telephone conversation and trying to figure out what the person on the other end of the line is saying?)

The social context, including therapist, client and the setting in which they meet, in addition to what they say in response to each other, helps both parties together to construct meaning from the dialogue. According to Bakhtin, "no utterance in general can be attributed to the speaker exclusively; it is the product of the interaction . . . and, broadly speaking, the product of the whole complex social situation in which it has occurred" (1927, quoted in Todorov, 1984, p. 30).

Bakhtin's perspective leads to the idea that the relations between therapist and client continue to alter in the very process of the conversation. There is no ready-made meaning that is transferred or handed over from one to the other. Rather, meaning develops or takes form in the process of interacting. A message is not transmitted from one to the other but "constructed between them, like an ideological bridge; it is constructed in the process of their interaction" (Bakhtin, 1928, quoted in Todorov, p. 56). Unlike Freud, Saussure, and Bandler and

Grinder, who dealt with the transmission of meaning by means of a ready-made code with fixed, determinable meanings, Bakhtin dealt with living speech, where meaning is "created for the first time in the process of transmission, [because] ultimately there is no code" (1970/ 71, quoted in Todorov, p. 56). Rush Rhees put it this way:

> To think of language as a system, or as a kind of method (cf. 'a method of representation', 'method of projection'), almost as a kind of theory, is wrong if only because language is something people speak with one another. In this way it is not at all like mathematics. (1970, p. 84)

At about the same time, in Cambridge, Wittgenstein was crossing the same bridge.[2]

> Philosophers very often talk about investigating, analysing, the meaning of words. But let's not forget that a word hasn't got a meaning given to it, as it were, by a power independent of us, so that there could be a kind of scientific investigation into what the word *really* means. A word has the meaning someone has given to it.
> There are words with several clearly defined meanings. It is easy to tabulate these meanings. And there are words of which one might say: They are used in a thousand different ways which gradually merge into one another. [And some whose different uses do not merge.] No wonder that we can't tabulate strict rules for their use. (The Blue Book of 1933/ 34, Wittgenstein, 1965, p. 28)

Beginning to undermine his own early emphasis on form or structure, Wittgenstein had come to the conclusion that "the . . . sentence gets its significance from the system of . . . [sentences], from the language to which it belongs. Roughly, understanding a sentence means understanding a language" (Wittgenstein, 1965, p. 5). The meaning of a sentence does not come from merely adding up the meanings of all the individual words in the sentence nor does meaning come from somehow adding up the meanings of all the sentences (in the sample), but rather meaning comes from people's use of language. To use Wittgenstein's favorite analogy: A word is not like a move in a chess game;

---

[2]There is every reason to suppose that Mead, Wittgenstein, and Bakhtin had no knowledge of each other's work.

rather, a word is akin to placing a piece on the board. A sentence, then, is like a move in a chess game, but the move can only be understood within the context of a game of chess. Thus, even a sentence has no meaning in isolation: Understanding a sentence is to understand language or the context in which the sentence occurs—a "language-game" (in the Blue Book of 1933/34, Wittgenstein, 1965). This, of course, does not mean that words are meaningless because they are not sentences. The chess piece's position on the board is not a move in the game but, rather, a condition or precondition for the game. Which square the piece is on determines which moves it can make.

Clearly, a way across Lacan's [w]hole can be developed by using Bakhtin's Bridge. Actually, this "bridge" might be more descriptively called "Wittgenstein's Wobbly Planks across the Quagmire." But Bakhtin actually used the term "bridge" as a metaphor for meaning, for making sense happen or being constructed in dialogue—between people. And, "Bakhtin's Bridge" has a nice ring to it, so it is the term I will use.

UNDERSTANDING/MISUNDERSTANDING

> This does not suppose that the mark [sign] is valid outside its context, but on the contrary that there are only contexts without any center of absolute anchoring.
> —Jacques Derrida (1982, p. 320)

Given that the meaning of a word is often or usually delayed and deferred, "understanding" (or making sense of something) in a dialogue is also subject to delay and deferral and thus making sense of something is a cumulative process rather than a specific act limited to a particular moment. Therefore, at any particular moment, misunderstanding is more likely than understanding (de Shazer, 1991). Furthermore, such misunderstandings constitute conversations and, in fact, misunderstandings make conversation possible. That is, if we simply (radically) understood each other, we would have nothing to talk about.

If a client were to say "I am depressed" and we *understood* what he meant (i.e., the common sense view), there would be no reason to ask him any questions. We would know precisely and exactly the past, present, and future of his condition. Without saying a word, we could give him a prescription, chemical and/or behavioral, he would say "thanks" and that would be all there would be to it. Fortunately, even our field's most positivistic endeavors (such as the DSM) recognize that things are not that clear-cut. So we ask questions because we know that we do not understand what our patient means when he says that he is depressed.

"Depression" is clearly not something simple. Clients' descriptions usually involve a conglomerate of troublesome thoughts, feelings, behaviors, attitudes, and contexts, including other people. None of the words or concepts that the client includes in his description are simple and therefore we do not understand what he says that leads us to asking further questions. And, of course, none of our words and concepts are simple, and thus the client asks us questions because he does not understand us. All of this conversation is based on the idea that understanding is possible even though we know it may be improbable. Norris (1989) develops what might be called an interactional or conversational "principle of charity" that seems to fit this situation: "Understanding simply couldn't get off the ground unless there existed [a] general willingness to assume, first, that other people make sense of experience in ways not radically unlike our own, and second, that the attitude of holding-true — of attaching a particular significance to sentences that get things right — is as important for them as it is for us" (p. 60).

Of course the client knows what she means (at that particular time), but we cannot know. Suppose you ask a client about what she means by the term "depression" and she starts by telling you that she has not been sleeping enough. Can you have any confidence whatsoever that her not sleeping enough has prompted her to choose the term "depressed"? Or was it your question that led to her answer? Regardless, when she starts to make her private meaning public through talking to you about her depression, the making sense of something that develops is automatically interactional: In the therapeutic setting, whatever understanding that develops is a joint product of the conversation between therapist and client. Interestingly, searching for the meaning of the term "depression" in effect constructs the meaning of the term "depression" and, at least sometimes or even often, accidentally reinforces the feelings of "depression."

Knowing exactly what is meant by the term "depression," is impossible: behind and/or beneath every meaning or interpretation lurks another interpretation or guess. Therefore, searching for "the one true meaning" is at least useless when it is not deleterious. As a result, it seems more useful to just accept the situation as it is and thus to use our joint misunderstandings toward helping the client construct a solution. Of course, "one should not understand this compulsion to construct concepts . . . as if they enabled us to fix the real world; but as a compulsion to arrange a world for ourselves in which our existence is made possible . . . the world seems logical to us because we have made it logical" (Nietzsche, 1968, p. 282).

Since the meanings of words/concepts are flexible, variable, and at times even undecidable, critics of this point of view frequently jump to the conclusion that we are saying "anything goes," i.e., absurdly, "depression" could mean "tree." However, logic, grammar, rhetoric (in a classical sense), use, context, and importantly, the concept's opposite (non-depression) serve as constraints on the range of potential meanings. In particular, what the depression is *not* usefully limits the possible meanings of the term. Whatever might be attended to in "non-depression" we call "exceptions," "miracles," etc. (de Shazer, 1985, 1988, 1991).

Talking with the client about what the problem/complaint is not, i.e., "non-depression," is one of the ways of using misunderstandings in a creative fashion. Focusing on "non-depression" allows therapist and client together to construct a solution, or at least begin to construct a solution, based the clients' experiences that are *outside* the problem area. Thus, a solution is a joint product of therapist and client talking together about whatever it is that the problem/complaint is not. Of course, we do not and cannot understand what the complaint is not any better than we can understand what the complaint is. Fortunately, talking about whatever the complaint is not (and again this is not something simple) seems to be useful and valuable to most clients. As they continue to talk about the non-problem/non-complaint, they are doing something different rather than more of the same, something that has not worked. The more they talk about "exceptions," "miracles," etc., the more "real" what they are talking about becomes.

POWER

It is not so much "power" that corrupts as the myth of "power."
—*Gregory Bateson (1979, p. 223)*

Of course this dialogic or interactional view does not mean that any two people in a conversation have equal influence over the meanings or understandings that develop. Each person's role, status, etc., and the context in which the conversation takes place all have some impact on the results of the negotiation. One party, A, brings to a particular conversation, in a specific context (x), his own point of view (A), and the other party brings her own point of view (B): the result for A might be Ab(x), while for B it might be aB(x). The dialogical or interactional view suggests, however, that it is at least unlikely that A will shift all the way to B or that B will shift all the way to A. That is, neither person has unilateral control over the results of the negotiation.

Bateson

The family therapy discourse is replete, perhaps beyond the point of overflowing, with interpretations (and interpretations of these interpretations), or better, overinterpretations of Gregory Bateson's thinking and writing about systems theory in general and about power and control in particular.

Bateson argued against having a concept of power. The reasons behind this become clear when one situates his theory within the theological arena he saw as both *appropriate* and *correct* (see Chapter Five). But just what did Bateson mean when he used the term "power"? What concept of "power" was it that Bateson saw as corrupting?

From Bateson's point of view,

"power," like "energy," "tension," and the rest of the quasiphysical metaphors are to be distrusted and, among them, "power" is one of the most dangerous. He who covets a mythical abstraction [i.e., the myth of power] must always be insatiable! (Bateson, 1979, p. 223)

When talking about relationships, a concept such as "power" (unilateral control by one person in a relationship) is necessarily incomplete without a linked, complementary concept describing and/or labeling the responsive behavior of another person, i.e., what Bateson calls the beginning of a pattern description. However, unilateral control is deemed to be impossible because "the part can never control the whole" (Bateson, 1972, p. 437), which does not mean that all parts have equal control. It is a question of power over whom or what and under what conditions? If someone tries to have unilateral or simple lineal control, he or she needs to find out what the responses have been, i.e., whether his or her efforts were successful. Thus the would-be controller is actually *responsive* and must modify his or her efforts accordingly. "Therefore he cannot have a simple lineal control. We do not live in the sort of universe in which simple lineal control is possible" (Bateson, 1972, p. 438).

> In the field of psychiatry, the family is a cybernetic system . . . and when systemic pathology occurs, the members blame each other, or sometimes themselves. But the truth of the matter is that both these alternatives are fundamentally arrogant. Either alternative assumes that the individual human being has total power over the system of which he or she is a part. (Bateson, 1972, p. 438)

> . . . no part of such an internally interactive system can have unilateral control over the remainder or over any other part. The mental characteristics are inherent or immanent in the ensemble as a whole. (p. 315)

Since, in Bateson's view, the system predetermines, predestines things, "power" is everywhere and yet nowhere. This religious milieu is headed by a very Calvinistic god: the system. From Bateson's perspective, there is not only no need but also no possibility for a concept of unilateral-power/lineal-control within systems theory. Within Bateson's theology, there is no possibility for there to be something outside power, no opposite concept, no "non-power," and therefore no possibility of such a thing as a concept of power. Attempts at unilateral control can only lead to "systemic pathology."[3]

Foucault

Bateson's position, interestingly, is rather similar to Michel Foucault's (1980): For both there is no outside to power's inside and for both, "power" is just another name for the concept of "relationship."

> According to Foucault (1978), power must be understood in the first instance as the multiplicity of force relations immanent in the sphere in

---

[3]Bateson uses the alcoholic to illustrate this point while Foucault would use Hitler or Stalin.

which they operate and which constitute their own organization; as the process which, through ceaseless struggles and confrontations, transforms, strengthens, or reverses them; or on the contrary, the disjunctions and contradictions which isolate them from one another; and lastly, as the strategies in which they effect. (pp. 92–93)

Simply put, for Foucault as well as Bateson, power is also just another name for "relationship" or "system." Nancy Hartsock points to an interesting conundrum in Foucault's theory that is suggestive for reading Bateson.

[For Foucault] at the same time (and perhaps contradictorily) power relations are both intentional and subjective, although Foucault is careful to point out that there is no headquarters which sets the direction. His account of power is perhaps unique in that he argues that wherever there is power, there is resistance. (p. 168)

For Foucault, power is "omnipresent" (Foucault, 1978, pp. 52–53): Individuals are always and everywhere in the same position, one of simultaneously undergoing, exercising, and resisting power in a net of systemic relationships among a net of systems. "Resistance" is the other term necessary for beginning a pattern description.

Emerson[4]

Foucault's concept of power-resistance was anticipated by R. Emerson (1962, 1964) who developed and studied a "power-dependency theory," which can be summarized as follows:

1. POWER: The power of actor A over actor B is the amount of *resistance* on the part of B which can potentially be overcome by A.
2. DEPENDENCE: The dependence of A upon B is (a) directly proportional to A's *motivational investment* in goals mediated by B, and (b) inversely proportional to the *availability* of those goals outside the A-B relation.

---

[4]See: de Shazer (1986) for an earlier version of some of this material.

3. The power of A over B is equal to, and based upon, the dependence of B upon A. (Emerson, 1964, p. 289, emphasis added)

Emerson's concept seems to fit rather well with both Bateson's and Foucault's points of view. Power-dependence is an attribute of a relationship which Emerson describes as changing or re-balancing in a couple of ways:

1. WITHDRAWAL: Decreased motivational investment on the part of the weaker member [B].
2. NETWORK EXTENSION: Increased availability of goals for the weaker member outside the relation (extension of the "power network" through formation of new relations). (Emerson, 1964, p. 290)

Most simply, B is seen as potentially "resistant" to A's use of power. This resistance develops when A's suggestions run counter to B's desires. Thus, Foucault's term "power-resistance" seems more descriptive and closer to Bateson's point of view than Emerson's terms of "power-dependence." For Bateson, Emerson, and Foucault, the dependence, as a necessary part of any relationship, is seen as mutual or reciprocal, i.e., A is dependent on B while simultaneously B is dependent on A. Implicitly, "power" and "resistance" reside in each other's "dependency." This does not mean that A and B are necessarily equal with regard to either "power" or "resistance." But it does mean that neither has unilateral control.

In Emerson's terms, the more or less traditional therapeutic relationship would be seen as unbalanced, i.e., the therapist has a power advantage since the client hires her as an expert, an authority to help in some way. Therefore, in some ways at least, the client would necessarily be seen as dependent upon the therapist. And, in some different way (or ways) the therapist is also dependent on the client. Furthermore, if the therapist were to be seen by either the client or the therapist or both parties as more "powerful," then it is natural, expectable, and even predictable that the client is going to be seen (by the therapist and/or observers) as "resisting" that influence when the therapist's point of view leads to suggestions that go against his or her desires. This fits with Bateson's, Foucault's, and Emerson's points of view. Termination would come about when either the clients' goals were met outside the context of therapy and/or new significant relationships were formed outside of therapy and/or other things were to happen that decreased the client's motivational investment in the therapy.

Of course, when the therapist focuses on what it is exactly that the client wants and lets that be the guide, there is no need for a concept of "resistance" (de Shazer, 1982, 1985, 1988). This also minimizes the need for a concept of "power." This is not to say that the therapist does not have influence. Clients, in fact, hire therapists in order for the therapists to have influence. Rather, following Emerson, if the amount of power necessary is dependent on the amount of resistance necessary to overcome it, then when there is cooperation rather than resistance, the need for power is obviously diminished accordingly.

> Plato has said: All virtue is knowledge. Francis Bacon added: All knowledge is power. Spinoza concluded: Therefore all virtue is power.
> —*David Bidley (1962, p. 283)*

PART II

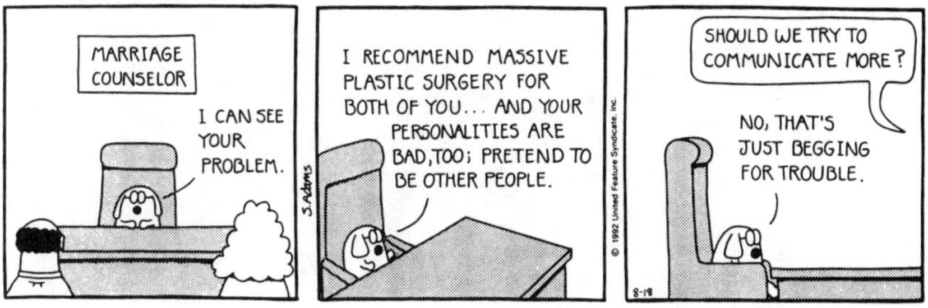

DILBERT reprinted by permission of UFS, Inc.

Chapter Seven

PROBLEM-TALK | SOLUTION-TALK

All of the facts belong only to the problem, not to its solution.
—*Ludwig Wittgenstein (1972 #6.4321)*

THERAPISTS ARE INTERESTED IN the *doing* of therapy and, at least in a certain sense, only the observation of sessions or watching videotapes of therapy sessions can give them the "data" they need. However, in a book, transcripts of therapy sessions are the only way to present these "data" to therapists. Without such "data" therapists can be expected to be shocked, to disagree and to argue when presented with ideas, descriptions, theories, etc., that they cannot make fit with their own ideas, descriptions, theories, etc., and "data" from their own clinical experiences.

Therefore, we turn our attention now to reading excerpts of transcripts from various therapy sessions involving therapists from different schools of thought. Comparing and contrasting the work of Nathan Ackerman, James Gustafson, and John H. Weakland will illustrate some of the ways language is used in therapy. The Ackerman and Gustafson transcripts were originally chosen simply because these two transcripts were in the first two books I found in my personal library that contained transcripts. Serendipitously,[1] the differences between

---

[1]It is deliberate not accidental I that kept these two examples while discarding two others that proved not to be as useful.

them led to some ways to illustrate how some of the conclusions to be drawn from the earlier, more theoretical chapters can be applied to the doing of therapy.

In some ways the therapist's job of listening and observing can be compared to the job of a reader. What the client says can be seen as similar to a text. At least in part, reading a transcript can be compared with observing a session from behind the see-through mirror. Ackerman's approach can be seen as a pure example of a reader-focused (or theory-driven) one, and Weakland's can be seen as a pure example of a text-focused approach. Gustafson's approach, while primarily a reader-focused one, nonetheless pays careful attention to the text.

As a tool for contrasting Ackerman's session with Gustafson's session, and both of those with Weakland's, I will set up the concepts "problem-talk" and "solution-talk" as a binary opposition,[2] which will allow us to follow Wittgenstein in setting up another expedient binary opposition between "facts" and their opposite, "non-facts." "Non-facts" is a conveniently broader term than "fictions," thus allowing us to include "fantasies, hopes, fictions, plans, desires," etc., as opposites to "facts." It is, of course, not this simple, as Weakland's session will undermine the rather clear-cut "problem-talk" | "solution-talk" distinction used with Ackerman's and Gustafson's sessions. Furthermore, the comparison of these three approaches can be used as a base upon which a further comparison can be built to look at the transcripts in the following chapters.

Problem-talk

As Part One of an experiment, imagine that you have spent the previous half-hour talking to Mr. A about all of the problems in his life, focusing particularly on his feelings of depression. How do *you* feel after this half-hour?

When I have asked therapists this question, they have talked about how, while listening to people describing their problems and searching for an explanation, "fact" piles up upon "fact" and, as a result, the

---

[2]This is only a temporary expedient, since the "inside/outside" of binary pairs cannot be guaranteed; the boundary is not a barrier.

problem becomes heavier and heavier for the therapist. After 45 minutes, the whole situation starts to feel overwhelming, complicated, and perhaps even hopeless to the therapist.

If this is the way therapists feel, can you imagine what the client must feel like after 45 minutes?

Solution-talk

As Part Two of this experiment, imagine that you have spent the previous half hour talking to Mr. B about all of the things that have gone well in his life, focusing particularly on his feelings of success. How do *you* feel after this half-hour?

When I have asked therapists this question, they have talked about how, while listening to people describing their successes and accomplishments, "fact" piles up upon "fact," which makes the situation more and more pleasant for the therapist. After 45 minutes, the whole situation starts to feel remarkable and stimulating to the therapist.

If this is the way therapists feel, can you imagine what the client must feel like after 45 minutes?

READING: NATHAN ACKERMAN

The following is the start of a session Nathan Ackerman (1966) had with a family. Each speaking turn (or unit) will be numbered to simplify subsequent reference.

[1] Dr. A: Bill, you heaved a sigh as you sat down tonight.
[2] Father: Just physical, not mental.
[3] Dr. A: Who are you kidding?
[4] F: I'm kidding no one.
[5] Dr. A: Hmmm
[6] F: Really not. . . . Really physical. I'm tired because I put in a full day today.
[7] Dr. A: Well, I'm tired every day, and when I sigh it's never purely physical.
[8] F: Really?
[9] Dr. A: What's the matter?
[10] F: Nothing. Really! (Ackerman, 1966, p. 3)

Reader-focused reading

Ackerman reads Bill's sigh as a signifier of something being wrong, a problem. Ackerman comments that father's response is evasive and that his own response, unit 4, is "further pressure for a more honest response" (p. 3). Bill, the author of the sigh, says that Ackerman's reading, based on Ackerman's own concerns and not Bill's, is simply wrong. Ackerman uses his own experience as an author of sighs to give himself more authority as an expert in sighs, suggesting that Ackerman thinks that the meaning of a sigh is both fixed and determined, if not predetermined. However, Bill continues to say that his own experience is different.

What is behind Bill's sigh? After all, as Wittgenstein puts it, "An 'inner process' stands in need of outward criteria" (1958, #580). When attempting to get at meaning during any conversation, outward criteria for an inner process include the circumstances, observable in the behavior of an individual, which, when present, would lead others to agree or disagree with his avowals. It is the context of a family therapy session (a particular type of conversation) that, at least in part, gives Ackerman some grounds for his reading of Bill's sigh as part of "problem-talk" rather than just a plain, simple sigh signifying Bill's having had a hard day at work.

From Foucault (1980) comes the idea that power and knowledge, in particular professional knowledge such as Ackerman's about nonverbal codes, are always inseparably linked; and in Christopher Norris's view (1989) this leads to the notion "that what counts as truth . . . at any given time is a reflex of the various social, political and disciplinary interests that dominate the field . . . [translating] the effects of power into a 'knowledge'—a set of rules, conventions, ethical and professional codes—immune to questioning by virtue of its sheer coercive force" (p. 128)—clearly a reader-focused rather than a text-focused approach. From both Emerson (1962, 1964) and Foucault (1980) come the idea that power is also inseparably linked to resistance: We can see how Ackerman's use of power is linked with Bill's resistance. Ackerman's interpretation of the sigh simply does not fit within Bill's desired interpretation.

[11] Dr. A: Well, your own son doesn't believe that.
[12] F: Well, I mean, nothing . . . nothing could cause me to sigh especially today or tonight.

[13] Dr. A: Well, maybe it isn't so special, but . . . How about it, John?
[14] Son: I wouldn't know.
[15] Dr. A: You wouldn't know? How come all of a sudden you put on a poker face? A moment ago you were grinning very knowingly.
[16] S: I really wouldn't know. (Ackerman, 1966, pp. 3–4)

Ackerman continues his reading of what happens in the room, including nonverbal behaviors, as facts, as part of "problem-talk," by interpreting (guessing that) the son's "grinning very knowingly" was a sign that the son agreed with Ackerman's interpretation of father's sigh. Ackerman comments, about unit 11, that the "therapist now exploits son's gesture, a knowing grin, to penetrate father's denial and evoke a deeper sharing of feelings" (p. 3): But where does Ackerman get this idea that son disagrees? Certainly not from anything *said* so far. Again, it is Ackerman's professional knowledge about nonverbal signs that leads to this interpretation and the son's resistance. Of course, the son's switch from "grinning very knowingly" to "a poker face" is new material for Ackerman's interpretive efforts (guesses).

[17] Dr. A: You . . . Do you know anything about your pop?
Son: Yeah.
Dr. A: What do you know about him?
Son: Well, I don't know, except that I know some stuff.
[20] Dr. A: (to John) Well, let's hear.
Son: My . . . well, I . . . (laughs.)
F: He's nailed down.
Dr. A: He's a man?
S: Yeah.
[25] F: Come on, come on, come on. Dr. A. wants information from you.
S: Eh, all right. I'll tell you, Dr. A.
Dr. A: Your father uses his hand, you know, not like your mother.
F: Give, give, give.
Dr. A: Mother's gesture is this, and Pop's gesture is give.

"Therapist dramatically enacts the contrast of father's and mother's gestures (mother's being an accusing forefinger—father's a demanding gesture with his open palm)—in effect: *give!*" (p. 5).

[30] S: Ah, I don't have much to say, to tell the truth. I can't . . . He's
   just a normal man, I mean, he's my father. He's a good guy.
Mother: May I make a suggestion?
Dr. A: What's your suggestion?
M: Well, uh, I have been keeping an anecdotal record of the time that
   has elapsed since we were here. Not ever minute of the time, but
   anything that I think is important enough to relate.
Dr. A: Um-hum.
[35] M: Now, I think this is good for many reasons. When you read it,
   you sort of get a better view of things, and, uh, if you'd like me to
   read it, I will. If you feel you'd rather ask questions, you can. But
   that's my suggestion.
Dr. A: Well, I'm glad you called my attention to that notebook in your
   lap there. You come armed with a notebook . . .

While mother attempts to focus the conversation on the "real life"
between sessions, Ackerman reads her "notebook" as a "dossier on
family" and reads mother as "armed with this notebook" which, in his
interpretive comments, he calls "a weapon" (p. 6). Mother's "notebook"
(a signifier or a Surface Structure of a type) leads to Ackerman's giving
this notebook rather strong, problematic meanings of dossier, arm,
weapon (the signified or the Deep Structure or unconscious), rather
than, say, a diary or data.

M: . . . and I've been keeping this record since last week because I
   think it's very important. You forget very quickly what people say
   and how they say it unless you write it down right away. Now, this
   is something I do for children in my class, that I do for case histor-
   ies, and I think it's a wonderful idea.
Dr. A: Well now, what you there? A "case history" on your whole
   family?
M: Yes.
[40] Dr. A: Marvelous! How long is it?

Ackerman's interpretive remark: "Therapist is amused. Injects a
note of ironic humor" (p. 6).

M: It's not that long. I just started it. (To father) There's some here
   that you didn't see last night.
F: Oh, you cheated!

M: I didn't cheat. I just didn't tell you there was more to it, that's all. You read the front of the book. . . .

F: That's cheating.

[45] M: Oh, no, it isn't. So if you would like me to read it . . . It's sort of a little resume of my thinking in the last week.

Given what has happened thus far in the session, how could father not give mother's behavior a negative interpretation?

Dr. A: Fire away!

"Therapist's choice of phrase dramatizes mother's weapon" (p. 7). However, the term "weapon" is based solely on Ackerman's own reading rather than anything anybody in the family has said.

M: But I was quite disturbed last week; in the middle of the week, very disturbed.

Dr. A: You're picking your finger-nails, Bill.

F: No, I was . . . I had a little hangnail.

"Therapist calls attention to father's urge to pick on himself" (p. 7) rather than paying attention to whatever mother was saying.

[50] M: That's a nervous ailment of his. He picks at his feet, at a rash there, and he picks at his fingers. That's a nervous ailment of his.

"Mother instantly picks this up to accent her critical attack on father's bad habits" (p. 7). However, she is just following Ackerman's lead, since he is the one who picked on Bill's hangnail-picking behavior rather than paying attention to what mother wanted to say.

S: Pretty disgusting.

Mother and son, like father before them, have now joined in on Ackerman's reading of everything as negative, problematic.

Dr. A: Pretty disgusting, you say?

S: (to mother) How about your nervous habits?

M: I have quite a few.

[55] S: Yeah, like sitting . . . never mind. Quite a few.

M: I said I have a few.

S: Yes, and they're pretty bad.

M: All right.

Dr. A: What's the matter? Are you sore at Mother because she's picking pieces out of Poppa's fingers?

[60] S: So what? So he has a nervous habit. So don't we all?

[61] Dr. A: What kind of piece would you like to pick out of Momma?

[62] S: She has some pretty disgusting habits.

Unit 61: "Therapist's choice of words hints at son's defensiveness
concerning his erotic interest in mother." Unit 62 Ackerman reads as
"a veiled allusion to the link of dirt and sex" (p. 8). Whoa, this reading
of units 61 and 62 is certainly not based on anything any of the family
members has said in the session.

Dr. A: Well, what are they?

M: I'll tell you what they are.

[65] F: Now wait a minute. . . .

Dr. A: She's talking.

About unit 65: "The tendency to cut in, cut down, and cut out one
another is characteristic of this family" (p. 8) and, one might add, (based
on the evidence of this transcript), of Ackerman himself.

Later:

[93] M: . . . Well, some of this stuff [she wrote in her notebook] is
pretty rugged. I mean, it's what I think and it's not complimentary
in some respects. And he read it. And for the first time since we're
married, which is twenty years, he didn't get angry.

F: More, dear.

M: All right, it's a little more than twenty. He didn't get angry. And I
can honestly say that's the first time that he ever acted like the
kind of man I hoped he was. He didn't get angry at what was in
this notebook.

"Mother now talks down to father" (p. 10) and yet it is also a compli-
ment: As far as mother is concerned, something has changed for the
better.

[96] Dr. A: Well, my, my—that's quite a bit of progress. Last week
   you said he wasn't a man at all.
M: . . . The first time since we're married. It was a pleasure to see him
   not get angry at something that was the truth.
Dr. A: Look at his tongue, look at his tongue.

"Therapist again makes use of father's nonverbal gesture. He is sticking his tongue out in hidden ridicule of mother" (p. 11). Again, Ackerman's interpretation of nonverbal behavior takes priority over what
mother was saying.
   As far as Ackerman is concerned, whatever the family members say
and do is subject to his interpretation as signs or symptoms of the
problem(s) and his knowledge of the nonverbal code. As a doctor, as
an expert, Ackerman's reading carries a lot of weight with mother,
father, and son; as a result, after some initial resistance, they follow
his lead and "cut in, cut out, and cut down" one another.

> There are various criteria for the right interpretation: e.g., (1) what
> the analyst says or predicts, on the basis of his previous experi-
> ence; (2) what the dreamer is led to by *frier Einfall* [free associa-
> tion]. It would be interesting and important if these two generally
> coincided. But it would be queer to claim (as Freud seems to) that
> they *must always* coincide.
> —*Wittgenstein (1972, p. 46)*

Clearly, the reading of nonverbal behaviors, which are seen as both
literal and universal, dominates Ackerman's agenda: Nothing is what it
appears to be. As a result, Ackerman, mother, father, and son have
together constructed a problem (or problems) based on a sigh, a grin, a
notebook, a hangnail, a tongue, and belches.
   This reading of Ackerman's reading certainly clarifies what led him
to use the label "troubled families" and to look for a "clinical theory of
family" (p. 40) without seeing his part in the construction of the trouble. Like Lacan, Ackerman does not see therapy as interactional or
as a conversation between therapist and client(s). Here the target of
intervention is the isolated, individual automatic thoughts and/or irra-
tional beliefs of the clients.

This interview shows the therapist in the process of undercutting the
tendency of the marital partners to console themselves by engaging in

mutual blame and punishment. Ultimately, he stirs hope of something new and better in the relationship. He pierces the misunderstandings, confusions, and distortions, so as to reach a consensus with the partners as to what is *really wrong*. (p. 39, emphasis added)

"The family was initiated into family therapy following the crisis situation in which the younger child, Peg, eleven years old, threatened to stab her brother and her two parents with a kitchen knife" (p. 4). Whatever it is that is "really wrong" must be found well below the surface of things, suppressed and repressed into the family member's individual unconscious, and perhaps into some sort of collective family unconscious. Obviously, whatever is on the surface is nowhere near as important to Ackerman as what is beneath.

READING: JAMES GUSTAFSON

Haley: I'm still interested in the way you approach symptoms. You seem concerned solely with the symptom and how to handle the symptom rather than what's behind it.
Erickson: Remember the symptom is the handle to the patient. What are you going to do with the pot? You take hold of the handle . . . You keep your hand on the handle, and whatever you do with the pot you still have your hand on the handle.
                                                            —Jay Haley (1985, p. 71)

Let's see how another therapist, James Gustafson[3] (1986, p. 173) deals with some nonverbal behavior:

Doctor: Are you a little annoyed with me for stopping you there?
Patient: Well.
Doctor: You smile?
Patient: I have been annoyed with you at various times, here when
             . . .
Doctor: Right now.

---

[3]In this first example, Gustafson is illustrating the way he thinks Sifneos would have worked with this client. In the second example, Gustafson is illustrating how he thinks Davanloo would have worked with this client. Thus, the interviewing technique is not necessarily representative of Gustafson's approach.

Patient: When you push me like that but I know it is necessary . . .
Doctor: OK, but then you go and explain my behavior for me. I asked
  you how you felt.
Patient: Ya, you annoyed me when you were pushing me.
Doctor: I was annoying you just now.
Patient: Ya.
Doctor: OK, but you see, you smile when you tell me that, about your
  annoyance.
Patient: Ya.
Doctor: Right.
Patient: Ya.
Doctor: So you're a little uncomfortable. Usually when people smile
  at me like that, they are uncomfortable. So you're annoyed with
  my pushing but you're uncomfortable telling me you're annoyed.
  Right?
Patient: Ya.
Doctor: OK.

Here the reading of the patient's smile, the therapist's guess or interpretation—including the authority of other "people" who smile at the
therapist—is confirmed by the conversation. Unlike Ackerman, Gustafson does not seem to assume that the meaning of the smile is both
fixed and determined; his approach, although reader-focused in many
ways, also takes the text (what is actually said) into account. He only
seems to assume that the meaning of the smile is determinable.

> Nor does the subject in [Lacanian] analysis remember what hap-
> pened as a child; instead it is the always-present structure of
> thought that is investigated and it is in that thought, not in the
> past, that his [sic] problem must be solved.
> —*Andrea Nye (1988, p. 137)*

Another example, from a different case of Gustafson's (1986), involves a case of severe migraines "which were not being controlled by
the usual pharmacological methods" (p. 183):

[1] Doctor: . . . . Your resentment—you start to tell me and then
  you're shrugging and smiling and saying, "Oh, it's nothing," you
  see? That's how you lose your feelings.

[2] Patient: Well . . .

[3] Doctor: What?

[4] Patient: Is that bad?

[5] Doctor: And then you get apologetic, you see? I'm just trying to tell you as a matter of fact . . .

[6] Patient: Um, hmmm.

[7] Doctor: It's not a criticism, it's just a statement of fact, but then you feel you have to apologize . . . (pause). And then you wait for me to take the lead. See, that's another way you do it, become very passive, you see?

[8] Patient: Ya. I know that. (p. 184)

Meaning here is being developed through the equation: (a) Shrugging and smiling while (b) talking about resentment equals (c) losing feelings. Over a half-hour later in the interview:

[9][4] Patient: I know. (Long pause) I don't know where to start. It's like, it's a very insecure feeling . . .

[10] Doctor: Go ahead.

Patient: I know, I'm thinking. It's so strange, but it feels like you're attacking what I am, which is not real good. (Patient covers face with hands.)

Doctor: Um, hmmm.

Patient: I don't like that.

Doctor: How does it make you feel. (Patient sniffs.) You've just had a feeling, didn't you?

[15] Patient: Ya.

Doctor: And you tried to get rid of it.

Patient: I am trying very hard to get rid of it.

Doctor: Well, let's stay with it. You just started to have a feeling about me, you feel as though I'm attacking who you are.

Patient: Um, hmmm.

[20] Doctor: What does that feel like to you?

Patient: It doesn't feel good.

Doctor: You're trying to push off your tears, aren't you?

Patient: Ya. (Pause) (Patient cries. Therapist hands her a Kleenex.)

---

[4]Since the full transcript is not available, this number is arbitrary.

Doctor: You don't want to look at me now do you?
[25] Patient: No.
Doctor: Why not?
Patient: Because.
Doctor: Why?
Patient: If I don't look at you then maybe I can be, remain *in control.*
[30] Doctor: But if you do this we're not going to get anywhere. (Patient barely suppresses grin, covers mouth with hand.)
Patient: I know. But you asked *why,* and I told you.
Doctor: See, there it is again. I'm not criticizing your response.
Patient: I know.
Doctor: I mean, you take my observation as an attack again. You're trying to stay in control, which is like a wall, just when you and I are starting to get in touch with who you really are and what you really feel. You really want to put up this wall.
[35] Patient: Ya. I do.

Gustafson uses the various nonverbal cues to serve as a context for what the patient says, which helps to determine what the client "really feels" (a Deep Structure or unconscious). In Gustafson's reader-focused approach, the text (and the author of the text) are used to confirm his reading.

Again, over a half-hour later in the session:

Doctor: It's more than fear. You were starting to cry and that was painful.
Patient: And it still is.
Doctor: You mean, it's right there.
Patient: Um, hmmm.
[40][5] Doctor: What is that pain? There's something very painful about being attacked for who you are. That was your phase. That hurts you a lot.
Patient: Ya.
Doctor: Okay, tell me how that hurts.
Patient: Well, it's like what if I don't like what I find and that's what

---

[5]This numbering is again arbitrary, just for ease of reference.

I'm afraid of. (Hand in front of face, waving something away, covering mouth, right side of face. Very shaky.)

Doctor: That you don't like? (Pause)

[45] Patient: Well, ya, it doesn't really matter what anyone . . . no, it does matter to me what other people think.

Doctor: Yes, you're very sensitive, you're very aware of whether I'm liking what I find.

Patient: That's right.

Doctor: So there's something painful here about not being accepted, not being liked for who you are.

Patient: Ya. Probably because, um, when I was in, I don't remember, but elementary school, junior high and all that, people didn't like me . . .

[50] Doctor: Hmmm.

Patient: It really wasn't too nice.

According to Gustafson, "this reaches her pain, put behind the wall for over ten years" (p. 189). "We had gotten far enough. The torment in the face had been connected to an extreme sensitivity to not being 'liked.' The migraine trigger was as clear as could be to both of us" (p. 191). This connection had been jointly constructed by the patient and the doctor through the conversation about the meanings of the juxtaposition of verbal and nonverbal cues. "So the patient began brief therapy . . . many more episodes of migraine were understood, because it became apparent how threats of 'not being liked' were coming up in many areas of the patient's life. . . . Follow-up six months after brief therapy showed her almost completely free of migraine, an enormous shift from where she began with us" (p. 191).

The sequences from the conversation (extracted above) clearly shows a developing, inductive logic, almost an arithmetical progression,[6] that leads to the inevitable logic of the conclusion drawn from units 43 through 51. Clearly, it seems most logical that the migraines are caused by the patient's not having been liked, being attacked for who she is, as far back as elementary school, at least ten years earlier.

---

[6]It all adds up: It is almost as if the various units can be added together $(1 + 7 + 11 + 14 + 29 + 30 + 34 + 40)$ which must produce this conclusion of units 43 through 51. Like a bunch of random object on a table: If we fool around with them long enough, we can find a pattern.

However, as Wittgenstein (1972) puts it, "If you are led by psychoanalysis to say that really you thought so and so or that really your motive was so and so, this is not a matter of discovery, but of persuasion" (1972, p. 27).

Although both Ackerman and Gustafson pay a lot of attention to nonverbal parts of communication, they approach them differently. Ackerman takes the approach that nonverbal signs are transparent, fixed, and determined. In effect, Ackerman behaves as if he has a codebook that gives him the one, single, true meaning for a sigh, which far outweighs the beliefs of the author of the sigh. Gustafson, on the other hand, behaves as if he knows that a smile and a shrug mean *something*, but only the patient can tell what they "really" mean — through confirmation of the therapist's interpretations, guesses.

Both Ackerman's and Gustafson's interviews illustrate different ways that problems get constructed during therapeutic interviews.

* * *

In general, problem-talk appears as if based on the traditional Western view of "truth" and "reality." As one "fact" follows another in the sequence of conversation, we start to feel forced to look behind and beneath, forced to assume causal links and interconnections between these facts. This leads to the idea that the "underlying, basic problem" — whatever is behind and beneath — must be worked on first, before the clients can tackle other problems (which are on the surface).

However, a poststructural view suggests that the way we use language can and frequently does accidentally lead us astray. It is easy to forget that making a description has to be done in language, and that the English language (at least) necessitates a sequential ordering of the words used in a description. Mistaking *descriptions* for *causal explanations* is a result of our being imposed upon or even duped by our language to the point of our forgetting how our notions developed from figures of speech[7] and the interactional process of therapist and clients taking turns talking together, that is, asking for and being given a description. It is important to remember that neither therapist nor

---

[7]More formally, we accidentally confuse ontology and grammar.

clients are doing something wrong when this happens. Rather, the fault—if there is any—lies in language itself.

Of course not all talk about problems is problematic. Sometimes, in fact, it is useful. For instance, if the client has never talked to anyone about the problem, then talking about the problem is doing something different. Talking about the problem can also be useful if the client has not found anybody prior to the therapist who would listen attentively and take seriously what the client says.

READING: JOHN H. WEAKLAND

Talking about the problem and how it is maintained (i.e., "attempted solutions") with a focus on interrupting "these attempted solutions, either by replacing them with new and different behaviors, or less often, by reevaluation of the original behaviors of concern as 'no significant problem'" (Weakland, 1993a, p. 141) is frequently a useful approach. Weakland's reading is clearly text-focused and his emphasis on getting as many details as is possible reflects his desire to stay within what the client says and within the client's logic.

The following is a verbatim transcript of a session John H. Weakland did with a woman and her ten-year-old son at BFTC in January 1991.

[1] John H. Weakland: Obviously, we've never met before and I don't know anything about you, so would you just tell me what the difficulty is or problem that brings you here?

[2] Mother: Well, we've been having a lot of problems as far as Neal, you know: paying attention, minding his school work. He's been getting into a lot of trouble and stuff lately.

[3] JHW: What sort of things have you been having trouble with, about him minding you?

[4] M: Well, whenever I say something to him, he gets this attitude and he doesn't want to do it, you know. He's real hard headed. If I leave instructions for him to do something, it's like I didn't leave any.

[5] JHW: You would leave written instructions?
M: No, I give them verbally.
JHW: How would you put it to him, so I can get the picture?
M: Well, I would say "Neal, make sure your room is cleaned up" or

something like "straighten up the house," you know, "before I get back" or something like that.

JHW: How does he answer to that?

[10] M: "AAAAAAAAAAAAAAAAAAAAAAAAAhhhhhhhhhhhhhh" And stuff like that, and then he, you know, in school he won't—I know he's capable of doing the work and stuff, but he's just having problems goofing off and stuff, you know, and failing. Just a lot of problems. Just last week he got charged with fourth-degree sexual assault.

JHW: Well, we'll get into that, but one thing at a time. Since I'm completely new on the scene, never met Neal before, so I'm at a point of ignorance: How do you know he's capable of doing his school work?

M: Because I went and talked to his teacher and stuff and they say he's very capable.

JHW: OK.

M: You know, just kinda sitting down and work there, when I can see what he's able to do, but he's just not making the grades.

[15] JHW: But you got their statement, and they ought to be in a position to tell, and that's their business.

What part of all this are you most concerned about? What's the thing that you would most like to see changed?

M: His attitude.

JHW: OK. But he's got an attitude about school; he's got an attitude about what you tell him to do.

M: An attitude thing towards life.

JHW: OK. But you can't very well start everywhere at one, so where would you most like to see his attitude change? Where you could see some concrete shift in things?

[20] M: As far as I'm concerned, the way he treats me.

JHW: OK. About how he doesn't mind you or something else?

M: About how he doesn't mind me when I say something to him. He always smart-mouthing me back and things like that.

JHW: Give me an example of what you might say and how he would smart-mouth you back.

M: I'll say, "Neal, I thought I told you to clean up the kitchen." "I did clean up the kitchen, I cleaned up the kitchen"—and he hasn't done it. Let me think of another example. You know, if I just bring something up like "I thought you were going to do good in school today," or "Where's your daily report?" or something like that. "I don't know what happened to it" and I'll say, "Now you know you gotta bring that stuff home." He'll say, "I forgot it, God, I forgot it." That's the way he talks.

At this point Weakland has developed at least a beginning of a focal point: The interaction that results in the son bad-mouthing mother whenever she wants him to do something. It is beginning to be clear what it is that mother wants to change. This way of talking about the problem is clearly designed to find out what the client wants to see changed rather than exploring how things got the way they are. Weakland's approach so far might be summed up in this way: *Things are the way they are; therefore, what does the client want to see change?* In contrast to both Ackerman and Gustafson's approaches, Weakland's approach involves text-focused reading.

[25] JHW: OK. Let me shift gears and check things out. I think it's pretty plain, Neal, that your mother is concerned about how you behave. I'd just want to check things out with you. You see any problems with the way you behave or anything else in the family? [Neal nods.] You do? Like what?
Neal: Messing up at school and stuff.
JHW: How do you see yourself messing up at school?
N: Sometimes I don't finish my work. I get bad grades.
JHW: Well, I know this isn't a question that I can really ask you to answer in front of your mother, but is getting bad grades a problem for you? [N nods.] Why?
[30] N: I can't pass grades.
JHW: I'm just asking you in terms of yourself, not anybody else. So what? What difference does that make to you?
    I'm obviously at an age where I don't have any kids in school and from all I hear, there are plenty of kids who say "Why bother?" But you say you're concerned about getting bad grades. How does that bother you? I don't exactly see why it should. Well, OK. In any case, it's not the kind of thing you could come right out and say in front of your mother and an audience that grades don't matter to you anyway. Well, you wouldn't want to say that even if it was so.

Weakland switches to talking about the problem in a way that has become the trademark of the approach developed by him and his colleagues Richard Fisch and Paul Watzlawick[8]: What has mother done about trying to get what she wants? The focus is not on the problem but rather it is on attempted solutions that have failed.

[31 cont] What have you tried to get your son to mind you better?

M: Punishments, taking things away from him.

JHW: What sorts of things?

M: No phone calls—he can't use that anyway. No TV.

[35] So you tried that but it doesn't really work.

M: Mm hm.

JHW: Well, I ought to mention, I should have mentioned it before, that I'm not just asking what works, I'm also asking about what you tried that doesn't work, because that's just as important to know. No point to doing more that doesn't work.

M: I tried everything. I tried whoopings, taking things away from him, punishments, talking to him, and I don't know: He's OK for a couple of days and after that he goes back to the same way.

JHW: So, he will change for a couple of days and then it's just as if it didn't happen, at least it looks like it. Actually, you do get improvement for a couple of days.

[40] M: Mm hm. Just a couple days.

JHW: So, you talk to him, you ask him, "Neal, why didn't you do what I told you to do?"

M: I asked him what's on his mind and stuff, if he has a problem or something that he needs to talk to me about. "I ain't got no problem." "There ain't nothin' wrong." Actually, one time he told me he hated me. I asked him what that means. He said, "I just said that because I was mad."

JHW: How much did that get to you, though?

M: When he said he hated me, it really got to me [begins to tear].

[45] JHW: That's about as tough a thing as a mother can hear, I guess. I was just wondering whether, if you found a way to, well, let's not say to get tough, but get firm within a way that would work, would

---

[8]At the Brief Therapy Center, Mental Research Institute, Palo Alto, California.

you be in danger that he might say some more that he hated you? What do you think?

M: Sometimes I worry about him hating me.

JHW: Think that might get in your way of handling him effectively?

M: Sometimes.

JHW: Well, here again it's a question I shouldn't bring up in Neal's presence, but do you think there is any possibility he might be aware that he can sort of get to you by saying he hates you and if he might even make some use of that?

[50] M: Well . . .

JHW: Might he use that sort of power tactic against you?

M: I don't know, I don't really believe so.

JHW: Well, that might be one of those things that's best not even to think about too much, the idea that your son might be trying to pull something on you to increase his power and to lessen your rightful power as a mother.

Mother and son then calmly talk about the "sexual assault" episode at school which had occurred after she arranged to start therapy. She was satisfied with the way the school and the police had handled things and was quite confident that he son had learned his lesson from this brush with the law. (Several weeks later, in a subsequent session, she tells the therapist that the whole episode was blown out of proportion and now dropped.) After this discussion, the son was excused from the room:

[101] JHW: You've been having a hard time trying to control your son and raise him right. Seems like he doesn't listen very well. The impression I get is most goes in one ear and out the other. He doesn't give you much response at all or maybe he uses some sassy remark like "I already did it" when he didn't. Some kids say "Yes, yes" but then they don't follow through. Does he do any of that?

M: All the time. Maybe it's got a lot to do with me, you know, raising him by myself . . . 'cause a lot of time I just can't be there.

JHW: Were you raising him yourself from the beginning or was his father around for a while and you split up or what?

M: Ever since he was conceived, he's been in and out.

[105] JHW: In and out, back and forth?

M: In and out, back and forth.

Later:

[110] JHW: You'd like to see Neal behave better, listen to you better, mind you better, but it's not likely that he's going to improve totally, all at once, overnight. More likely to be gradual, step-by-step. But what would be the first sign of his improvement, to you? What, if you saw it happen . . .

M: [Interrupting] I just want him to be responsible.

JHW: . . . You'd say, OK, I think it helps to think about things as specifically as you can. What, if you saw him do it? You'd say to yourself, "He's made a first step of improvement"? Think as small as you can because things are likely to start small and build rather than big changes overnight.

M: School work.

[115] JHW: School work.

M: Improving in school.

JHW: OK. What would you need: Would you think about positive words from one of his teachers? Or, something on his report card? Or seeing him do something different at home, homework, or what?

M: Well, basically, a good report from school and he should do him homework. That would be the first sign of improvement.

JHW: OK. But the school, you mean you might talk to one of his teachers, or his report card?

[120] M: His report card.

Later:
Weakland now switches to mother's taking things away, which she reported did not work.

[130] JHW: Would I be right, when you take things away you sort of point out to him that you are doing this as a lesson to him?

M: Mm hm.

JHW: Sometimes there is more impact if something just disappears for a while, mysteriously. But that's getting a little ahead of ourselves.

Later:
Weakland now focuses on mother's reactions to her son's saying "I hate you," which is something else that has not worked very well.

[140] JHW: I'm thinking again of something else. It sounded to me before—correct me if I'm wrong—that certainly if he says "I hate you" and maybe even something in that direction, like "I don't like you," "I'm not with you," I get the impression that that sort of pushes your button somehow, does it?

M: Yah, it does.

JHW: How does that get to you?

M: It makes me wonder, why am I trying so hard? I mean, sometimes just the way he looks at me. Oh, it just tears me up.

JHW: Tears you up? How?

[145] M: Well, I guess it just, I really can't explain. It makes me angry, you know. Make me feel like he really just don't care.

JHW: Something like: You've been working hard, in difficult circumstances, to be a good mother and it looks like nothing's come of it?

M: Right.

JHW: That must hurt. I'm wondering what you might be able to do about it, 'cause I can understand the hurt, but—whether he is intending it or not—he's using that in a way that makes him more powerful and you weaker. And that's not a good thing when you're raising a kid.

Later:

[151] JHW: Sounds like even when he's not pushing your button, maybe you're pushing your own button, putting yourself down as a failure as a mother, that sort of thing. I think it's much more of a case: You've been in a very difficult situation, you've been trying hard and I think that's very impressive to me how hard you've been trying in a very difficult situation. Kids are difficult enough to raise in the best of circumstances.

I'll tell you something that—I don't know if you can do it, but if you can do it—it would start to make a difference in the situation. It might be a step in getting him to turn around—I don't know if you can do it; it will probably make you think it's a wild idea and so you couldn't do it. It might be, I know you're sincere, but it might be too much to ask you to even think of this, or wonder if it could be useful to him. That would be, next time he—I hope he doesn't say "I hate you" pretty soon, but it wouldn't have to be that. It could just be if he did something like gave you a bad time or he even gave you that real dirty look—if you could respond to that by saying "Neal, you certainly are getting on me. Apparently I deserve it 'cause I guess I've been a bad mother." I wouldn't be asking you to believe it, but only to say that to him.

M: [Smiling broadly] I guess it's worth a try.

JHW: Well, it probably wouldn't be easy.

This "little task" has been developing since early in the interview (units 42–52 and 140–148), when the son's saying "I hate you" is described as being something hard on a mother and just the kind of thing that gives the boy more power and mother less. (See Chapter Twelve for an example of a client's reinventing the same task during the course of a session.)

* * *

Clearly, John Weakland's interview is different from both Nathan Ackerman's and James Gustafson's. Weakland makes every effort to "just read the lines," to stay focused on the text itself, to take nothing for granted, and to not make any assumptions. The question the interview focuses on is not "What's wrong?" but rather, "So, given something is wrong, what are you going to do about it?"

Weakland's focus is not on the problem at all. Rather, it is on resolving that problem. All of the attention paid to the details of the failed attempted solutions is meant to (1) find out what did not work, so as not to repeat it, and (2) find out what really counts (in this case, emotionally) to the client.

* * *

Obviously, Bateson's abstract, Ackerman's interview, Gustafson's interview, Weakland's interview and a poem (one of Dylan Thomas' for example) are vastly different activities in strikingly different contexts. And yet, all of these activities use language and are embedded in language. Language in poetry and abstracts for professional journals is used rather deliberately and more carefully than language is used in psychotherapy sessions.

Paul de Man (1986) raises a point about language that is at least interesting if not provocative (in the sense of irritating as well as arousing) when looking at language use in therapy sessions (although he limits his scope to literature):

> Literature is fiction not because it somehow refuses to acknowledge "reality," but because it is not *a priori* certain that language functions according to principles which are those, or which are *like* those, of the phenomenal world. It is therefore not *a priori* certain that literature is a reliable source of information about anything but its own language. (de Man, 1986, p. 11)

Given Lacan's [w]hole, it is also not *a priori* certain that therapy sessions are a reliable source of anything but their own language because "what we call ideology is precisely the confusion of linguistic with natural reality, of reference with phenomenalism" (de Man, 1986, p. 11). Henry Staten (1984), paraphrasing Wittgenstein (in his study of Wittgenstein and Derrida), expresses this conundrum quite clearly: "Language is what bewitches but language is what we must remain within in order to cure the bewitchment" (p. 91).

De Man's use of the term "ideology" seems rather different from the Frankfurt school's use (Geuss, 1981) and so to minimize our difficulties here, I refer to the dictionary which points to a family resemblance between the uses:

> **ideology,** 1. the study of ideas, their nature and source. 2. the theory that all ideas are derived exclusively through sensation. 3. thinking, speculating, or theorizing, especially when the theory or system of theories is idealistic, abstract, idle, impractical, or farfetched. 4. the doctrines, opinions, or way of thinking of an individual, class, etc.

It is an open question whether the conclusion reached by Gustafson and his client is a result of

1. the natural, logical sequence of a conversation, or
2. one attempt after another to find the missing pieces, stopping only when he believes that "We had gotten far enough" (Gustafson, 1986, p. 191), which might mean that they got to the bottom of the problem, or
3. having "gotten far enough," which might mean simply that they now have enough information to stop searching for missing pieces, or

4. a Theory that determines ahead of time and for all time that it is necessary to look to the (memories of the) past for causation, or
5. events in (what de Man calls) "the phenomenal world."

But, given Lacan's [w]hole, how can Gustafson be certain that they "had gotten far enough"? Is it not possible that going even "further" or "deeper" might not be going too far? Where does the certainty come from when he says: "The migraine trigger was as clear as could be to both of us" (p. 191)? Is it Theory, conversation, logic, all three, two of the three, or something else altogether?

On the other hand, it seems clear that the conclusions drawn from Ackerman's interview are ideological and driven by Theory rather than by the anything in the "phenomenal world." That is, they are based on his doctrines, opinions, or way of thinking as an expert interpreter: a reader-focused reading. There is little or nothing based on the conversational aspects of the interview. Rather, the thinking is based on an theory or system of theories that is not at all obvious to us as readers.

In contrast, it seems clear that the conclusions (i.e., what's going on and what to do about it) drawn from Weakland's interview are at least closely related to the natural, logical sequence of the conversation itself, and the client's descriptions of events in "the phenomenal world," which is a result of a text-focused reading.

* * *

There is a striking shift in the therapist-client relationship from Ackerman's to Gustafson's to Weakland's session and in the organization of the session itself. In fact, the definition of therapy[9] (an event, a series of events, a practice) constructed by the participants is almost discontinuous, perhaps mutually exclusive. That is, if Ackerman's session is used as a defining prototype, then Weakland's session would likely fall outside that definition and vice versa. The construction of each of the participants, client, therapist, and reader, in each of the three cases is radically different. As a reader we experience the interaction, the client's position as well as the therapist's in each case, in very different ways.

---

[9]See Chapter One.

In Ackerman's case, the therapist is constructed as a powerful interpreter of obscure signs, which suggests that only he and not the client
knows what is really going on. The therapist is constructed as an expert
and the client as someone who is ignorant about what she is doing.
Thus, in this case, the resistance that is constructed is necessarily as
strong as the therapist's power.

In Gustafson's case, the position of the client is quite differently
constructed. While the therapist is again constructed as an expert with
special knowledge, the client's position is rather collaborative in contrast to the client's situation in Ackerman's case. The client is constructed as having all of the information necessary to understanding
the clinical problem and the therapist is constructed as having the
knowledge about where to look for that information. The therapist, as
expert, knows exactly where to look (the past) and what to look for
(unpleasant or traumatic events constructed as causal to the current
problem). As a result, the resistance constructed is minimal (in comparison to Ackerman's case), since the client's agreement is constructed
as necessary to the success of the therapy.

Both the therapist and client are constructed differently in Weakland's case. While the therapist is constructed as having special knowledge (about how problems are maintained), the client is constructed
as having all of the information/knowledge necessary for resolving the
problem. The therapist is constructed to be a detective who just follows along wherever the client's clues lead. Thus the client's construction is privileged and taken seriously, in contrast to the situation in
Ackerman's case where the client's construction is disqualified and the
therapist's is privileged.

Chapter Eight

GETTING TO THE "PROBLEMS" OF THE SURFACE

"All tore down, sir, but get in anyway"—He opened the rear door
of the cab for me—"and I'll run you down to number seven"
[Bloom's home, #7 Eccles Street] "except, you understand it's not
there, but no charge, sir, can't charge for an address that doesn't
exist, can I?"
—*Dublin Taxi Driver*[1]

NUMBER SEVEN ECCLES STREET was the Dublin address of a fictional
character, Leopold Bloom, invented by James Joyce. Thus, one might
say, it never existed and yet someone is looking for #7 and the taxi
driver is willing to take him there—without charging because it does
not exist! Or does it? (As Gertrude Stein is reputed to have said about
Oakland, California, "There's no there there.")

USING NUMBERS TO BUILD A BRIDGE

Life is the art of drawing sufficient conclusions from insufficient premises.
—*Samuel Butler*

---

[1]C. Barnard (1993) O'Ireland! *Modern Maturity*, Feb/Mar issue.

To paraphrase Wittgenstein (1958, #43): For a large class of topics
or themes — though not for all — in which we employ scaling questions,
the meaning of a number is its *use* and, in particular, its use in *relationship* to the other numbers on the scale.

As anyone who has played around with numbers knows, like words,
numbers are magic. As is our usual practice, we took a cue from some
of our clients' spontaneous use of scales and developed ways to use
scales as a simple therapeutic tool. Unlike most scales used to measure
something based on normative standards (i.e., a scale that measures
and compares the client's functioning with that of the general popula-
tion along the bell curve), our scales are designed primarily to facilitate
treatment. Our scales are used not only to "measure" the client's own
perception but also to motivate and encourage, and to elucidate goals,
solutions, and anything else that is important to each individual client.
John Weakland points out that our scales are used:

> When there's something that's not concrete, you concretize it in a way
> that, from a distance, looks very damn strange: You invent one of these
> scales. By inventing one of these scales, you can take a whole, damn,
> amorphous thing and reduce it to a number; now it's real and concrete.
> In a logical sense, that's an impossible task. But you do it, and now it's
> real . . . [thus] when it's global, general, amorphous, and vague — you give
> it a number. (Weakland, 1993b)

Scales allow both therapist and client to use the way dialogue works
naturally by developing an agreed upon term (i.e., "6") and a concept
(i.e., on a scale where "10" stands for the solution and "0" for the
starting point, "6" is clearly better than "5") that is obviously multiple
and flexible. Since you cannot be absolutely certain what another person meant by his or her use of a word or concept, scaling questions
allow both therapist and client to jointly construct a bridge, a way of
talking about things that are hard to describe — including progress toward the client's solution.

For instance, a young woman thought that she was halfway toward
her goal "10" (vaguely defined as "feeling better") and therefore gave
herself a "5." When asked about what would be different when it was
"6," she simply said, "I will feel more sixish." Of course, the therapist
would have liked to have more concrete and specific descriptions of
"5" and "6," but the client was unable to describe things concretely,

even though she was sure she would know when she was at 6. Scales give us a way to creatively misunderstand by using the numbers as a way to describe the indescribable and yet have some confidence that we, as therapists, are doing the job the client hired us to do.

The meanings of "5" are constructed in the process of therapist-client interaction. "5"'s meanings are not in any way transmitted from one person to another. In fact, therapist and client frequently can and do have different and perhaps even contradictory meanings. Through the use of numbers, the client's meaning(s) are privileged and accepted without question and thus teaching "the client to recognize the contextual cues that would enhance their behavioral control" (Efran & Schender, 1993, p. 74) is unnecessary, uncalled for, and perhaps disrespectful. For the client and the therapist the "5" gets its meanings principally from the scale to which it belongs: "5" is better than "4" while it is not quite as good as "6."

Scaling questions were first developed to help both therapist and client talk about nonspecific, vague topics involving feeling states such as "depression" and obscure topics such as "communication." All too frequently people talk about topics like these as if the experiences depicted by these terms were controlled by an on-off switch; one is either depressed or not and couples communicate or they do not. However, fortunately, it is not that clear-cut. Even people who say that they have been depressed for years will usually be able to describe times (minutes, hours, days) when they were less depressed. By developing a scale, the range of depressed feelings, as well as both the complaint and progress, is broken down into more or less discrete steps. For instance, if a scale is set up on which 0 stands for the most depressed a client has felt in recent weeks (or better, 0 stands for how the client felt at the time of the original phone call seeking therapy) and 10 stands for the day after the problem(s) that brought them to therapy are miraculously solved (which includes being free of depressed feelings or, at least, not being aware of any depressed feelings and therefore being able to do something that the client now feels unable to do), then any rating above 0 says not only that the complaint is less bothersome but also that things are already better and progress is being made toward the solution. The solution, in this situation, no matter how vaguely and nonspecifically described, is not just the absence of depressed feelings; rather, it is the achievement of 10. The numbers allow for this simultaneous double meaning without becoming either ambiguous or contradictory. That is, a "6" simultaneously means that the client is 60% of the way toward his or her solution and that the complaint is 60% less bothersome. Thus the complaint is only 40% as "influential" as it once was.

The great majority of the scales we use are set up as going from 0 to 10, with 10 standing for the desired outcome. This is based on the idea that a change from 100% to 99% is only a 1% relative change. However, a change from 0% to 1% is mathematically approaching infinity. Ideas of change and progress (and even "magical" numbers) naturally grow by having something added to them. Progress added to progress leads eventually to enough progress. The scales are constructed and manufactured purposefully in order that they be extended. Neither client nor therapist can know ahead of time what these extensions involve. The details do not pre-exist and thus the miracle question (de Shazer, 1985, 1988, 1991) is used to help clients figure out just exactly what kinds of things they might count as extensions on the various scales.

Scales can be thought of as "content free," since only the speaker knows what she means by 5. Other people, such as therapists, just have to accept this fact. The therapist can discuss how the client's life will be different when she moves from 5 to 6. The natural follow-up to this question's response is to ask what the client needs to do to move from 5 to 6. ("When you move from 5 to 6, what will be different in your life? Who will be the first to notice the changes in you? What will your mother do differently when she notices the changes in you?")

We have found that scales can be used with small children, developmentally disabled adults, and even those who tend to be very concrete. That is, anyone who grasps the idea that 10 is in some way(s) "better" than 0 and that 5 on this sort of scale is better than 4 can easily respond to scaling questions.

For example, a cute little eight-year-old child was brought to therapy in the aftermath of having been molested by a stranger in a shopping mall. During session four the therapist drew an arrow between a 0 and a 10 on the blackboard, with 10 standing for the time when therapy was finished. The therapist asked the child to indicate how far she had come in therapy by drawing an "x" on this line. The child drew her x at about the 7 mark. She was next asked what she thought it would take to go from x to 10. After several minutes, during which she shifted her weight from side to side, she hit upon an idea and said, "I know what!" "What?" asked the therapist. The little girl replied in a rather somber voice, "We will burn the clothes I was wearing when it happened!" The therapist, amazed at this creative idea, said, "That's a wonderful idea!" Soon after this session, the child and her parents had a ritual burning and then went out to dinner in a fancy restaurant to mark the occasion (the end of therapy).

ANSWERS/QUESTIONS

> The stupidity of people comes from having an answer for everything. The wisdom of the novel comes from having a question for everything. The novelist teaches the reader to comprehend the world as a question. There is wisdom and tolerance
> in that attitude.
> —*Milan Kundera*[2]

Like Kundera's novel(ist), we take nothing for granted and thus have questions for everything, including miracles: "Suppose that tonight after you go to sleep a miracle happens and the problems that brought you to therapy are solved immediately. But since you were sleeping at the time you cannot know that this miracle has happened. Once you wake up tomorrow morning, how will you discover that a miracle has happened? Without your telling them, how will other people know that a miracle has happened?" Of course, this is unrealistic and impossible: Most people do not believe in miracles. Even for those who do believe in miracles, such occurrences are very rare indeed. Obviously, the most realistic thing a therapist can expect a client to say is "I don't know." (This is, in fact, a rare occurrence.)

This "miracle question" is a way to begin constructing a bridge between therapist and client built around the (future) success of the therapy. The phrasing of the question includes a radical distinction between problem and solution, which is a result of our noticing that the development of a solution is not necessarily related to the problems and complaints in any way (de Shazer, 1985). The absence (of the complaint/problem) is a given and the client is being asked to describe an effect, i.e., the morning after the miracle or the day after success

---

[2]Quoted in Madigan, 1993, p. 219.

that is either without a cause or at least without a known or knowable cause. (A miracle can be defined as an effect without a cause.) The client's answers to the question, the descriptions of the day after the miracle, give both client and therapist some sense of what it is that the client wants out of therapy.

Of course a (transcript of a) solution-focused interview will "seem strangely *unconversational*" (Efran & Schenker, 1993, p. 72) when it is compared to a "normal" conversation two people might have over lunch, because the therapeutic conversation has a clear and distinct focus and purpose. A conversation with an architect about your dream home will focus on where you want the doors, windows, fireplaces, stairs, walls and so on. This conversation will also seem unconversational because of its focused purpose. At the end of your conversation with your architect, your satisfaction should come from you thinking, feeling, and believing that you got what you wanted, while the architect's reward (in addition to his fee) comes from doing the best job he or she can helping you to get what you want. There is nothing in the nature of this kind of conversation that demands that it be "fun" (Efran & Schenker, 1993, p. 72) for the architect.

In recent years there has been a great deal written about questions in therapy and many, many times I have heard the comment "What a great question!" This reflects the field's developing focus on the linguistic, interactional, and conversational aspects of doing therapy. Questions, once thought of as functioning primarily to gather information, have been re-thought as interventions. For instance, Karl Tomm, a questioner of questions, sees the therapist's *reflexive* questions as "formulated to trigger family members to reflect upon the implications of their current perceptions and actions and to consider new options" (1988, p. 9). Other types of questions (lineal, circular, strategic, etc.) are seen to work in different ways. At least in part, the distinctions between the various types of questions are based on the therapist's assumptions and intentions (Tomm, 1987, 1988). It is, of course, valuable and necessary that we look at the relationship between assumptions and intentions, theories and practices. Otherwise doing therapy might become confused with having just any old garden variety conversation.

Tomm (1988) gives the following example of a *reflexive question*: "Let's imagine there was something that he was resentful about, but didn't want to tell you for fear of hurting your feelings, how could you

convince him that you were strong enough to take it?" which is intended to elicit a *reflexive answer*: "Well, I'd just have to tell him I
guess" (Tomm, p. 9). Certainly both the therapist's assumptions and
intent are clear enough in Tomm's example.

This leads to some questions:

1. What is it about the client's response that makes it *reflexive?*
2. Is it *reflexive* solely because it is a response to what the therapist
   intended to be a *reflexive question?*
3. What is it about the therapist's question that makes it a *reflexive*
   question as such?

Of course therapists want clients "to reflect upon the implications
of their current perceptions and actions and to consider new options"
(Tomm, 1988, p. 9). But does the therapist's intent have any control
over what happens? Does a therapist's intent have more control over
the client's response than an author's intent has over a reader's response? Probably not. It is not altogether clear that things are this
simple and straightforward. In fact, it is quite clear that therapist intent
has little or no control over the client's response. The reader's response
is not determined by the author's intention and the client's response is
not determined by the therapist's question. On the one hand, questions open up possibilities for various types of answers while, on the
other hand, they simultaneously constrain and limit possible answers.

As an experiment, let's look at some segments of an initial interview
(Deutsch & Murphy, 1955) beginning with the client's first speaking
turn: [unit 2] "Well, I've felt fairly good, Doctor. (Pause) Much better."
This looks like a "great answer" and, logically, it should have been
preceded by a "great question." What was the doctor's question?

Interestingly, the doctor's question was: [unit 1] "Could you tell me
how you happened to come to the hospital?"! The doctor takes the
client's answer [unit 2] at face value and so his next question is: [unit
3] "Much better, in what way?" (Deutsch & Murphy, 1955, p. 29).

It is only when the answer is useful that we can say that the (so-
called "great") question was a useful one. In fact, we frequently find
that what the question actually meant can only be known by the answer it triggers. That is, we can tell more about what kind of question
a question was by looking backward from the answer. A question can
only become "great" when it preceded a "great answer." A "great an-

swer" is judged to be "great" when and only when it is useful to the purpose of therapy.

IN COLOGNE

This consultation session was done in front of a large group of therapists as part of a seminar. Since the couple spoke only German, an interpreter was involved. In this situation scales really come into their own, not only as a bridge between therapist and client but as a bridge across the differences in language (including both words and concepts).

[1] de Shazer: So, just pretend they [the audience] aren't there.

First of all, I want to thank you both for coming today. I hope that it will be useful for you but there are no guarantees on that. I'm more sure that it will be useful for those invisible people out there. We'll try to make it as useful for you as we can.

My first question is: Let's say that "10" stands for what you hoped to get out of therapy and "0" stands for how things were before you started therapy. Where would you say you are between "0" and "10" today?

[2] Mrs. K: "5"

[3] Mr. K: "8"

[4] SdeS: "8," you've gone from "0" to "8" [pointing to Mr. K] and you from "0" to "5."

[5] Mr. K/Mrs. K: Yeah.

[6] SdeS: How did you do that?

[7] Mr. K: "0" is completely helpless, no freedom. The goal "10" would be feeling free in whatever you are doing and thinking.

[8] SdeS: OK. How did you get from "0" to "8"? How did you do that?

[9] Mr. K: By self-reflection, a little egoism.

[10] SdeS: OK. Go on, how else?

Mr. K: Jumping off from being a man who was brought up in very close norms and rigidity, and doing what I want, actually want to do.

SdeS: OK. What about you? [to Mrs. K] How did you get from "0" to "5"?

Mrs. K: I live outside the hospital. I have a child.

SdeS: Mmmm. Good. And what else?

[15] Mrs. K: I begin to live.

SdeS: What are you doing differently now that you are at 5 that you were not doing at 0?

Mrs. K: Taking more responsibility for myself.

SdeS: OK, good. Good. In any particular times and situations?

Mrs. K: No. In my whole life.

[20] SdeS: Your whole life.

Mrs. K: Ja.

SdeS: Good, good, good. He says 8 and you're saying 5. How come? What do you think he sees that says to him it is "8" compared to your "5"?

Mrs. K: He was not as much down as I was.

SdeS: OK. What do you think? How come you are at 8 and she's at 5? How come you are 3 points higher?

[25] Mr. K: I can't say if it's really 8, it was just a self-description.

SdeS: Of course, sure.

Mr. K: It depends on how you think about the two diseases we have. I can't say which one is more serious.

It is clear that they both are answering in terms of themselves as individuals rather than as part of a couple. Thus their being in therapy must be due to either her problem(s) or his rather than due to a "relationship problem." Obviously the question (unit 1) is open for either or both readings.

SdeS: That's a point. What are you doing differently at 8 compared to 0?

Mr. K: I had to do an effort of will, in the beginning, and this was my first step. I don't know if she was able to do that. I was.

[30] SdeS: [to Mrs. K] If I had asked you to guess what he'd say, would you have said "8"?

Mrs. K: Ja, ja.

SdeS: Ja. Well, same question. If I'd asked you to guess . . .

Mr. K: Maybe even 6.

SdeS: Interesting, interesting. Has it been a lot of work or just a little bit to go from 0 to 5, 0 to 8?

[35] Mrs. K: Very much work. I was a make-up artist at an opera house and a dancer. I went to school. I used to be really somebody in the society and then suddenly I was nothing at all any more.

SdeS: Umm hmm. What do you say: A lot of work or just a little?

Mr. K: Very much.

SdeS: OK. I've a strange question: Do think it's going to be more work or less to get to 10 than it was to go from 0 to 5, 0 to 8?

Mr. K: I don't think I have to reach 10. Probably I cannot.

[40] SdeS: OK. OK. So, is 8 good enough?

Mr. K: It could always be better, but ja.

SdeS: What about you? What do you think? Is it going to be more work or less from 5 to 10?

Mrs. K: Less.

SdeS: Good, good. Glad to hear that.

Let's suppose that you get really lucky and tonight there is a miracle and you get to 10 while you are sleeping. But you can't know this miracle has happened because it happens while you're sleeping. How will you discover tomorrow morning that you got to 10?

[45] Mrs. K: I would know this for sure, because every morning when I wake up my illness is there.

SdeS: Right, and after the miracle it is gone.

Mrs. K: Ja.

SdeS: What would be there instead?

Mrs. K: My own love for myself.

[50] SdeS: And, as a result of that, what would you do differently?

Mrs. K: I would accept myself.

SdeS: Hmm hmm. Right. And, how do you think he would know? Without your telling him?

Mrs. K: He would see that I get up and go to school.

SdeS: Umm hmm. [to Mr. K] Same question: How would you discover that there's been this miracle?

[55] Mr. K: I would not notice it inside myself, but in how other people act.

SdeS: How's that? What would you notice?

Mr. K: It is so difficult to live with this disease in this society. When you're down, even then they are stepping on you. And when you are 50/50, some will still give you a kick and others will let you get up. I will notice a change in how others will treat me.

SdeS: Umm hmm. How will she know that you have had this miracle?

Mr. K: I don't believe that she would notice. It might be and it could be that, if the miracle happened, we both would know if we belong together or if we should go separate ways.

[60] SdeS: OK, OK. Two possible miracles.

Mr. K: Ja, if she went to school I wouldn't notice it as a miracle because she wants to do that now too.

SdeS: Right, right. But she would *do* it rather than just talk about it.

Mr. K: She wanted it even when she was very ill.

SdeS: I see. Are there days, or parts of days, that you remember, when things were like they will be at 10?

[65] Mrs. K: For him, ja.

SdeS: Ja? How close to 10?

Mrs. K. Close.

SdeS: 9?

Mrs. K. Even more.

[70] SdeS: Even more? 9.5? When was the most recent time?

Mrs. K: Four months ago.

SdeS: Four months ago. You agree?

Mr. K. Ja, even closer the last time.

SdeS: From your side

[75] Mr. K: There were also days when I was at 2 or 3.

SdeS: Sure, sure. OK. What do you think, where you two are now at 5 and 8, how can you succeed in at least maintaining that? How can you maintain 8?

Mr. K: A healthy egoism. I don't let myself be seduced.

SdeS: Umm hmm. How do you do that?

[80] Mr. K: The past six years, I had the feeling that I lived my life the second time. Childhood is very important. As a child, you have to do everything that parents want. All that made me, made my decision very strong not to allow . . . to send me to war anymore, to nobody and . . .

SdeS: Wow. How did you do that? That's a big . . .

Mr. K: I have to fight for it every day.

SdeS: Um hmm.

Mr. K: And I long for the day when I don't have to fight for it anymore.

[85] SdeS: Absolutely. [to Mrs. K] How about you? What do you think you need to do to maintain where you are now at 5?

Mrs. K: I have a pension [receives a disability check] and I feel strapped down by that.

SdeS: Sure. So, what are you going to do?

Mrs. K: Other people have decided for me.

SdeS: Ja, so, what are you going to do?

[90] Mrs. K: I'll fight against the disease to my last gasp.

SdeS: Ja, good. Are you going to fight against the people that gave you the pension, too?

Mrs. K: Ja!

SdeS: Will he help you?

Mrs. K: Ja.

[95] SdeS: Who else will help?

Mrs. K: My daughter, I think.

SdeS: Sounds like a big job you have given yourself. [Long pause] Could we bet on your winning this fight?

Mrs. K: Ja.

SdeS: Ja? Good, good. Obviously, when things get to 10, they are not going to just be at 10 and stay there, right? There is bound to be some fluctuation. How far down from 10 will it still be "OK," just a part of the normal fluctuation?

[100] Mr. K: Down to 1, because I find it normal for me.

SdeS: Oh, OK. How about you?

Mrs. K: Not lower than 5.

SdeS: No lower than 5. OK. So, you are at the bottom right now of what you think is normal.

Mrs. K. Ja.

[105] SdeS: OK. So, if I got this right, if things were to be no worse than this, for both of you, over the next six months, then that will be OK, at least?

Mr. K: It even could be a bit lower, I have to live with that.

Mrs. K: I don't want things to go worse, since I was totally down.

SdeS: No worse. That would be OK?

Mr. K/Mrs. K: Ja.

[110] SdeS: Good. Congratulations. That means that you've done a good job. [Shakes their hands and the hands of the therapist.] [To therapist.] But actually, they are the ones that did it. [Long pause.]

But the question now is: How confident are you that you can stay within this normal range for the next six months? Very confident equals 10, not so confident equals 0, or somewhere in between?

Mr. K. As for me, I'm sure that I can keep that and live with the ups and downs.

SdeS: Right. And you?

Mrs. K: About 5.

SdeS: 5. And where would your daughter say? How confident is your daughter that you can stay at 5, at the lower part of "normal"?

[115] Mrs. K: Completely confident.

SdeS: Does she know you better than you know you? [Everybody laughs.]

Mrs. K: Ja.

SdeS: Do you think we should believe her?

Mrs. K: Ja.

[120] SdeS: You say 5, she would say 10, so we should believe her 10?

Mrs. K: Ja.

SdeS: You agree?

Mr. K: Ja, ja.

SdeS: Ah ha!

Does this sequence mean that Mrs. K is underestimating herself at 5, since she now says we should believe her daughter who would rate her at 10? Has this sequence, units 114–124, reframed the whole situation? This is a wonderful example of a great answer, but does that mean that unit 114 was a great question?

[125] Mrs. K: She is a wonderful girl!

SdeS: Um hmmm. So, if she were here today, what would she suggest that you two do to get to the next point up the scale?

Mrs. K: She would be interested in everything that is going on here. She is only three.

SdeS: I know that. [Everybody laughs.] Pretend for a moment that she could make suggestions.

Mr. K: She would leave us like we are. [Mrs. K nods.]

[130] SdeS: OK. Good for her. What about your best friends, where on the scale would your best friends say you are?

Mrs. K: We don't have any friends, except for one woman friend.

SdeS: What do you think she would say?

Mr. K: She lives in Switzerland. She would agree with our daughter.

Has the 5 now been reframed at 10 through the daughter and the woman friend?

SdeS: OK. Is there anything else that you think we should talk about today before we take some time off to think about things?

[135] Mrs. K. I would like to ask you something. Can schizophrenia be completely cured, is that possible? Or, is it possible to lead my own life?

SdeS: You are doing that now.

Mrs. K: Ja.

SdeS: I'll think about your question. Anything else?

Mrs. K. What do you think about medication? Are you for it or against it?

[140] SdeS: Neither. If it is useful . . .

Mr. K: Who knows?

SdeS: Ja, who knows?

Mrs. K: To me they are not useful. I have to do it by myself.

SdeS: It's hard work.

[145] Mrs. K: And I have to get healthy.

SdeS: OK. So, let's take about 10 minutes. You can go walk around, have some coffee.

The scaling questions, dominant throughout the interview, make staying on the solution side of the distinction easier for everybody. In fact, the scales are set up in such a way that all the numbers are on the solution side. That is, "1 to 10" is used to mean success while "0" is just meant to mark the point before the start of the therapy. Since clients frequently perceive some positive change or changes prior to the start of therapy, the first therapy session can then be put on the solution side through the use of scales.

While we can have no idea what "5" or "8" actually represents in terms of behaviors, thoughts, feeling, perceptions, etc., these numbers depict the clients' perception of difference, change, progress, and movement toward solution. For instance, at one point in the session, I ask Mrs. K about how confident she was that she would stay above "5" and, therefore, that the solution would continue to develop and she said "5." And then I asked her about her daughter's confidence that the solution would continue to develop and she said "10." Obviously, Mrs. K thinks her daughter has more confidence in her than she herself does. I then ask if we should believe her three-year-old daughter rather than her! Both mother and father agreed that we should. At this point, I have used the difference between her perception of her confidence ("5") and her perception of her daughter's confidence ("10") to help her increase her level of confidence: She said that her daughter's "10" was more credible than her own "5"!

After the Pause

SdeS: Well, again I'd like to thank you for coming today. I have certainly been impressed with how far you have come. And the hard work you have put in; that's really impressive. And I think I agree with you that the next part will be easier than the first part was. But that does not mean that it will be easy, it could be just less hard. I have a couple of suggestions for you, but before I do that, I'll answer your questions.

I can only answer your questions in terms of research rather than talking about you individually. The research says that, over the long term, in effect, "schizophrenia is 'curable'"—that is, people can lead a normal life. And also this research says—in answer to the second part of your question—that the majority of the people stop taking medications as they become more successful. Whether that is true for you, in this case, who knows?

OK. I have a couple of suggestions that came to me that I think you might perhaps find useful. [To Mrs. K] The main thing you need to do is to continue doing what you have been doing because it has worked so well so far. [To Mr. K] And you, particularly since you are saying it is higher for you that, what you need to do is more of that.

And, I think you both have a sense of humor?

Mrs. K/Mr. K: Ja, ja.

SdeS: I thought so. So, I have a suggestion for you [Mrs. K] I think might be useful. And that is, get yourself a coin, and each night before you go to bed, you toss the coin. [Demonstrates] And if it comes up this side, that means that the next day you should pretend to be at 7 instead of at 5. Pretend, secretly, to be at 7. And don't tell him about this. Don't tell him what the coin said or that you're pretending to be at 7. OK? [She nods.] And the other days, when it comes up the other side, you don't have to pretend. And see if you can fool him with the pretending.

[To Mr. K] And when you become convinced that she is at 7 and not just pretending, the minute you get that idea, that means that 24 hours after that, you'll be going to give her some sort of reward. You understand? [Both nod.]

I want to wish you both the best of luck and thank you for coming today.[3]

Since Mrs. K's "5" was the bottom of what she would consider a normal range for herself, "7" represents the middle of the range from "5 to 10." Mrs. K, through her daughter, had become quite confident that she could and would reach "10." Nobody, including her, knows what exactly this "7" represents in terms of thoughts, feelings, behaviors, etc. All we all know is that it can be used to depict noticeable improvement. Interestingly, she does not actually have to do any pretending for the task to be effective: All that needs to happen is that Mr. K. *perceives* her doing something that indicates to him that she is either (a) pretending to be at "7" or (b) is really at "7." But, how can he tell the difference? After all, the assignment requires her use of her sense of humor to try and trick him into either (a) believing that she is only pretending to pretend or (b) believing that she is only pretending to be "7" while still at "5" or (c) being at "7" on a day when she is not required to pretend. That is, it is clear that on days when she gets "heads" she is to pretend to be at "7," but it is not at all clear what she is to do on days when she gets "tails," since on those she "does not have to pretend." Does it mean that on days when she gets tails she does not have to pretend to be "7" and therefore she acts as though she is where she is at "5" or does it mean that she should really be at "7" without pretending?

Regardless, on some day when he thinks things are "really" better for her, on some day when he thinks she is not just pretending things are better for her, he is asked to give her a reward. So, whatever he does for her that she thinks might be a reward for really being better works to reinforce her being better—again regardless of whether or not that was the intention behind his doing something for her.

Thus the task sets things up so that each of them can interpret

---

[3]According to Doctor Thomas Keller, the therapist, after this session Mr. K decided he did not need any more therapy and so he stopped coming. Mrs. K had five more sessions within the next six months. During this period she stopped the medications slowly and, after some hectic days, found stability by herself. She is talking more to people and feels that she has made progress in developing an adult relationship with her parents. In general, things seem to be much better and to have stabilized.

whatever the other one does as an indication that things are continuing to get better.

*   *   *

"Schizophrenia" is a word that psychiatrists (and others) use to represent a patient's extreme deviance from a hypothetical norm.[4] This norm does not exist as such: Each individual deviates from this norm to a greater or lesser extent and each individual's degree of deviance may vary at particular times and/or in particular situations. But no individual is ever completely normal at any one particular moment in time. The concept "normal" is actually empty: There is always only deviance.

At some point in time, Mrs. K was diagnosed by some psychiatrist as "schizophrenic" or as having "schizophrenia." That is, he or she thought that Mrs. K was "extremely deviant" at that particular time in that particular place. According to Thomas Szasz (1970), "the diagnostic label imparts a defective personal identity to the patient. It will henceforth identify him to others and will govern their conduct toward him, and his toward them. The psychiatric nosologist thus not only *describes* his patient's so-called illness, but also *prescribes* his future conduct" (p. 203). Regardless of the psychiatrist's intent and regardless of the official psychiatric meanings of the word "schizophrenia," Mrs. K has read this diagnosis as meaning "once a schizophrenic always a schizophrenic." She does not like this idea and wants a cure but she does not know if a cure is possible.

On the other hand, her diagnosis of herself is that she is now at "5," which means to her that she is at the bottom of what she considers "normal," which is significantly better than "0." From my perspective, her staying at "5" or moving further up the scale is her job. The therapist's task is to help her accomplish that by continuing to focus on

(a) what is happening,
(b) what she is doing,
(c) what her husband is doing, and
(d) what the therapist and therapy is doing

to help keep things within the "5 to 10" range.

---

[4]Of course, this is not the only use psychiatry has for the term "schizophrenia." Other uses are beyond the scope of this chapter. See, for instance, Szasz (1970).

For her "normal" is the range from "5 to 10" which includes the normal ups and downs of everyday life. Of course her "normal," like everyone's, including yours, mine, and the diagnosing psychiatrist's, is deviant from the psychiatrist's hypothetical norm. Each individual's normal is always already deviant!

As long as her normal is satisfactory for both her and her husband, then whether or not the diagnosing psychiatrist would think her normal is "normal enough" is irrelevant.

"Schizophrenia" started out as the name of a concept and subsequently has become reified and thus is frequently[5] read or interpreted as static, as not changing over time. The term is usually read to mean that cure is impossible: Only remission is possible and therefore relapse is always lurking around the corner. Mrs. K's own diagnosis is, however, fluid and changeable (from "5 to 10").

The differences between the psychiatrist's diagnosis and her own diagnosis points to the radical distinction my colleagues and I draw between "problems" and "solutions" and to the distinction between "reader-focused reading" and "text-focused reading." Prior to her mentioning the term "schizophrenia," there was no indication during the interview of any extreme deviance. My hunch is that if she continues to see herself as staying within the range from "5 to 10" she will no longer have to meet with any psychiatrists. Therefore, she will no longer be in any situations where a psychiatrist will be able to read her deviance as being extreme and thus, in a very real sense, she will no longer "be schizophrenic" and she will no longer "have schizophrenia." This is "true" if for no other reason than the fact that someone who does not see psychiatrists fits within their hypothetical norm (de jure if not de facto). That is not to say that should she run into a psychiatrist after five years of staying within her normal range he or she might not still find her deviance to be extreme. But if this normal range remains satisfactory for her and her husband that is really all that matters; if she has no complaints about her life, then she will have no need to seek out another psychiatrist.

---

[5]Some psychiatrists and the field of psychiatry may have other ways of reading the term "schizophrenia" which are beyond the limited scope of this chapter.

Chapter Nine

LISTENING, OR TAKING WHAT THE CLIENT SAYS SERIOUSLY

It is a capital mistake to theorize before you have all the evidence.
It biases judgment.
— *Sherlock Holmes (A Study in Scarlet)*

John H. Weakland (JHW): Yeah. I think that sounds very simple, but I don't think it is simple . . . I think it's a very complicated operation.

Steve de Shazer (SdeS): Yeah, it is. It's so easy to "read into" . . . You've got to watch out for this. People, therapists in particular I guess, are taught to "read between the lines" . . .

Michael Hoyt (MH): "Listen with a third ear" . . .

SdeS: Diagnosis, interpretation, understanding . . .

JHW: "Perceptiveness" . . .

SdeS: Yeah. To me, however, the danger of reading between the lines is that there might be nothing there. So, you've just got to listen to what the client says. Just stick on the lines of things. The client says that getting out of bed on the south side makes for a better day than getting out on the north side. Well, then, goddammit, tell him to get out of bed on the south side! As crazy as that may sound.

MH: If it works, don't fix it.[1] Do more.

---

[1]Which also clearly means, "If it is not broke, don't break it" (G. Miller, 1993).

SdeS: Yeah, do more of it. I had one case like that. He moved the bed over so he couldn't get out on the north side. He'd run into the wall trying to get out on the north side of the bed.

That would be a different challenge to have—instead of "perceptivity training," have a "simplicity training," or a "beginner's mind" or "denseness training."

MH: "Keep it simple."

SdeS: "Stupidity training."

MH: Maybe the fact that you weren't trained in psychology originally
. . .

JHW: That's a great help.

SdeS: I think that my training in music helps.

JHW: (To MH) Ask him a little more about "taking it seriously," because I have this feeling that it doesn't just mean one simple thing, that it may mean, maybe, a lot of variations on that point: "Taking it seriously." And I got your example; that's clear. But I don't think it always means the side of the bed, that sort of thing.

SdeS: Exactly. A counterexample of "taking it seriously" is when clients come in and tell you "This is the problem. And it's a big, heavy, monstrous problem." To you, it looks trivial. And you go and tell them about all these other people who really have problems.

JHW: Yeah, yeah.

SdeS: That's a counterexample. . . . Clients tell you they've got a problem; then they've got a problem, and you'd better take it seriously. You also better take it at face value if they tell you they ain't got no problem. That's the other side of it.

He [a client] comes in, and somebody sent him because he drinks too much. He says he doesn't drink too much or that it's not a problem. Leave it alone: Take it seriously.[2]

*   *   *

---

[2]This transcript is part of an interview with John H. Weakland and me organized by Michael Hoyt that took place December 3, 1992. The complete interview appears in Michael Hoyt (1994), *Constructive therapies* (New York: Guilford).

While doing therapy, my colleagues and I attempt to pay close attention to exactly what the clients say and how they say it, while simultaneously refusing to take anything on trust alone (which sometimes means asking what are apparently stupid questions). At the same time, we attempt to follow a conversational "principle of charity." This means that we are willing to assume that other people make sense of their experience in ways not radically unlike our own. That is, anybody who was in the *same* situation as the one the client describes would probably describe the situation in much the same way. Furthermore, this principle of charity includes the assumption "that the attitude of holding-true—of attaching a particular significance to sentences that get things right—is as important for them [i.e., the clients] as it is for us" [i.e., therapists] (Norris, 1989, p. 60). "Taking it seriously" also means that what the clients say should be treated with due respect and construed responsibly by paying attention to details.

Each interview is build around three major concerns: (1) What can the clients tell us (what can we know) about that they (and we) will find useful in constructing a solution? (2) What can clients (and their therapists) reasonably hope for? and (3) For clients and us alike, what ought we to do?

BUILDING HER OWN MIND

> When patients come into my office, I greet them with a blank
> mind and I look them over to see who and what and why they are
> without taking anything for granted.
> —*Milton H. Erickson (Haley, 1985, p. 114)*

To attempt to follow Holmes' and Erickson's advice to "greet them with a blank mind," I have found that it is usually best to force this blankness on myself by only knowing the basics, i.e., the client's name, address, age, occupation (if any), etc.

[1] Client: I've been at the . . . company for a year and a half.
[2] Steve de Shazer: Mm hm.
[3] C: And I've been at the . . . part-time for like six months . . .
[4] SdeS: Which is better for you?
[5] C: I like both.

[6] SdeS: OK ... and would you prefer I call you Candace, or Candy?

[7] C: It doesn't matter really.

[8] SdeS: What do your friends call you?

[9] C: Candy.

[10] SdeS: Candy. OK. Then [laughing] maybe I should call you Candace.

C: [Laughing] Candace.

SdeS: OK. Um, let's see. OK. Well, should we jump right in? What brings you in? Oh, before you start that, after about a half-hour or so, I am going to take some time out to figure out, think about what you've been saying, and maybe if some of my team is back there, talk with them about that. And ... then I'll come back and let you know what our thinking is. Before I forgot to tell you that. So, what brings you here today?

C: Mmm. I've been having problems really.

SdeS: Mm hm.

[15] C: Adjusting to my situation.

SdeS: Mm hm.

C: I was, I was married for like nine years and now it's over.

SdeS: Mm hm.

C: And, you know, I end up living with my mother.

[20] SdeS: Ah. OK.

C: So, now I'm not getting along with anybody at all.

SdeS: Ah ha. OK. So, how long has it been since you were back living with your mother?

C: Ah, ummmmmm, I say about seven months now.

SdeS: Mm hm. That's not easy.

[25] C: No.

SdeS: No.

C: Not at all.

SdeS: Yah, OK. and ah, ...

C: I'm not a good talker.

[30] SdeS: No?

C: No, I can answer your questions and try to explain myself, but I'm not good at just talking.

SdeS: OK, well, I'm not either, so ... I'm much better at listening. [Both laugh.]

C: Heh.

SdeS: So your mother . . . to answer my other question, your mother
   is taking care of the kids, when you're working?
[35] C: Some of the time, sort of.
SdeS: Sort of. Mm hm.
C: She does and she doesn't.
SdeS: Mm hm.
C: You understand?
[40] SdeS: Well, no but ah, . . .
C: Well, OK, it's, it's, OK—when I work she says she is going to keep
   'em herself but . . . she keeps em, yah, she does.
SdeS: Mm hm.
C: I'd say yah. Either her or their father keeps them.
SdeS: OK. So their father is still in the picture. Mm hm. And you'd
   rather he wasn't I guess from what you said . . .
[45] C: Right.
SdeS: And the face you are making.
C: [Nods]
SdeS: Mm hm, OK. [Pause]

Her facial expression is, of course, part of her language and how
she is using it needs to be checked out rather than assumed. Her words
and her facial expression fit together; one confirms the other. At this
point in the conversation it seems clear enough that what brings her
in to see me is the sort of thing that brings people in to see a therapist.

As I see it, complaints are sort of like subway tokens. That is, they
get the person through the gate but that does not determine which
train he or she will take, nor does it determine which stop he or she
will use to get off. Where the person wants to go is not predetermined
by where they start out.

The fact that both of us paused after I said "OK" [unit 48] suggested
to me that it was now my turn to talk, since she did not either continue
talking about the children's father or introduce a new topic.

The Day after the Miracle or "Where Are We Going?"

[48 continues] So, now, this may be a strange question for you, but,
   ah, I am going to ask anyway. Suppose one night there is a miracle.
C: Mm hm.

[50] SdeS: And the problems that brought you in here today are solved. OK? This happens while you're sleeping so you can't know it's happened.

C: OK.

SdeS: OK? The next day, how would you discover there'd been a miracle? What would be different that would tell you . . . that a miracle has happen?

C: [Long pause] Mmmm . . . I don't know. [Long pause]

Nothing other than "I don't know" is really an appropriate answer to this "miracle question." Therefore, I just wait in silence, giving her a chance to think. Since any conversation involves turn-taking, my not taking a turn means that it is still her turn. There is no need to push by either expanding the original question or finding other ways to ask the same question.

[53 continued] I can't really say . . . um . . . for one thing I'd get up and not hearing my mother argue about anything would be relief.

SdeS: OK. What would she do instead of that? What would she do instead?

[55] C: Tell me "good morning," and ask how I'm doing.

SdeS: Mm hm. OK.

C: And act like she cares about my kids.

SdeS: Mm hm. OK.

C: And, I don't know, I think it'd be a much brighter day, too.

[60] SdeS: In what way?

C: I don't know, I think I'd get up feeling much more happier about myself.

SdeS: Mm hm. OK. And what would you do then? What would be different, if you're feeling brighter and happier, what would you do that would be different then?

C: I don't know, I'd probably lose my mind.

SdeS: Well, maybe, yah. How would it show up? What would you do . . .

[65] C: Ummmmm.

SdeS: that you don't do now?

C: Ummmm. I don't know, I think I'd smile a little more.

SdeS: OK.

C: And my attitude would be different.

[70] SdeS: Right.
C: Mmmm, I don't know, I think I'd be a much more happier person.

So far, so good. We have a beginning picture of what it is she wants from the therapy. The next step is to expand this to her immediate context and her interactions with other people.

[72] SdeS: Mm hm. OK. And, ah, being happier and smiling more, and so on, would make some difference in how things go for you . . . with other people?
C: Mm hm.
SdeS: And if your mother's happier, what else? Ah, OK. So what else would somebody else see? What would your mother see? What would your mother see different about you after this miracle?
[75] C: I don't think my mother will see anything at all. I mean, I can go and win a million dollars and it still wouldn't change her attitude about me at all.
SdeS: Mm hm.
C: So, I don't think she'll see anything.
SdeS: OK, but if she *could* . . . what would she see, what would she see if she wanted to or could?
C: I'm a much more happier person.
[80] SdeS: Mm hm.
C: Better to get along with.
SdeS: Mm hm.
C: I'd have more weight. Ah . . .
SdeS: Um hm?
[85] C: Let's see, ummm, I guess that's it.
SdeS: OK. Well, if the children could tell us, what would they tell us about what they might see the day after the miracle?
C: What would my children see? A much more fun mom.
SdeS: Mm hm.
C: Spend more time with them.
[90] SdeS: Mm hm. OK. More fun with the kids, more time with them. What else would they notice?
C: That's all, really.
SdeS: OK.
C: That I can think of.

SdeS: Right, right. What about their father? What would he notice
different about you do you think?

[95] C: Mmm, he'll see how much more happier—no stress, or anything.

SdeS: Mm hm.

C: I think that's it, 'cause right now he hates me.

SdeS: Mm hm. Mm hm. Well that doesn't mean he can't see something different about you if you change, does it? . . . just because
he hates you.

C: I guess.

[100] SdeS: Sometimes it . . . sometimes . . . it makes a difference.
OK. So, ah what about people at work? What do you think they'd
notice the day after this miracle?

C: Basically everybody would just see that I'm much more happier,
much more relaxed, and ummm, just relaxed, happy.

Now that we have some beginning pictures of life without the prob-
lem(s) that brought her to see me, we need to find out something
about her experiences with being happier, more relaxed, smiling more,
etc. If we find out that she has had such experiences, then we can
have some confidence she will know when she has them again.

Constructing Exceptions or "When Has That Already Happened?"

[102] SdeS: Mm hm. So, when are the times now when you're a little
bit more relaxed and happy?

C: When I'm with my boyfriend.

SdeS: Mm hm. OK.

[105] C: Sometimes.

SdeS: Sometimes. OK. What would he tell us about that? The day
after the miracle? What would he say?

C: Ummmm, he'll see that I'm much more happier, . . . like hey, everybody would see I'm much more happier,

SdeS: Yah.

C: and little more at ease,

[110] SdeS: Mm hm.

C: You know.

SdeS: Is there anything he might see you do that would tell him for sure that there'd been this miracle, that you're happier, something you'd be doing that would signal this?

C: Talking with confidence in myself.

SdeS: Mm hm.

[115] C: Actually knowing who I am, what I like, and what I want.

SdeS: OK.

Thus far, how she has described the day after the miracle both in terms of how she will know and how others will know has been rather vague and global. Interestingly, none of her descriptions involve the absence of a "problem"; rather, they involve the presence of something desirable. Although more details would probably be useful so that she might know more exactly what she is looking for, what she has said so far indicates that she is looking for the kind of things many clients look forward to getting out of coming to therapy.

[117] C: I'm a helpless case.

SdeS: What do you mean?

C: I'm, you know, just weird.

[120] SdeS: What do you mean?

C: I am. I don't know, I, I, I don't know if I'm confused or what. Ah, I don't know.

SdeS: What do, er, well, what gives you that idea that you're confused?

C: Because.

SdeS: That you're a hopeless case?

[125] C: Because, I know what I want, but, but, knowing what I want and doing it is two different things for me.

SdeS: Mm hm.

C: I mean, I can say it and mean it but, doing it is like a whole new thing.

SdeS: Yah. So what do you want?

C: I want to be left alone.

[130] SdeS: By whom?

C: My husband . . .

SdeS: Mm hm.

C: My mother.

SdeS: Mm hm.

[135] C: And my sisters.

SdeS: Mm hm.

C: That's all.

SdeS: OK. So if you want to be . . .

C: Actually I just need to get away.

[140] SdeS: Mm hm.

C: You know, I just, mmmm, just like I, I never have time for myself, until I left him.

SdeS: All right.

C: And it is like, now that I'm not with him, I feel a little better about myself, and it's like I want some . . . independence.

SdeS: Mm hm.

[145] C: You know,

SdeS: Mm hm.

C: Want to do stuff for myself now.

SdeS: Mm hm. Right.

C: Be on my own for a while.

[150] SdeS: Mm hm, but?

C: But, nobody thinks I have a mind of my own to do that and everybody want to say "You shouldn't do this, you shouldn't do that," and "Do it this way and do it that way," but, no one wants me to take that chance, you know, and see if I can do it for myself.

SdeS: Mm hm.

C: Or not.

She is clearly giving me very strong hints to be very careful about telling her to do anything. In fact, it is obvious that making suggestions about what to do is exactly the wrong thing for me to do. Therefore, taking the hint, I ask her about what *she* is going to *do* rather than attempting to tell her what to do.

[154] SdeS: So what are you going to do?

[155] C: I don't know. Run away I guess. I don't know.

SdeS: OK. Maybe. Well, if you run away, what are you going to do?

C: Well, I don't even know where I want to go.

SdeS: Mm hm. OK. Yah.

C: [Pause] I don't know, see I told you I'm weird.

[160] SdeS: Well, I don't know about weird, but ah, but maybe, we'll see if I agree later on.

C: Heh.

SdeS: But, you say you'd like to run away, you'd like to be alone. You'd like for people to . . . respect you.

C: Yah.

SdeS: So ah, ahhhh, . . . if you did, where would you run to? So, what else could you do instead of running?

[165] C: Ahhh, . . . scream?

SdeS: Scream.

C: I don't know.

SdeS: Mm hm. Have you tried that?

C: No.

[170] SdeS: No. Have you ever tried running away?

C: Yaaah.

SdeS: Yah?

C: It ain't worth . . .

SdeS: OK. OK. Have you tried screaming?

[175] C: MMM. [Nods her head]

SdeS: At whom?

C: At myself really, because, to sum it all up, all I want to do is just be happy, you know?

SdeS: Sure.

C: It just seem like it just so impossible for me to be happy or no one wants me to be happy, that's what it is.

[180] SdeS: Mm hm.

C: It's like, it's wrong for me to want something for myself, or want myself to be happy or

SdeS: Mm hm.

C: Do what I think will make me happy.

SdeS: Right. OK. You think that your husband, mother, and so on think you shouldn't be happy, or you don't know . . .

[185] C: Well, they, I mean, they have that attitude like, I mean, when I left my husband, I left my husband for a reason.

SdeS: Sure.

C: And, it's just that all the while we been married it's been terrible, you know, I been sick in bed, you know and it just kept going on and on and on until I just got tired, you know. And I left.

SdeS: Mm hm.

C: OK, I left and I was just gonna be on my own, you know.

[190] SdeS: Right.

C: I'm too old to be living with my mother in the first place with kids.

SdeS: Sure.

C: So, she was like, don't, I mean "move in with me for a while and then," you know, "until your husband cools down," you know, "and then you can move into your own place." But, now, you know, we don't get along. It's like nothing I can do pleases her.

SdeS: Mm hm.

[195] C: Everything I do gets on her nerves.

SdeS: Mm hm.

C: And she can't seem to sit down and talk to me, you know. Nobody ever sits down and just talks to me.

SdeS: Mm hm.

C: You know, everybody just wants to tell me but no one wants to talk to me.

[200] SdeS: OK. And if they would talk to, what would you be saying?

C: I mean I'd be telling them how I feel.

SdeS: Mm hm.

C: But no one cares to hear how I feel, so, I just go on.

SdeS: Mm hm. So, could you get your own place?

[205] C: Now, you, . . . um, yah, I can.

SdeS: Mm hm. Would that make it better?

C: I think it would help a lot.

SdeS: Mm hm.

C: A lot more, I mean, get me going a little more than now because, like now, just staying there with mother, it's not working, I'm depressed and I'm upset and I'm angry and

[210] SdeS: Um hm. Um hm.

C: I just can't deal.

SdeS: Um hm. You know, you know, when you go back and live with your mother, . . . 30 years old and it starts to feel like you're 17 again, doesn't it?

C: Mm hm.

SdeS: . . . "Come in on time" . . . and all that stuff.

[215] C: Um hm.

SdeS: Yah. So, you could get, it might be difficult, but you could get your own place.

C: Um hm.

SdeS: Um hm.

C: It'd be unsafe for a while too, but . . .

[220] SdeS: Um hm.

C: . . . until my husband drops off the face of the earth. Then I'd be OK.

SdeS: Mm hm. So, you're afraid he might do something?

C: Well, I, he, he at this point says he can't live without me and I'm the only person in the world for him, and he don't want to make a start over with no one else . . .

SdeS: Mm hm.

[225] C: And, when I just, you know, tell him "I don't want to be bothered, just leave me alone, go away," then he wants to threaten me.

SdeS: Mm hm.

C: And so, I had to leave for a while, me and the kids, and my job and everything, because he was threatening to come up there and beat me and you know, or have someone else beat me, or

SdeS: Mm hm. Mm hm.

C: Whatever. He has beaten me over and over again

[230] SdeS: So, that has happened.

C: Yes.

SdeS: Mm hm.

C: And it's like, he just won't leave me alone.

SdeS: Mm hm. OK. So if you're going to . . . does it make it safer for you then to live with your mother? Is that part of it?

[235] C: Ah, she thinks it is. I don't think so because the last time he beat me, it was at my mother's house.

SdeS: Mmmm.

C: So.

SdeS: Mm hm.

C: And she wasn't there so I don't see any difference . . .

[240] SdeS: Mm hm.

C: You know.

SdeS: Right. Right. So, did you get the police involved and all that, too?

C: No.

SdeS: No. Um hm. How come you chose not to?

[245] C: Um, I don't know, I was just scared and all I could think of was just leaving, and just going away.

SdeS: Mm hm. OK.

C: So he couldn't harm me.

SdeS: Mm hm. But you didn't get far enough away? . . . or what?

C: Yah, I got far enough away, but my mother, you know, she knew where I was at and you know, she would call me every day and then she was like, she didn't like the conditions where I was at, so she wanted me to come back.

[250] SdeS: Mm hm.

C: And stay with her.

SdeS: Mm hm.

C: My mother, I don't know, we, it something, I mean, she acts like she cares but she don't.

SdeS: How so?

[255] C: Because, it's like she wants me there with her.

SdeS: Right.

C: But she don't. It's like, um, I can't really explain it, it's, she, I mean, she complains about every little thing I do, you know, "Every grown person needs their own place," but then when I say, "I'm going to look for a place," then she says, um, "You know it's not safe for you to move just yet," you know, "Why you want to rush your life? why you want to get out there so he can hurt you?" and you know, like that, but . . .

SdeS: Mm hm. Mm hm.

C: Staying there with her, she, I mean we don't get along, we don't talk, we don't speak to each other too much.

[260] SdeS: Mm hm.

C: You know it's like, I told her she hates me because she won't talk to me,

SdeS: Mm hm, I see, so, . . . it's just as difficult for her to have a kid come back I suppose, as it is for you to go back.[3]

[263] C: Not really, because . . .

SdeS: Yah?

[265] C: I have, I still have two sisters left there that lives with her and she just cherishes one of them.

SdeS: Mmmm. Mm hm.

C: That's her favorite . . . or whatever.

SdeS: Oh yah, OK. So, what can you do that's going to make it safe enough for you?

---

[3]A mistake: Arguing before the data.

C: Just get a restraining order, I don't have.

[270] SdeS: But if you get a, yah.

C: . . . just move.

SdeS: Will he pay attention to a restraining order?

C: I don't know, he acts crazy sometimes.

SdeS: Um hm.

[275] C: I mean, he really goes off.

SdeS: Um hm.

C: I don't know. If he'd just drop off the face of the earth, I'd be safe.

SdeS: Yah. But that's . . .

C: . . . No.

[280] SdeS: Probably . . .

C: . . . not going to happen.

SdeS: Not going to happen.

C: No.

SdeS: So you've got to do something else.

[285] C: And all I can think of is just getting a restraining order.

SdeS: OK.

C: That's all.

SdeS: OK. So, have you taken some steps toward doing that?

C: No, 'cause he hasn't bothered me too much anymore, he was like, "OK, I'll give you what you want. You want a divorce, I'll give you this divorce and I won't bother you."

[290] SdeS: Mm hm.

C: But, I don't know, I mean, he hasn't like threatened me or anything . . .

SdeS: Hmmm.

C: or whatever.

SdeS: OK.

[295] C: He's just . . .

SdeS: OK.

C: He's like, see, he's really sneaky so I never know . . .

SdeS: OK.

C: what to expect.

[300] SdeS: But he said now, that he's going to give you the divorce and leave you alone.

C: Mm hm.

SdeS: And since that time, has he left you alone?

C: Mmm, yah.

SdeS: Yah.

[305] C: I mean he hasn't bothered me or anything, he still calls and check and see what time I come in.

SdeS: Mm hm.

C: You know,

SdeS: Mm hm.

C: And all that stuff.

[310] SdeS: But he hasn't threatened you recently since that point, since he said he wouldn't do it?

C: No. He hasn't threatened me . . .

SdeS: [For] how long . . .?

C: He just . . .

SdeS: How long ago was that?

[315] C: Oh, I'd say about two weeks ago.

SdeS: Mm, mm hm.

C: Maybe.

SdeS: OK.

C: He just likes to call and tell me how wrong I am.

[320] SdeS: Mm hm. Mm hm. OK. Yah. And ah, that doesn't make life any easier.

C: No.

SdeS: No. It's easier than getting beat up by him.

C: Yah. Mm hm. That's no fun at all.

SdeS: No . . . no. OK, so, somehow, in order to do what you want, and be who you are, do what you like to do, somehow you got to get yourself safe.

[325] C: Mm hm.

SdeS: Do you feel safer at mother's than you might alone?

C: I, well, I mean, I . . .

SdeS: Whether it really is or not, do you feel safer or not?

C: No, I'm, I'm not afraid or anything like that, I'm, I'm used to being by myself so that's not the problem and feeling safe or whatever, is not the problem, *being* safe is.

[330] SdeS: No, yah, right. But you're saying it's no safer there as far as being safe, you're not necessarily safer at your mother's than you would be somewhere else.

C: Right.

SdeS: That's why I was asking about feeling safer.

C: Mm hm.

SdeS: But you don't feel any safer there, either?

[335] C: No.

SdeS: No, OK. OK. So, what are you going to do?

C: I don't know. [Long pause] I don't know what to do. I know what I want to do, but ah, I don't know what to do.

SdeS: Yah, you want to, well, what is it you want to do?

C: I think, I, what I want to do is just be on my own for a while.

[340] SdeS: Right.

C: Just move to my own place and just be on my own for a while.

SdeS: Mm hm.

C: To relieve some of this tension I have built up in me.

SdeS: OK. OK. Is this move, being on your own for a while, is that you and your kids or just you?

[345] C: Yah, me and my boys.

SdeS: Yah, OK. OK.

C: I think we'll be much happier.

SdeS: OK, so what steps do you need to take to do that?

C: Um, just find a good enough area for to raise them, I mean I have like, little boys.

[350] SdeS: Yes.

C: And, just finding a place, you know, an area or whatever, safe enough for us.

SdeS: Mm hm.

C: And then, trying to get a good general idea of what my income's gonna be like every month to pay rent.

SdeS: Right. Right.

[355] C: And, I have to clear up my credit, since he done put every-thing in my name. Now the creditors call me every day to remind me that I have bills in my name, thanks to him . . .

SdeS: Mm hm.

C: . . . that I have to pay for.

SdeS: Mm hm. Mm hm. Ah, I can see why you're thinking about running away.

C: That's just half of it. [Long pause]

[360] SdeS: I'm sure. [Pause] So, how close are you to starting to take these steps, finding a place that's safe enough?

C: Um, I'm getting closer. I, I want to just go, and . . .

SdeS: Yah.

C: . . . just do it.

SdeS: OK.

[365] C: But ...

SdeS: So what's stopped you from just doing it?

C: I don't know, I don't know if I'm afraid now or what.

SdeS: Mm hm.

C: I shouldn't be afraid though, because that's something I want to do so bad.

[370] SdeS: Mm hm.

C: I don't know. Maybe if I had somebody to kinda like, support me, maybe ...

SdeS: Mm hm.

C: ... I'd just go on and do it.

SdeS: Support you in what way?

[375] C: You know, just say, well you know, say, "You can do it," you know, "This is what you want to do, you can do it," you know.

SdeS: Mm hm.

C: Keep letting me know I can do it, until I can feel that confidence ...

SdeS: What about your boyfriend?

C: Yah, I don't know. I mean, he's good, he does that.

[380] SdeS: Mm hm.

C: But, I think, ah, he has problems too now, and ...

SdeS: Mm hm.

C: Trying to deal with mine and trying to help him, that's not going to work.

SdeS: No. No. OK. Ah, what about women friends?

[385] C: No. No. I have no friends ...

SdeS: Um hm.

C: ... at all.

SdeS: How's that?

C: See, I have, well see, I had a lot of um, I don't know how to say, a lot of bad experiences with woman friends,

[390] SdeS: Mm hm.

C: Because of my marriage, so I don't care for woman friends at all.

SdeS: OK. What about people through the church, your church?

C: Yah, but my husband has been through the church too, so ...

SdeS: Mm hm. Mm hm.

[395] C: There's no one there either.

SdeS: Mm hm.

C: So I have nobody . . .

SdeS: Mm hm.

C: . . . but myself.

[400] SdeS: Just yourself.

C: Am I weird yet? Nah?

SdeS: [Shrugs, pause] But, so, OK, you get these ideas, you know what you want to do, you think you should do, so you're going to have to talk yourself into it. If nobody else is going to do it.

C: That's not easy. Nobody else listens to me, then I feel like why should I listen to myself.

SdeS: Yah, right, exactly. How do you convince yourself that you should listen to yourself?

[405] C: Yah, I don't know. See, that's why I need somebody to be on my side or something.

SdeS: Mm hm.

C: Nobody's on my side or nothing, everybody just tells me how wrong I am or what they don't like about me, but I don't have nobody to say, well, "There's a good part of you, do this," or "You do have a mind of your own, so why don't you try it and see." I don't have anybody to do that.

SdeS: Mm hm. Mm hm. In that case, you have to do it yourself.

C: Yah, but that not easy,

[410] SdeS: No, no.

C: Because, I can't do it, I mean I can tell myself, and then, I don't do it.

Constructing a Bridge between the Future and Past Success

SdeS: But, so, so far you don't believe yourself, when you tell yourself. I see. I see. So, have there been times in the past when you told yourself these things and you did these things?

C: Yes. When I finally left my husband.

SdeS: Mm hm.

[415] C: I, I ah, kept saying over and over again that I was going to do it and it took me a while, but I did it.

SdeS: Mm hm.

C: And I feel good about it.

SdeS: Mm hm.

C: You know.

[420] SdeS: OK.

C: So, I'm doing good a little bit.

SdeS: Mm hm.

C: But...

SdeS: OK. so that's what you think—that you talked yourself into that, and that that was a good thing to do.

[425] C: Mm hm.

SdeS: And, although it's not perfect, things are better for you since you did that.

C: Mm hm.

SdeS: OK. How about before that, were there times in your life where you talked yourself into doing something, that...

C: I didn't even have a mind before then, I mean I just, it was like, I just listen to what everybody say, and do this or do that, and you know I was just too busy trying to please everybody else, trying to do what everybody else, what makes everybody else happy, and not what makes me happy.

She has just described a major exception: one time when she sees herself as having used her own mind. She decided what she ought to do and did it and, importantly, she sees that it made things better for her. This is exactly the kind of thing she is looking for; this is what she wants more of in her life. Now we have a better picture of where she wants therapy to go and we also know that she has the necessary skills, etc.

[430] SdeS: Mm hm. Mm hm.

C: It was like I didn't have a mind of my own.

SdeS: Mm hm.

C: To tell myself anything.

SdeS: So if that's true, then you've come a long way already?

[435] C: Yah.

SdeS: ... OK. Now you've got to ... you might be finding yourself confused now or then, but at least you've got a mind of your own.

C: Yah.

SdeS: Good for you. OK. So, you're really going to have to get on your own case, aren't you? Boy. How are you going to do that? Well, you're going to get a lot of noise from these other people, aren't you?

C: Mm hm.

[440] SdeS: Like . . . your mother, your sisters, I suppose.

C: Mm hm.

SdeS: You're used to listening to that.

C: Mm hm. See, I can listen, you see, you know I see I'm not good at just expressing myself or..

SdeS: Can you turn off your ears? Not listen even though they're yakking on about . . .

[445] C: I, I don't know, my feelings get hurt easily and fast.

SdeS: Mm hm.

C: You know, when, when it's somebody I care about, you know, and I just feel so badly if somebody I care deeply about and then, they can't seem to find anything good about me or help me.

SdeS: Right.

C: Or anything they say they want to help me, but you know,

[450] SdeS: Mm hm.

C: They want to criticize too much. I mean I hear more criticism than I—I don't even hear anything about, you know, what I can do or, "I'll help you do this," or anything.

SdeS: Right.

C: You know, I, I live with my mother, I try to do everything I can to please her but then she tell me I don't appreciate living there with her.

SdeS: Right.

[455] C: And . . .

SdeS: Right, OK.

C: It's hard.

SdeS: Yah, yah. And you listen to that.

C: Yah.

[460] SdeS: And you end up getting hurt by that, you said. What would happen if you didn't listen?

C: Then I have "an attitude" according to her.

SdeS: Mm hm.

C: I just don't want to listen or whatever.

SdeS: Mm hm.

[465] C: I been trying to ignore her, you know. It's not easy. I have to leave then, you know, and I don't like that, just up and leave and don't say where I'm going or anything. Then when I . . .

SdeS: Right.

C: . . . finally do come back, then she's upset because I left and didn't say I was going anywhere or when I was coming back or whatever, but I have to leave and, I been crying too much, I been crying for nine years and I'm tired.

SdeS: Mm hm. Mm hm.

C: You know, I'm tired of crying, I just want to be happy, you know, I just . . .

[470] SdeS: Sure. Sure.

C: Want things to work for me sometimes.

SdeS: Sure. Sure. Sure. Mm hm. OK, so

C: Do you understand me?

SdeS: Well, no, I'm not sure yet.

[475] C: [Laughter] You're not sure yet?

SdeS: I'm not sure yet.

C: I don't understand myself.

SdeS: I think that, um . . .

C: That I'm confused?

[480] SdeS: No, I don't think you're confused, I think that you're just, ah . . .

C: Scared?

SdeS: . . . learning how to be you.

C: Oh.

SdeS: Still learning how.

[485] C: That's true.

SdeS: And you were saying before, you're just getting a mind of your own, or listening to it at least.

C: Mm hm.

SdeS: Listen to yourself for the first time.

C: Do I need help?

[490] SdeS: Do you? You say you do.

C: Yah.

SdeS: Hm, well, if you say you do, then maybe you do.

C: But you don't know?

SdeS: I don't know.

[495] C: Oh.

SdeS: I guess what I don't know is whether you need the help, or you just think you need the help.

C: Oh. Ohhhh, I think it's both.

SdeS: Both. OK. I'll take your word for it. So, the question I have though, is, ah, how you're going to do this, as you get more of your mind, you use more and more of your mind, and ah, listen to yourself and do what you're telling yourself what you should do and want to do, what you're going to do about these ears of yours, they are so sensitive about what other people are saying?

C: I don't know, I mean, I been hurt so much it seems like I should be immune to it and just tune it out, but it's like, it's rough when you're in the corner by yourself and you have people you care about, and, and love and they can't find it nowhere to, you know, to try and help you or . . .

[500] SdeS: Mm hm.

C: See how you feel about anything.

SdeS: Mm hm. Mm hm. Well . . .

C: I don't know what to do.

SdeS: Yah.

[505] C: And I don't want to hate them.

SdeS: No.

C: I don't know what to do. Run away, I guess.

SdeS: Well, you said that, you, you ran away. Where would you run?

C: Umm, I don't like different places, I don't know. I don't know. I don't know where I want to go.

[510] SdeS: Mm hm. It doesn't do any good to run away unless you are running away to something.

C: Right.

SdeS: Or somewhere at least.

C: I don't know, all I just know is I just want to go away. Go away anywhere, it don't matter.

SdeS: Don't matter, OK. So, why don't you do that?

[515] C: I don't know where to go.

SdeS: Well, you just said anywhere.

C: See, I'm confused, I don't know, I just want to go away, but I don't know where.

SdeS: Mm hm. Mm hm.

C: Then I say "anywhere."

[520] SdeS: Right.

C: But I don't really want to be just "anywhere."

SdeS: Right. You want to be?

C: Mmmm, I guess just somewhere by myself.

SdeS: Mm hm.

[525] C: For a while.

SdeS: Mm hm. Even if that's here in Milwaukee?

C: Mmm, yah. Yah, here.

SdeS: Mm hm.

C: I pretty well feel safe here, more than going to a different city where I don't know anything or anyone.

[530] SdeS: Right, right.

C: But then why should I like it here, nobody cares about me anyway? So it's like being somewhere where there's no knowing anybody or know . . . no help for me.

SdeS: Mm hm. Well, so you're going to have to do something.

C: Yah, but I don't know what.

SdeS: Well [pause]. So I suppose that, before I take some time to think about this some more, I have some other questions I guess. Um, so has your husband tried to talk you into coming back?

[535] C: Yah. He's been doing that since I left . . .

SdeS: Mm hm.

C: . . . when he beat me.

SdeS: Mm hm. And is your mother trying to talk you into going back to him, or,

C: In a way, she wants me to go back there, but, I don't see why she would say that, I mean, he, this like the third time he done beat me, I mean . . .

[540] SdeS: Mm hm.

C: My common sense tells me that if I go back he's gonna do it again. Why she . . .

SdeS: That's what the statistics say, yah.

C: Why she don't understand that, you know, if I go back, he's gonna do it again, you know?

SdeS: Mm hm. Mm hm.

[545] C: I'm not happy there, I don't want to be there.

SdeS: Right. OK, is there anything else I should know before I take some time out, anything else that comes in your head that might be important for me to know today?

This final question is often useful because (1) a "no" gives the conversation a place to stop, a finishing point, and (2) something that the client has not yet said that she thinks is important will also serve as a place to stop, a way to complete the interview. At times this will mean that the interview needs to continue a little while longer; however this still marks the end of this part of the session.

[547] C: Um, no.
SdeS: OK. I'll be back in five, ten minutes. You just relax. OK?
C: Mm hm.

As an experiment pretend you were behind the mirror. From behind the mirror, what would you want to point out to me that I should pay particular attention to? What should I ignore? What should I do? What should I be sure not to do? What came most strongly to your attention? What step(s) toward constructing a solution have been taken? How best can I help her use what she has already done and already knows? If you had been the therapist, what would you do next? Take at least 15 minutes, but no more than 30 minutes, to think about this before continuing to read.

Where Candace wants to go can be summed up as *having her own mind*. This means thinking things out for herself, deciding what to do, and then doing it. Achieving this will allow her to have a life more like the one she described as "after the miracle" has happened. She'll be happier, smile more, talk with confidence, be more relaxed, and be a more fun mom [units 48 through 115].

As she sees it, her feeling confused is one of the things that gets in her way. Therefore, I introduced the idea that confusion might be a "symptom" of having her own mind. It is, of course, both. In either case or in both cases, when she knows her own mind she does not feel confused.

After the Pause

[550] SdeS: OK, I'll tell ya. Really, I'm impressed with how far you've come in developing your own mind. Ah, I think you have done very well with that project.
C: You do?
SdeS: Mm hm. Mm hm. And, you're feeling better than before, because you developed your own mind, hmh?
C: Yah.
SdeS: And you followed your own ideas about what's good for you. And I think that that's a big step forward; maybe not just one step,

more than one step in there. And I think you're on the right track
with that, and I think that your feeling confused right now about
what to do is a good thing.

[555] C: It is?

SdeS: And I bet you think that's weird, right?

C: Yah.

SdeS: I'll tell you why I think it's a good thing. Because, being confused, right now, prevents you from doing something before you
are sure it's the right thing for you to do. It's part of having your
own mind that you get confused sometimes, until you know what
to do, until it's really clear. It prevents you from making mistakes.
And, ah, so don't force yourself to do something before you are
sure it's right for you. Just let yourself be confused until you've
made up your own mind, what to do is clear to you. Ah, well, as
you say, people are going to tell you what to do and ah, telling you
what to do is not something you want to do, so you shouldn't listen
to them either. So, for right now, what I suggest you do, don't
fight this confusion. Just let it be. And what I want you to do, I
think would be helpful, to learn more about your own mind, is to
observe the times when you feel less confused during the week,
and observe, watch what you're doing then, what's going on, where
you are and what other people around you are doing in those
times. So keep track of that and bring that with you next time.

C: OK.

[560] SdeS: OK. Let's go out front here and figure out when would
be a good time. . . .

At this point, we made sure that she had all the available information on the various programs for women in her situation. As usual, she
knew as much or more about these programs as we did.

Although I deliberately used the phrase "what I want you to do"
several times, I nonetheless did not tell her what to do. I only told her
to watch for times when she is using her own mind and to observe
when she sees herself thinking more clearly which, I gathered, has
something to do with the times when she was not confused. For me,
the question was: Under what conditions is she more likely to see
herself as having and using her own mind and therefore having days
somewhat like the day after the miracle?

Chapter Ten

"WHAT IS BETTER?"
AFTER THE FIRST INTERVIEW

> The problem isn't trying to adapt therapy to that particular [diagnostic] classification, but: What potentialities does the patient disclose to you of their capacity to do this or to do that?
> —*Milton H. Erickson (Haley, 1985, p. 126)*

IN GENERAL, THE PURPOSES of the second interview, or any interview after the first one, include (but are not limited to):

1. constructing the interval between sessions as having included some improvement,
2. checking on whether or not what the therapist and client did in the previous session is seen by the client as having been useful, i.e., leading or allowing the client to perceive things as having improved,
3. helping the client figure out what he or she is doing and/or what has happened that led to improvements so that the client can figure out what he or she should do more of,
4. figuring out whether or not improvements have led to things being "good enough" so that further therapy is not necessary, and finally,
5. when the client does not describe any improvements, preventing both therapist and client from doing more of something that did not work and, therefore, prompting both therapist and client to do something different.

SESSION TWO

[1] SdeS: I had an old friend come to town that I had to go to lunch with, so thank you for being kind enough to come a couple of hours later.

[2] C: That's OK.

[3] SdeS: So . . . what is today? 22nd . . .

[4] C: 23rd.

[5] SdeS: 23rd. I always get confused about that. Can't count very well. [Pause] So what, ah, what's better since last time you were here?

At the end of session one, I used her word "weird" to apply to me and now I used her word "confused" to apply to me. Thus, I do not see either "weird" or "confused" as being necessarily "bad."

[6] C: What's worse.

[7] SdeS: Well, let's start with what's better.

[8] C: Nothing.

[9] SdeS: Are you sure about that?

[10] C: I'm positive.

SdeS: How can that be?

C: It just is. Nothing is positive at all.

Constructing Improvement

SdeS: Tell me about, since you were here last . . .

C: Tuesday.

[15] SdeS: Tuesday, OK. So, how did Tuesday go after you left here?

C: Ah, it went OK.

SdeS: Yah.

C: Just OK.

SdeS: How did you get that to happen?

"Just OK" is at least slightly better than "worse" and so I want to find more about Tuesday because she and I may want to use whatever happened as material for constructing at least some minimum success.

[20] C: Well, I talked a little bit more than I usually do.

SdeS: Mm hm.

C: To my friends.

SdeS: Mm hm.

C: And that was it. . . . I just got to talk a little bit more.

[25] SdeS: Mm hm.

C: That's all.

SdeS: Mm hm. Mm hm. OK, what about Wednesday then?

C: Wednesday, ah, actually things did go well, Wednesday, Thursday, Friday, up until Sunday.

SdeS: Mm hm.

[30] C: Everything was OK, I talked and I was just on my own.

SdeS: Mm hm.

C: To do whatever I want.

SdeS: Mm hm.

C: And then, Monday was, I mean Sunday.

[35] SdeS: OK. So Sunday was, what about Monday, did you pick it back up on Monday?

C: No.

SdeS: Today?

C: Been crying today.

SdeS: Mm hm.

[40] C: All day, off and on, really.

SdeS: Mm hm. OK, but Tuesday, Wednesday, Thursday, Friday and Saturday were OK?

C: Mm hm.

SdeS: Er, at least OK?

C: Yah.

[45] SdeS: Mm hm. OK. So how did you do that? You said you were talking more, what else?

C: Ah, I, I, it, it was better because nobody bugged me, I mean got on my case about what I should be doing or what I'm not doing,

SdeS: Right.

C: You know, all that, I was just pretty much in control of my own self and my own mind.

SdeS: How did you do that?

[50] C: How did I do that? I have to get angry or intimidated to get like that.

SdeS: Mm hm.

C: And that's the only way, so if they like get next to me, I just like, forget it, I do what I'm gonna do.

SdeS: OK.

C: And can't change my mind or whatever.

[55] SdeS: Mm hm.

C: So I have to get pushed to that limit and then,

SdeS: Right.

C: So,

SdeS: OK. And that was OK for you though, you were. . . .

[60] C: Mm hm.

SdeS: OK. So, you were, you knew your own mind and you stuck to it.

C: Mm hm.

SdeS: Wednesday, Thursday, Friday, and Saturday.

She is describing Tuesday, Wednesday, Thursday, Friday, and Saturday in ways that a very similar to the way she said that she wants things to be.

[64] C: Mm hm.

[65] SdeS: OK. OK, and ah, were you feeling less confused too?

C: Uuummm, yah. I don't think I was confused at all really.

SdeS: Hmmm. The whole week! Since the last time you were here?

C: Right, since the last time I was here.

SdeS: How come?

[70] C: I don't know, I think it was just good for me to talk to somebody, somebody to listen to me.

SdeS: Mm hm.

C: You know. I think that,

SdeS: Yah, but ah, you had a whole week to get, be confused again. And how come you didn't get confused?

C: Um, I don't know.

[75] SdeS: Hmm. OK, but. . . .

C: You don't understand me?

SdeS: Not yet. [Laughing]

C: [Laughter]

SdeS: It's OK. You're paying me not to understand.

[80] C: [Laughter]

SdeS: So, well, so Tuesday, Wednesday, Thursday, Friday and Satur-

day, you knew your own mind, you stuck to it, and were not confused at all. Somehow.

C: Mm hm.

SdeS: I'm still wondering how you did that.

C: OK, I don't know, I'm just weird I guess.

[85] SdeS: OK, well, OK, maybe. But, how do you go about being
weird then?

C: Um.

SdeS: If you knew how you did that . . .

C: I, I don't know.

SdeS: . . . you could do it all the time.

[90] C: I know, but, I don't know, I, I guess when people just upset
me. You know.

SdeS: Mm hm.

C: I don't know.

SdeS: Mm hm.

C: I don't know how I did that, I just did.

[95] SdeS: OK. OK, and ah, can you do it again?

C: Hmm?

SdeS: Can you make tomorrow pretty much like last Wednesday?

C: Mmmmm.

SdeS: Would you know how to do that?

[100] C: No.

SdeS: So you don't know how you do that?

C: No, I just do it.

SdeS: You just do it. OK. Could you bet on doing it tomorrow?

C: No. No.

[105] SdeS: No. So you just have to be lucky?

C: Yah.

SdeS: Yah, oh gee, that's terrible. [Pause] OK, so well, let's try it this
way for a minute. Wednesday, Thursday, Friday and Saturday. If
most days for the next six months were like that, would that be
OK with you?

C: That'd be fine.

Her saying at the start of the session that things are "worse," about
which I expressed some doubt, does not apply to the whole interval
between sessions. Rather, "worse" just applies to Sunday, and perhaps
to Monday and Tuesday (up until the time of the session). Throughout

this period she reports not having been confused; she knew her own mind and stuck to it. (Frequently, when clients say things are "the same" or "worse" at the start of a session, it turns out that this evaluation does not apply to the whole interval between sessions.)

Her report about not being confused all week will lead some people to read my suggestion from the previous session, i.e., "for right now, what I suggest you do, don't fight this confusion. Just let it be" as a "paradoxical intervention" that worked or that I had a "paradoxical intention" behind what I said. However, that was not the point of the suggestion at all. Rather, the purpose was "to learn more about your own mind, to observe the times when you feel less confused during the week, and observe, watch what you're doing then, what's going on, where you are and what other people around you are doing in those times." This is what she did. At least in this case, the idea of a "paradoxical intervention" or "paradoxical intention" comes from reading-between-the-lines or is part of a reader-focused reading rather than a text-focused one. It comes from an interpretation rather than from reading only what is on the lines.

Inventing a "Success Scale" or Constructing Success from a Different Point of View

[109] SdeS: OK. Well let's call that, oh, I don't know, let's call that 10. OK?

[110] C: Mm hm.

SdeS: And, the worst day recently, say before you came here last Tuesday,

C: Um hm.

SdeS: That was zero. OK, and where between zero and 10 was Sunday.

C: Zero.

[115] SdeS: OK. And Monday? Where would you put that?

C: Mmmm, Monday was like 5.

SdeS: OK, and um, today?

C: Today, I don't know what today is. Mmmm, like 5.

Although the scale and the number concretize things, what is concretized remains multiple. For instance, the client may have many, many ways to pull herself up to 5 from 0, and they are all covered by these numbers.

At various points during the session, scales are used to help the client draw distinctions, compare and contrast various aspects of her situation and how she wants things to be different when the solution has been constructed. Not only are scales used in this way during the interview, but at times they can also be used in the same fashion as part of a homework task.

The scales are used to help draw a distinction between Sunday and Monday/Tuesday and to help her see that somehow things changed between Sunday and Monday. Things began to turn around and got all the way up to 5. In this way, the whole interval is now in the process of being constructed as "progress." Since there are likely to always be days when things are nearer to zero than to 10, the question naturally becomes how to recover from a bad day.

[119] SdeS: OK. Now, tomorrow could be, do I understand what you are saying, that if you're lucky you could be 10, if you're not lucky, you could be zero and you can't do anything about it?

[120] C: I don't have no control, or something, I don't know.

SdeS: Hmm. OK. So, how did you get then, from Sunday at zero, to Monday back to 5? How did you do that?

C: I'm just lucky I guess.

SdeS: Lucky?

C: [Laughter] I don't know.

[125] SdeS: Mm hm. Do you think you might have had something to do with it?

C: No.

SdeS: No. Going back . . . did you have something to do with it being 10 last week?

C: Well, yah, yah, a little bit.

SdeS: Mm hm.

[130] C: Because . . .

SdeS: OK.

C: Then, I mean, it was like, I just didn't care about anything.

SdeS: Mm hm.

C: Nothing at all, and . . .

[135] SdeS: Except you.

C: Whatever I said I was going to do, I just did it.

SdeS: Right, OK, so the only thing you were paying attention to is your own mind, but other people were . . .

C: Um hm.

SdeS: OK. OK, anything else that you had to do with it?

[140] C: Um, no. Not really.

SdeS: OK. Then, but you found somebody, some people to talk to?

C: Just friends.

SdeS: Ah ha. And ah, if you decide to go talk to those friends, does that help most of the time?

C: Mm hm.

[145] SdeS: Mm hm.

C: Yah, it do.

SdeS: Mm hm. So is that part of it too? If you do that, say every day, would that help?

C: It helps a lot.

SdeS: Mm hm. Mm hm.

[150] C: Cause he [the boyfriend] the only one that listens, you know, and let me have an opinion whether it's wrong or right.

SdeS: Mm hm.

C: You know.

SdeS: Mm hm.

C: And if it's wrong, you know, we talk about it, you know. What's wrong with what I did, you know, why it's wrong, or whatever.

[155] SdeS: Right.

C: But everybody else, they just really don't care, you know, they feel that it's wrong, it's wrong, and that's it.

SdeS: Mm hm.

C: You know, or if it's right, and they don't, you know, whatever, it just whatever, they just go and you don't have anything to say about it.

SdeS: Mm hm. So is that what you got into on Sunday?

[160] C: Mm hm.

SdeS: People telling you that you were wrong again, putting pressure on again?

C: Mm hm.

SdeS: Mm hm. So, how come you listen?

C: That's my mother.

[165] SdeS: Your mother, oh, oh, oh, oh.

C: You have to listen to your mother, don't you? [Laughing] I mean . . .

SdeS: Well . . .

C: I mean I listen to her but I try not to disrespect her, and that's kinda hard to do both at the same time.

SdeS: Yah, yah, yah.

[170] C: And see, we had problems when I was little, but me and her can't sit down and talk about it. She doesn't want to hear about it.

SdeS: Right.

C: So I don't know, maybe it's a problem with her with me, or whatever, but, together we can't do it.

SdeS: Mm hm.

C: And then what happened last Sunday, was the kids' father called, and now he's supposed to be getting a lawyer to get the kids away from me, and now she wants to get on his side and say I'm an unfit mother, you know, and I don't feel I'm being unfit to them, I mean I don't beat them, I feed them, I, you know, I bathe them, I clothe them, I mean I do everything a mother do for her kids, you know, but . . .

[175] SdeS: Mm hm.

C: I don't know, she gets in her little attitude moods and then she feel like, um, I'm not good enough for anything.

SdeS: Mm hm.

C: And he's just mad right now, too, because he feels I'm not good enough for anything either.

SdeS: Right. OK, so you let that get to you.

[180] C: Yah, because then it seems like the whole world is just on their side and no one can see my point of view, or want to hear it, or care about it.

SdeS: Mm hm. Mm hm. So, did your husband try to pressure you?

C: He, um, I don't know, well not really. I mean, he just likes to yell and fuss all the time, and I don't want to hear that.

SdeS: Mm hm. Mm hm. You didn't feel threatened?

C: I'm starting to get out of that now.

[185] SdeS: Mm hm.

C: You know, his little threats or whatever. It is starting to wear off. It used to really do something to me, but now it really don't.

SdeS: Mm hm. Is he making less threats yet?

C: Ah, no.

SdeS: You were saying last time he was making less.

[190] C: Well he was but, he, he's still the same, just, I don't know, he's really sneaky like . . .

SdeS: Mm hm.

C: You know, it's like when he's around people, or whatever, I mean his threats aren't as bad as when he talks to me one on one, you know.

SdeS: Right, right. Mm hm. But you aren't feeling particularly threatened or scared about it right now?

C: Nah . . .

[195] SdeS: So, that was Sunday, but you . . . managed to, somehow,
get back up to 5 Monday?

C: Mm hm.

SdeS: So what's different between, say Monday, which was 5, and
Saturday, which was 10?

C: What's dif . . . ah, um, I don't know, I guess mainly being by myself,
just trying to get out of everybody's way, and just mainly stay to
myself.

SdeS: Mm hm.

[200] C: . . . Mostly leaving the house . . . not going . . .

SdeS: OK. OK. OK. All right, so that helps. What else helps?

C: Ah, well right now, just not being there,

SdeS: Not being there, yah. So what do you do? How do you make
. . . what do you do to stay away?

C: Um, sometimes I'm at work.

[205] SdeS: Right.

C: Sometimes I'm just out riding around.

SdeS: Mm hm. Mm hm. OK, and that helps?

C: Mm hm.

SdeS: Mm hm.

[210] C: 'Cause I don't have to hear anything.

SdeS: All right, right.

C: You know, how bad I am or wrong I am, or whatever.

SdeS: So, have you got yourself looking for or thinking about looking
for a place, on your own?

C: Mm hm. I'm not thinking about it anymore. I'm gonna do it.

[215] SdeS: You are?

C: Yah.

SdeS: Mm hm.

C: I have to.

SdeS: When do you plan to do it?

[220] C: As soon as possible.

SdeS: Yah.

C: Maybe by the end of the month or something.

SdeS: You got enough money?

C: I should have, by the end of the month, . . . anywhere, it don't
matter, a garage or whatever.

[225] SdeS: Mm hm.

C: It don't matter.

SdeS: So you've reached that stage?

C: Mm hm.

SdeS: Anywhere.

[230] C: Yah, anywhere.

SdeS: Mm hm. OK. So, how, how are, when you get the zero days like that, how are the kids affected?

C: Well, I guess they feel like I don't love them or don't care about them, or whatever. I, when I'm at those days, I don't like being around them really.

SdeS: Mm hm.

C: Because, you know, all I do is yell at them.

[235] SdeS: Right.

C: You know. I don't like that.

SdeS: And when things are at 5, what's different then?

C: I spend a little time with them,

SdeS: Mm hm. Mm hm.

[240] C: You know, I talk to them a little better, you know, I'm not yelling at them or anything.

SdeS: OK. And 10?

C: 10? I mean, we just buddies then.

SdeS: Mm hm.

C: We get along just fine.

[245] SdeS: Mm hm. Mm hm. [Long pause] It sounds to me like, ah, last time you were here you were saying you felt confused about things and what to do, and where to go.

C: Yah, am I getting better?

SdeS: Sounds better. You said you weren't confused all week. I'm beginning to believe you.

C: Hmmm.

SdeS: Sounds like you're not terribly confused right now.

[250] C: [Nods head.]

SdeS: So, I'm wondering what the next steps are for you. What do you think you ought to be doing next, looking for a place, and so on, but what else do you think you should be doing next?

C: Mm, I want to go to school.

SdeS: Mm hm.

C: I wanna try and get in school. I did that today.

[255] SdeS: Um hm?

C: Hopefully I'll be going to school.

SdeS: OK, and what school and for what?

C: Tech, and for microprocessor.

SdeS: Mm hm. Do you think that might be good for you?

[260] C: Well, yah, I think it be real good for me because I have three
boys to take care of and I need a job where I can take care of them.

SdeS: Right.

C: And . . . to take care of them and live by myself too.

SdeS: Right. So, you think you can make enough money that way,
more or less?

C: Mmmm, . . .

[265] SdeS: Mm hm.

C: I guess I can.

SdeS: You think it might be a good job you'd enjoy doing?

C: Um, I'm into secretarial work anyway, so I guess a little more knowledge will probably benefit me more.

SdeS: So school, and ah, . . . and looking for a new place to live, right.
What other steps?

[270] C: Mmm, after that I don't know, I mean, if I can accomplish
that far, then I'm doing good to myself.

SdeS: Mm hm. Mm hm. OK. Yah, yah, for somebody who didn't have
her own mind a year ago, that sounds like a lot, certainly heading
in the right direction. What about this—got some ideas what you're
going to do about this husband of yours?

C: I don't know, I just wish he'd just go away and leave me alone. I
mean he's saying he's gonna get this lawyer and he's gonna send
me the divorce papers and all that stuff and I don't know what the
deal is. He hasn't done it yet.

SdeS: He hasn't done it yet. Mm hm.

C: I think he just likes to bug me or pester me or just make life miserable for me.

[275] SdeS: Mm hm. Mm hm.

C: I figure the longer he can do it, he'll just keep doing it I guess, I
don't know.

SdeS: And ah, as long as all that he's doing is just pestering you.

C: Yah, so far.

SdeS: Mm hm. Mm hm.

[280] C: Yah, so far that's all.

SdeS: Is it likely to stay that way?

C: Not for long.

SdeS: No.

C: He'll find something else to get really upset about and then want to come after me again.

[285] SdeS: Mm hm. So what you going to do if that happens?

C: I don't know what to do. I'm just tired of running and tired of being afraid.

SdeS: Right. What do you think you can do?

C: Hm. I don't know.

SdeS: So, have you talked to other people who've been in that kind of situation?

[290] C: Not really.

SdeS: No.

C: I think I talked to my mother, but, some days she feel I'm right about getting away from him, and you know, that's why I'm there with her now.

SdeS: Right.

C: She feels I'm protected. But then, her other days it's like, he's right about everything and she want me to—I don't know if she want me to go back there with him or what.

[295] SdeS: Mm hm.

C: I don't know.

SdeS: Mm hm. I guess she was in that mood Sunday, huh?

C: Mm hm.

SdeS: That was one thing you seemed pretty clear about last time certainly, that you had no plans to go back.

[300] C: No, that's one thing I don't want to do.

SdeS: So how are you going to make sure you can accomplish that, and do it safely?

C: Now, that's something hard.

SdeS: Yah.

C: 'Cause I never know what he's up to next. He's a good con artist.

[305] SdeS: Mm hm.

C: . . . 'Cause it's like, one day he's really nice and just wants to do everything and is everything and then the next day, it's like, or the next minute, really, he just gone off the deep end.

SdeS: Mm hm.

C: I try to do things without getting him upset, but that don't work either.

SdeS: Yah. Does it work sometimes?

[310] C: Yah, sometimes.

SdeS: Mm hm.

C: Not a lot.

SdeS: But, ah, so far he's stuck to his word about that? This time.

C: Mmm, yah.

[315] SdeS: Hmm. But you aren't ready to believe that's forever?

C: No.

SdeS: So somehow, you have to figure out a way to handle this.

C: Mm hm. And it would be nice if I had somebody to help me or whatever, but no one, no one wants to do that, or I don't know they care or whatever.

SdeS: Mm hm. What about your boyfriend?

[320] C: He could do something, but his problem is he don't want to go to jail.

SdeS: Right.

C: And if he steps in and do anything, that's what's gonna happen so, as far as that part, he says I'm on my own with that and I have to take care of that by myself.

SdeS: Mm hm.

C: He can't help me with that.

[325] SdeS: Yah, well, I can see if he thinks he's going to end up in jail if he does anything, then he shouldn't do that. Might be other things he can do to help?

C: I don't know, I don't see what he can do, I mean 'cause my husband, he don't even want to talk to anybody. They finally met each other on bad terms but,

SdeS: Hmmm.

C: But, it's like he didn't want the guy to say, I mean he didn't even want him to say anything to him or anything.

SdeS: Right. Well, I guess I can understand that.

[330] C: It's hard though, like giving him a chance to do whatever else he wants to do, and now he don't want to do it.

SdeS: Mm hm. Mm hm.

C: He has everything and I have nothing and I don't know why he just can't be happy and you know, just leave me alone, but, I don't have anything, and he gonna see to it I don't never have anything or be happy or anything.

SdeS: But he didn't know the fact that you have your own mind.

C: No, he don't want to realize that, that I have a mind, but, 'cause he used to control it . . .

[335] SdeS: Mm hm.

C: . . . for about 13 years.

SdeS: Mm hm.

C: And to see that I, you know, don't want to listen to what he has to say anymore, or do what he say anymore, he don't like that.

SdeS: Right. So.

[340] C: That's the problem right there.

SdeS: Right, right. From his side.

C: Mm hm.

SdeS: Mm hm. So here you are, now you got your own mind, and,

C: Now everybody hates me.

[345] SdeS: Except you.

C: Yah, except me.

SdeS: And your boyfriend.

C: Yah, that's true.

SdeS: What about the kids?

[350] C: Ummmmm, they still love me, I think they just don't know when to love me, or they kinda confused.

SdeS: How?

C: Because from my days.

SdeS: Right.

C: You know.

[355] SdeS: Right, OK. So how do you, how do you, how are you getting used to yourself now with your own mind?

C: It's not easy, at all. I scare myself sometimes.

SdeS: Mm hm.

C: And sometimes I feel good about what I'm doing then, and sometimes I feel bad about what I do because when I do something that pleases me, sometimes it hurts somebody else, and you know, I don't like hurting people, I'd rather hurt myself than to hurt somebody else, but it make me feel good.

SdeS: Mm hm.

[360] C: Sometimes.

SdeS: Mm hm. So, you say most of the time that you like yourself? So, makes sense, but would you say that most of the time, you are, you know, surprising yourself, feeling good about having your own mind?

C: Mm hm.

SdeS: Mm hm. It's better than not having any at all, huh?

C: Right.

[365] SdeS: You were saying before, yah. So now you have to, ah, learn how to adjust to that, and ah,

C: And control it.

SdeS: And control it.

C: Mmm.

SdeS: And for . . . four days last week it was, at least those four days, you were controlling it pretty well.

[370] C: I was doing good.

SdeS: Now since, when . . . how you going to do that? How you going to change how you handle things like Sunday, so you don't let that go all the way back to zero?

C: That's what I . . .

SdeS: If that happens again.

C: That's what I been thinking about, and I don't know how I can do that. My mood changes a lot.

[375] SdeS: Yah.

C: I don't know, if I can get my mood at one place and stay there, I'll be OK.

SdeS: Yahhh, but have you ever been able to do that?

C: No.

SdeS: No. Do you think other people are able to do that?

[380] C: Yeah.

SdeS: Yeah?

C: Mm hm.

SdeS: OK, and how do you think they do it?

C: They just don't care, I mean.

[385] SdeS: Oh.

C: I have a sister, she don't care about anything, and I mean I barely see her unhappy.

SdeS: Mm hm.

C: 'Cause she don't care, I mean, she says she don't do this, she don't do this, and she don't care who it hurts, as long as it's not her.

SdeS: Mm hm.

[390] C: You know, and she is always on top of the world, you know I barely see her unhappy about anything, so.

SdeS: So how does she do that?

C: She just don't care about anything.

SdeS: Hmmm. Hmmm. Does that mean she doesn't have any fun either?

C: Hmmm?

[395] SdeS: She wouldn't have any fun either?

C: Well,

SdeS: Neither fun nor . . .

C: Well she does, I mean she just, she has it all together, she do what she want to do . . .

SdeS: Mm hm.

[400] C: . . . you know, and whether it hurts you or not, you know, if it makes her happy, she does it.

SdeS: Well, OK, I see.

C: I mean, she don't, she just don't care about nobody's feelings but her own.

SdeS: Mm hm. I see.

C: But me, I just, I don't know, I have this weakness with caring too much or something.

[405] SdeS: Is that something you want to change?

C: Not a lot, I mean, not a lot. I want to change a little bit because I don't think I'll ever get anywhere like that.

Inventing a "Caring Scale"

SdeS: Let's say, back to different numbers but, let's say 10, again, is as bad as possible, caring too much, the worst you can get on that, right?

C: Mm hm.

SdeS: And zero is ah, not caring at all about anything. . . . Ah, where would you like to be on that?

[410] C: A 2.

SdeS: Two, OK. And, um, how close were you on Wednesday, Thursday, Friday and Saturday?

C: I think I was at zero.

SdeS: You were at zero? OK, and on Sunday.

C: Sunday I was at 10.

[415] SdeS: You were all the way up to 10. Now, then today?

C: Umm, about 5.

SdeS: About 5, OK. So, if you could get to 2, that'd be, if 2 was about where you were most of the time, that's what you'd like to see happen?

C: Mm hm. I think I'd feel a much better person.

SdeS: Mm hm. Mm hm. OK. So, how, tell me what's the difference between zero and 2?

[420] C: Well, at 2, I mean, I care about people's feeling and stuff, but as long as it don't hurt them drastically, I really don't care,

SdeS: Mm hm. OK.

C: You know, it's like that.

SdeS: Mm hm.

C: I mean, I don't want to be where I don't care about other people's feelings, but you know, if it's no major thing like it's gonna kill them or whatever,

[425] SdeS: Right.

C: Then, I just don't care,

SdeS: Mm hm. Mm hm.

C: You know.

SdeS: Mm hm.

[430] C: You upset, you upset.

SdeS: Mm hm.

C: That's how I want to be.

SdeS: OK, and how would it be at zero?

C: At zero?

[435] SdeS: What would be the difference?

C: Well, at zero I just don't care whether I hurt you or not.

SdeS: Mmmmm.

C: So.

SdeS: Mmm hm. No matter how badly it might hurt somebody else. Is that true?

[440] C: Mm hm.

SdeS: OK. OK. Yah, OK, I can see a 2 would be better than zero, yah. Now, over the past few months, where have you been on that?

C: Umm, well since Friday I been out of town and I came back Sunday, and that's when everything just issshhh . . .

SdeS: Mmhm . . . mm hm.

C: Before then I was like in my own world, I mean I did whatever I wanted to do.

[445] SdeS: Mm hm.

C: And . . .

SdeS: Before you came here last time, where were you on this would you say?

C: Ah, um, I'd say about 5.

SdeS: About 5. Mm hm. OK. Now last time when you were here, you said that ah, you weren't used to talking, you didn't . . .

[450] C: Mm hm.

SdeS: And ah, talking like this is strange for you, new for you, and I'm wondering if, ah, you have said everything you wanted to say?

C: Yah.

SdeS: Yah. Last time and today too?

C: Mm hm.

[455] SdeS: OK, OK. So you haven't found it too difficult?

C: No.

SdeS: Not as difficult as you thought it was going to be?

C: No, mm mm.

SdeS: So, OK. Good. OK. I ah . . .

[460] C: It, it feels just, I still not good at just, still saying what I want to say.

SdeS: Mm hm.

C: I mean, as long as you ask me, I can tell you like that, but that's part of just saying this and then like that.

SdeS: Right.

C: I still can't do that.

[465] SdeS: So, is there, is there anything I forgot to ask?

C: No.

SdeS: Nothing that you know of? No?

C: Mm mm.

SdeS: OK, I can't think of anything. So, ah, I'm going to take some time out and think about this. And you can just relax and I'll be back in about 10 minutes.

[470] C: OK.

Thinking about Things

Since she describes the days when she knew her own mind (Tuesday, Wednesday, Thursday, Friday, and Saturday) as more a result of "luck" than anything else, achieving her goals is being constructed as a matter of chance! Both she and I know that she had at least a little bit to do with it, but she essentially sees this as "beyond her control." While undeniably other people and various events play some (perhaps large) part in having a "10" day or a "zero" day, the more aware she is of her part, the more control she will have and the higher the probability that she will be able to pick herself up again following days that are nearer zero than they are near to 10.

Since she began the session by saying things were "worse" (which seems to have been contradicted during the rest of the session) and not "better," we (the team and I) need to do something different. She had observed when she was less confused and, therefore, she is likely to do another task. In this situation, we need a task different from the observational task given in session one.

[471] SdeS: OK, now, the team and I are really impressed that, ah, now that you have discovered your own mind, that you can surprise yourself with it. And that's wonderful. And it's wonderful as I see it, that you were able to, you knew your own mind and you stuck to it last week for four days at least.

C: Mm hm.

SdeS: I think that, and the team agrees, your plan to pursue school makes sense, a good idea for you, and that finding a place of your own is a probably a good idea.

C: Mmm.

[475] SdeS: But, and ah, but I guess what puzzled us, what puzzled me, is ah, the good luck stuff.

C: Mmm. [Nods]

SdeS: And ah, so first of all, what we suggest you do is, you make sure you watch when you have good luck.

C: Mm hm.

SdeS: And that, we have a hunch that if you're watching for it, you have a better chance of having it.

So, what we'd like you to do, between now and next time you come, each night before you go to bed, OK?

[480] C: Mmm.

SdeS: Why don't you make a prediction, about where on this 10 to zero scale, with 10 being knowing your own mind and sticking to it, and zero being the opposite, OK?

C: Mm hm.

SdeS: So each night before you go to bed, make a prediction, where you're going to be on that scale the next day. And then before you go to bed the next night, think about where you were, all that day, and see how that matches with the prediction. And if they're different, try and figure out how come. Do that each day.

C: Mm hm.

[485] SdeS: All right. And maybe take notes of that so you can bring it along with you next time and see what maybe, you can learn something from that.

C: OK.

SdeS: OK. So what do you think, when should we get back together. What do you think—a week, two weeks, three weeks, what?

C: Two weeks.

SdeS: OK. Let's go up front and figure out when's best.

We could have, of course, used the "caring scale" with 10 standing for "caring too much" and 0 standing for "caring not at all." The scales seem related to each other and it probably would not have made any significant difference.

It seems to me that clients frequently are the best judge about how long the interval between sessions should be and, whenever possible, I try to follow their wishes. Would her picking one week have suggested less confidence in herself or would her picking three weeks have indicated more? Two weeks fit my schedule nicely, so I did not ask.

However, it turned out to be three weeks before the next session. By that time, she had begun school and had found herself a new place to live and had actually moved. She described herself as having had her own mind and sticking to it 85% of the time during the three-week interval (8.5 on the 0 to 10 scale). At the end of the third session, she decided that things were "better enough" for her to go it alone and thus no further sessions were scheduled.

Chapter Eleven

CONSTRUCTING
STORIES OF SUCCESS:
CONSULTATION INTERVIEWS

I make a point of never having any prejudices and of following
docilely wherever fact may lead me.
— *Sherlock Holmes (The Reigate Squires)*

ALTHOUGH MOST THERAPISTS do few consultation interviews, these one-time-only situations are frequently rather concise, well-structured, and sometimes simplified representations of my approach. However, because of the complexity of the context, consultation interviews are also highly ambiguous situations.

First of all, the members of the audience, the workshop or seminar participants, have paid good money to see me describe and demonstrate my way of working. Thus they have every right to expect that an interview done directly in front of them will be in some way at least representative. When an interview is done in the front of large group of therapists, the participants have to pretend to be invisible or at least to be just part of the wall of a typical room in which therapy is usually done. The context is slightly simpler when the participants observe the session through a see-through mirror or on a television screen.

Second, most therapists who bring clients into consultation interviews want to see how I might work with this particular client and thus to be able to draw some sort of comparison between their work and mine. (The therapist sometimes sees the case as "stuck" in some

156

way, but this is not a necessary part of the therapist's reason for bring-ing any particular client to a consultation interview.) The organizers of seminars want me to sell my approach to their colleagues (or, at least, to persuade their colleagues to look at a different approach). Usually the seminar participants are, reasonably enough, rather skepti-cal about the viability and usefulness of brief therapy in their contexts.

Third, the clients have every reason to expect that a consultation interview will be therapeutically useful to them, particularly when they are brought to see a "foreign expert." Regardless of what the therapist may have explicitly told them, the implicit message may well be that they are in some way(s) a difficult case and the therapist therefore needs some help. It would seem reasonable that they see themselves as exhibits under the microscope of the therapist, the consultant, and the seminar participants.

Finally, from my perspective, I first and foremost need to protect the clients from themselves and their expectations. Thus I usually open with remarks questioning the usefulness of the consultation in-terview. Second, I need to protect the therapist and to help him see the usefulness of his work. Thus I need to help the clients construct a description or a story in which things are getting better or have been getting better during the period they have been in therapy with this therapist. My assumption is that this will also be therapeutically useful to the clients, since this is exactly the type of story that my successful clients tell me.

Since my approach is the product that I am trying to sell the audi-ence or, better, to persuade the participants is useful with these (or any) clients, I need not only to demonstrate my methods of construct-ing a story of success, but also to use my methods to illustrate how this story automatically leads to a specific, particular message (including a task) at the end of the session.

Perhaps surprisingly, the situation is made easier for me when an interpreter is involved because this automatically forces both me and the clients to simplify things. None of us can make our usually auto-matic assumption that the other "understands." In fact, using an inter-preter helps to mark the context as one in which "misunderstanding" is far more likely than "understanding." Even more than when I work with English speaking clients, I tend to favor scaling questions in this context, since it is clear that all the clients need to "understand" is the idea that, on a scale from "1" to "10," "5" is better than "4." Thus we can construct an understanding or, at least, a mutual, workable misunderstanding.

IN BREMEN

Haley: What about all the other purposes that it [the symptom]
served? Whatever they may be?
Erickson: Your assumption is that it served other purposes. Have
you ever thought about symptomatology wearing out in serving
purposes and becoming an habitual pattern?
—Jay Haley (1985, p. 15)

This consultation interview was done in Bremen in 1991 at the Norddeutsches Institut für Kurzzeittherapie. The client is an English teacher and the interview was done in English.

[1] C: I'm a school teacher.

[2] Steve de Shazer: What age people?

[3] C: I, I'm retired. I retired some time ago, but, ah, it's not fixed, ah, if I go on or not. So at the moment I don't work. But my education is to be a school teacher in English and Geography.

[4] SdeS: With what ages?

[5] C: I had the ages from 12 to 19.

[6] SdeS: Ah ha.

[7] C: [Unintelligible] ... I've been with groups of students in the U.S., three times by the way, in Wisconsin.

[8] SdeS: That's where I'm from.

[9] C: Pardon?

[10] SdeS: That's where I'm from.

C: Oh, you're from?

SdeS: Wisconsin.

C: We went to a school in Stevens Point.

SdeS: Ah hah.

[15] C: North of Madison.

SdeS: Mmm.

C: You're from?

SdeS: Milwaukee.

C: Yes, Milwaukee. The beer city.

[20] SdeS: Yes, yes. So, do you want to go back to teaching, if you had the choice?

C: I'm not quite sure. Ah, some time ago I asked for retirement because, ah, of these disturbances I have, I was . . . neurotic depression and anxieties. I stopped teaching, but they wait for five years, they wait for five years to decide finally if I, ah

SdeS: Um hm.

C: If I can go on. At the moment I teach, so-called college of self-education.

SdeS: Right.

[25] C: But only two, ah, courses; four lessons.

SdeS: You enjoy it?

C: Yes I do, yes.

SdeS: Well, let me ask you this question. [Goes to blackboard] Now that you brought that up, we'll start with this one. My favorite question, one of my favorite questions, I guess. Let's say 10 stands for the problems that brought you to therapy . . .

C: Yes.

[30] SdeS: They're completely solved. And zero stands for, how things were before you started therapy. OK?

C: Yes.

SdeS: Where would you put yourself between 0 and 10 today?

C: So 10 is a bad state?

SdeS: No, no, 10 is . . .

[35] C: 10 is . . .

SdeS: This is the bottom [pointing to 0].

C: Ah, the bottom.

SdeS: Where would you put yourself?

C: I would put myself, ah, number 3 perhaps, number 3.

The client's saying that he "enjoyed" his teaching and his rating himself at "3" means that he sees himself as having made some progress since he began therapy. We need to find out as much as possible about the differences between 0 and 3. (His difficulty with the 0 to 10 scale, not an uncommon one in consultation sessions, led me to subsequently switch to a version using a range from −10 to 0 scale [see below] which seems to be less difficult for clients in consultation interviews. However, I have found that the 0 to 10 scale causes less difficulties during my therapy sessions than does the −10 to 0 version. The difference may be due to the fact that most models of therapy lead to sessions that are "problem-focused" and the "minus numbers scale" fits better when dealing with "problems" and getting rid of them.)

[40] SdeS: OK. Now, my next most favorite question. How did you do this? How did you get from 0 to 3?

C: That's a difficult question. I am not an expert.

SdeS: Yeah. But you did it!

C: Yes I did, but I'm not an expert so it is very difficult for me to explain that.

SdeS: Give it a shot, as we say.

[45] C: I mean, some of my problems go back to my youth.

SdeS: Sure.

C: They went back, when I was in school, ah, I can remember there were certain situations . . . similar situations I experience at the moment.

SdeS: Right. But, what I would like to see is: How did you get from 0 to 3? How did you do that?

C: You mean that's good progress?

[50] SdeS: Yeah, that's progress.

C: Well, I don't know if I started at the bottom, perhaps I started somewhere else, and then I went back from 5 to 3. Did I start at the bottom? I don't know. So . . .

SdeS: Things are better now for you than they were before you started therapy?

C: Perhaps a little bit better. The problem was me, always that I realize things that, or I have an insight in my mind of what is wrong, or where are the mistakes, but it is very difficult for me to put them into practice, to put the knowledge of, or to put the things I know, yes, into practice.

SdeS: Um hum.

[55] C: For instance, you can know a lot, but you, in practical life, make a lot of mistakes.

SdeS: Sure. So, what do you know about what to do right? What works for you?

C: What works for me? Maybe time works for me, I don't know. I read all kinds of books to help myself.

SdeS: Yes.

C: Scientific books and books for laymen.
[60] SdeS: Um hm.
C: And I go to therapy and I am in certain groups, self-help groups.
SdeS: Un ha.
C: Self-help groups for depressive people, for instance.
SdeS: Um hm.
[65] C: And I do other things. I take part in many courses, so I'm quite active.
SdeS: OK.
C: I'm quite active. Active more or less is the opposite of depressive.
SdeS: Oh, OK.

The client makes being active into the opposite of being depressed. At this point in the session I just mark this in my memory as something that will perhaps need to be clarified later.

C: I wouldn't be here if I were to feel, if I would be happy and be full of joy, etc., etc.
[70] SdeS: Probably not. That's true. So, what would it be like to be that happy, that you wouldn't need to come here anymore? What would you be doing then?

The client's level of activity, plus the fact that he enjoys teaching, plus the 3 on the progress scale, all suggest that there is a need to develop signs of progress, to find out what differences in his life will be significant for him. It is a bit of a puzzle that he goes to self-help groups for "depressive people" and yet he sees himself as "active," which he calls the opposite of depressive. How will he know when things are better? Perhaps his difficulty with the scaling question led me to abandon the scale too soon. Perhaps it would have been more useful to be asking about him about how he and others will know when he has reached 5.

[71] C: No, that would be a state of, ah, where I wouldn't have these symptoms. These symptoms, for instance, lack of self-confidence, low self-esteem, or inferiority complex, which is very strong.
SdeS: OK, when that's gone, what would be different?
C: What would I . . . I would enjoy life more, for instance.

SdeS: OK. How? How would that show up? How would somebody know you were enjoying life more?

Sometimes asking the client about how other people would know something, i.e., that they were enjoying life more, helps them to describe things more clearly and concretely.

[75] C: How? It concerns my feelings. Other people would see this, of course, but, ah, it's a matter which concerns me, and I just would feel better, to make it very easy.

SdeS: Yeah.

C: I just would feel better.

SdeS: Right. And, I guess I wonder, when you feel better, what will you do that you don't do now?

C: Then certain things wouldn't be there, for instance. There are now some anxieties which I have in certain situations, in groups for instance. I make mistakes, or so, that other people laugh at me, then certain things wouldn't be there and I wouldn't suffer from these things, so it would be a lack of suffering, perhaps.

[80] SdeS: Yeah. OK. And how would your best friend know, for instance, that you are happy and self-confident, without your telling him?

C: Maybe we would talk about different things. At the moment, ah, my best friend has similar symptoms. I know him from a self-help group. He has similar symptoms, depressive symptoms, and all the time we talk about this. I would ask him to talk about other subjects, not about depression and medicine all the time.

SdeS: Right.

C: And so on.

SdeS: You'd be talking about other things?

[85] C: Yes. But still at the moment, I do a lot of things. For instance, I am in the course for Latin and I teach two English courses; I go to lectures, etc. So I do other things apart from these symptoms.

SdeS: Exactly. That's why I am asking you. You are saying you're doing all these things, and that's why I am asking: What would you be doing different when things are better for you? I think it is important to figure that out so that you know what the signs are, you see?

C: Yes, for instance, I wouldn't be afraid in certain situations and certain events.

SdeS: Um hm.

C: Perhaps, which is a problem for me at the moment, so perhaps, no anxieties or less anxieties, perhaps.

[90] SdeS: OK. What kind of events, in particular, are you talking about?

C: I'm talking about groups. Groups, I don't feel good in groups, although I teach in these two groups, but there I am, concerning the subject, I am much better than the participants.

SdeS: Right.

C: So I feel quite strong. It's OK. I can manage. But in other groups, I always think the others are better than I am. That refers, of course, to my inferiority complex.

SdeS: Right.

[95] C: I always think they are better, so I am afraid of people whom I believe are higher than I am, whom I think are very good, very strong, etc.

SdeS: OK. And somehow or another, when you are up to 10, that won't be a problem anymore.

C: There would be problems if I am at 10, of course there would be problems, but there would not be the degree of suffering there is at the moment.

SdeS: Right. OK. So, suppose you went home and went to bed and to sleep. While you were sleeping, a miracle happened. The problem that brought you to therapy in the first place is solved, completely. But you couldn't know that it had happened, because you were sleeping at the time.

C: Um hmm.

[100] SdeS: So, when you wake up tomorrow morning, how will you know, how will you find out that there has been this miracle?

C: You are talking about the miracle which won't happen.

SdeS: Right.

C: So, it's not realistic for me.

SdeS: Well, just pretend.

The client's reaction "it's not realistic for me" is not unusual and, of course, the idea of a miracle of this sort is not realistic. It is, however, a useful way to help the client talk about what he wants to get out of the therapy.

[105] C: OK. Such a miracle happened, um, I would be a different person.
SdeS: What would you do?
C: More self-confident, more . . . not these anxieties, and not these neurotic symptoms or neurotic depression.
SdeS: Um hmmm.
C: Yes. I always say, "not," "not." It would be better if I would say it in a positive way.

Since he spends so much time talking about his "symptoms" with his best friend and going to self-help groups, it is hard to imagine what he might do instead. Having the anxieties go away is not a useful way for him to describe what he wants because there is always the question about what will be there instead of these anxieties. That is, once something is absent, there is a hole. But if there is a hole in his life, what will come to fill that hole? If he does not know what else to do or if he does not know what he would like to have fill that hole, then the easiest thing for him, or anyone, is to simply fill that hole once again with anxieties (often called a "relapse"). The end of anything is very hard to mark or to prove, since one can never know what will happen tomorrow. It is more useful, therefore, to work with the start of something, since whether or not something starts is much easier to know.

[110] SdeS: Right, right. That's what we're looking for. What would tell you that this miracle has happened?
C: You mean, how would I feel? Or how this miracle would have happened?
SdeS: What would you do? How would you feel after the miracle?
C: I would feel very good after the miracle, of course.
SdeS: Yes.
[115] C: Quite clear.
SdeS: Right.
C: Yes. I should tell you . . .
SdeS: Yes, and you'd feel more free . . .
C: Yes, I would have a high degree of freedom, freedom, of course. Right.

[120] SdeS: Right.

C: I wouldn't care for, I don't know if this is the right word, "care for" these symptoms all the time. Part of my day, much has to do with these symptoms.

SdeS: Right. So many hours . . .

C: Yes.

SdeS: Right. Now, when you don't spend those hours that way, what will you do instead?

[125] C: Yes. I would do a lot more positive things.

SdeS: Like what?

C: Like what? For instance, I had the idea and I wrote to some publishers that I want to write a book. And at first I thought nobody would agree to this.

SdeS: Yes . . .

C: Anyway, the second letter was successful and these publishers said they are interested in this book.

[130] SdeS: Um hmm.

C: The title of this book would be "How My Children Will Be Successful in School," which would be great in Germany, of course.

SdeS: Yes.

C: In USA too, perhaps.

SdeS: Yes.

[135] C: Right and yes, I would have more power and more energy for this.

SdeS: So, you would start working on this book the day after the miracle?

C: Yes. I would start working on the book, and do other positive things.

SdeS: OK.

C: Lots of positive things, you can imagine, but I do some of these positive things already.

Starting to work on his book is a much more useful way for him (and others) to know that things have gotten better for him. Certainly, working on a book will fill at least some of the hole left by the end of the anxieties. (This is not to say that writing a book is without difficulties or without anxieties of a different sort.)

However, the puzzle, developed through my text-focused reading, remains. As far as he is concerned, activities are the opposite of depression, and he is already doing some of these positive things, these positive activities. And yet he continues to see himself as having depressive symptoms. Should his rating be higher than 3? Lower? Is 10 unrealistic?

[140] SdeS: Right.

C: In spite of my disturbances or problems.

SdeS: It's amazing. How do you do that? How do you get yourself to do these things in spite of it?

C: Yes. I'm sure that I can't sit at home and do nothing.

SdeS: I know people who do. If you had been here a few hours ago, you'd know one too.

[145] C: That's just not my way of living. My wife tells me I even do, in spite of my disturbances, I do too many things concerning lectures and different things. And the University starts next week . . .

SdeS: Right, right.

C: Yes, so I am able to do these positive things, but still there are these depressive things.

SdeS: Right.

C: I take medicine, I have to take medicine.

[150] SdeS: So, how would your wife know that this miracle happened to you?

C: Yes. I talk very often about my symptoms, to my wife, and she would notice that I wouldn't talk about these symptoms so much, or I wouldn't talk about these symptoms at all.

SdeS: Not at all, they're gone.

C: Yeah.

SdeS: And so what would you talk about with her?

[155] C: Yes, what I would call positive things: geography, history, languages, etc., etc.

SdeS: What does she do? Is she working?

C: She is a teacher too.

SdeS: Teacher too.

C: Yeah.

[160] SdeS: What does she teach?

C: She teaches English and Home Economics.

S. English and Home Economics. When you talk together at home, what language do you use?

C: What language? German, of course.

SdeS: Well, not "of course" . . .

[165] C: Because when my wife had one of the examinations, they told her she should go for one year to England to improve her English a bit.

SdeS: Um hmm.

C: So, it wouldn't make any sense if we talk English at home, or so, wouldn't make any sense; perhaps it would make sense, but German is easier.

SdeS: Of course it would be.

C: Yeah.

[170] SdeS: Your English is going fine.

C: Thank you.

SdeS: Um hmm. Ah . . .

C: [Interrupting] Yes, but I don't know, I don't know apart from this riddle, apart from this miracle . . .

SdeS: Um hmm.

[175] C: . . . I don't know how to get rid of these symptoms, and I said these symptoms are lack of self-confidence, anxieties, and being in low spirits very often.

SdeS: Right, and spending a lot of time talking about them with other people and dealing with them in other ways.

C: Yes, talking . . . but suffering from it too.

SdeS: Of course.

C: It's not only a nice thing for spare time or for leisure time, I really suffer from these things.

[180] SdeS: You must be tired of that!

C: Must be?

SdeS: Tired of that, of suffering from all this.

C: Yes, then, my problem is, I think, I'm not completely the master of these symptoms. To a certain degree I can do something against it, but to a certain degree it comes from the inside. It is not quite clear if there is a genetic component, it's not clear.

The puzzle clears up a little bit here. He sees these various positive activities as part of a fight against the problem, sort of an anti-problem, an anti-depression, rather than as signs of progress or as part of a solution. Fighting against the problem is just as intolerable as the problem itself! That is: Problem + Anti-problem = Suffering. Sticking to a text-focused reading has allowed us, therapist/reader and client/reader, to make some sense of what we have been talking about.

[184] SdeS: Right.

C: Ah, a certain degree comes from inside and I can't do anything against it. It's biochemistry of the brain.

SdeS: Ah . . .

C: Biochemistry of the brain.

SdeS: Maybe. I wonder about that because you go to these lectures and all these other things, in spite of it.

C: Yeah.

[190] SdeS: So, how come? How do you do that? How do you get yourself to do that?

C: Maybe it is what Victor Frankl said when he used the term "self-transcendence" which means you forget your symptoms and do other things.

SdeS: You've been reading Frankl?

C: I've been reading Frankl for some years, yes, different books.

SdeS: Um hmm.

[195] C: So, I do good things, although I sometimes don't feel good.

SdeS: Um hmm. And, when you do these things and usually you don't feel good, would somebody watching you with a hidden camera, or something, would they know, could they tell whether you felt good doing it or not? Could they tell you didn't feel good? Would somebody else know?

C: Yes. I think other people, to a certain degree, other people can notice if I feel good or not. Sometimes people tell me that I'm too serious.

SdeS: Uh hmm.

C: And I don't laugh enough, but it's not so important for me, but I think other people could see a difference.

[200] SdeS: Your wife could?

C: She could, at any rate.

SdeS: What do you two do together that's good, that's fun, that you two enjoy doing?

C: My wife and me?

SdeS: What's the best for you two together?

[205] C: Perhaps traveling.

SdeS: Un hmm.

C: I think so. Today the holidays are starting and we will go for three or four days, until Sunday, to someplace nice in Germany.

SdeS: You both enjoy that.

C: Yes.

[210] SdeS: Good. Good. Now, during these holidays, these next three or four days, you will be doing things that you enjoy doing?

C: Yes.

SdeS: Whether you feel like doing them or not, right? Is that what you've been saying? You do these things anyway, in spite of how you feel sometimes?

C: I didn't get the question.

SdeS: Let me try again. Over the next few days, on these holidays . . .

[215] C: Yes . . .

SdeS: Are you going to have to do the things you enjoy in spite of the problems, or are you going to be just doing the things you enjoy?

C: I think the first one is correct. Do them in spite of the problems.

SdeS: OK. Now, if the miracle happens, then you would be doing them just because you enjoy doing them?

C: Yes.

[220] SdeS: How would your wife know the difference?

C: Yes. For instance, I wouldn't talk about these problems. That's one very important point. And I think my behavior would be different.

SdeS: In what way?

C: In a way that I would have, would have more joy.

SdeS: Uh huh.

[225] C: And when you have more joy, you laugh more. And other people see it in your face and your whole body and the way you talk.

SdeS: Right.

C: Different point, you know.

SdeS: So, that would be clear to her certainly.

C: Yes.

[230] SdeS: OK. I was thinking about how the people in your English class . . .

C: Yes, ah . . .

SdeS: How they would know . . .

C: I think, at the moment, the people in my two English classes — we have now had three lessons, three weeks —

SdeS: Right.

[235] C: I think they don't recognize that I have problems. For instance, I am teaching and giving a lot of privates lessons, different students, and I think they don't notice. One student even told me that I am very funny. She asked me if I'm always as funny as that.

SdeS: What did you say?

C: I didn't say anything.

SdeS: You should have said "Yes."

C: I should have said "Yes"?

[240] SdeS: You're too shy, though.

C: It was a surprise that other people don't recognize that I have some problems.

SdeS: Yeah.

C: And, I think, very often for other people, it is difficult to recognize.

SdeS: Your student, she didn't see it. She thought . . .

[245] C: Right. She thought I am very funny.

SdeS: Uh hmm.

C: Yes. But . . .

SdeS: Are you?

C: Yes, but towards one person I am very often in a different position. Or I behave differently from my behavior in groups.

[250] SdeS: Do you think that the other people in your English class think you are funny too?

C: In my English class? I don't seem like I'm funny. I want to be more funny in English class. The English class is OK, perhaps average, not very good, not very bad.

SdeS: Uh hmm.

C: It's OK.

SdeS: I wonder if they think you're funny.

[255] C: I don't think so because I don't laugh very much and I don't make jokes. Of course I am different in groups . . .

SdeS: Well . . .

C: . . . from . . .

SdeS: But she told you she thought you were funny and you didn't know that!

C: For me, this is a very rare experience.

[260] SdeS: Yeah.

C: Not many people told me.

SdeS: Do you believe her?

C: Yes, I believed her. She said it very seriously.

SdeS: Good. I think I believe her too.

[265] C: Uh hmm.

SdeS: Do you think that sometimes, like with her, you're funny and you don't notice it?

C: I've been told that sometimes it's called some kind of "dry humor" or whatever.

SdeS: Yeah.

C: Maybe it's true, but I think it's very seldom.

[270] SdeS: Hmmm.

C: And, ah . . .

SdeS: The difficulty with dry humor, it's very easy to miss it.

C: Uh hmm.

SdeS: If you're looking in the wrong direction, for a second, or not listening for a second, you might miss it.

[275] C: Um hmm. Um hmm.

SdeS: I wonder . . .

C: The point is I always am afraid of being rejected by other people.

SdeS: Of course.

C: Maybe these English courses or somewhere else. I always have a fear of being rejected or refused or not accepted.

[280] SdeS: Right. How do you handle that? You do these things anyway sometimes.

C: I just want to mention, it's young pupils whom I teach once or twice a week. They think I'm very good because I try very hard to teach them English or French and they think I'm very good. I feel good in these relationships.

SdeS: Um hmmm.

C: But I don't feel good in groups.

SdeS: Um hmm.

[285] C: But I . . .

SdeS: Well, I don't know if there is an answer. So, one more question. When was the most recent "best day" for you?

C: The best day for me, no. The last time . . .

SdeS: When?

C: Perhaps the first evening of my evening course, because we had stopped [for the summer] for some months.

[290] SdeS: Right.

C: I thought I wouldn't manage it, I wouldn't be able to teach that group. And then I saw I could teach it, I could do it perhaps average or so.

SdeS: Um hmmm.

C: And, yeah, I was very content with myself.

SdeS: Well, I have another one of those questions. 10 stands for, you would do any task that we might suggest to you that will help you reach your goal, while 0 stands for the only thing you are willing to do is hope and pray.

[295] C: Right.

SdeS: Where would you say you are today, between 0 and 10?

C: At 0 you pray,

SdeS: That's the only thing you do.

C: At 10, you fulfill a certain . . .

[300] SdeS: Do anything.

C: I think I would be perhaps at 7.

SdeS: The greatest majority of things we might suggest to you, you would do those?

C: Yes.

SdeS: Is there anything that pops into your head that you are sure you wouldn't do?

[305] C: Anything I would not do to solve this problem? To go to more doctors, I would not . . .

SdeS: OK.

C: They're not very efficient.

SdeS: And one of the things I believe in is efficiency. So, I am wondering if there is anything else you would want to tell us now that might be important for me to know today. Anything pop into your head? Anything at all?

C: I don't know how efficient I really am. I talk about this with my wife and with other people.

[310] SdeS: You'd like to be?

C: I have some friends, and on a scale from 0 to 10, I ask them where do I stand today.

SdeS: Um hmm.

C: And they tell me very often 8 or so . . .

SdeS: Um hmm

[315] C: And I am always astonished about such a high estimation . . .

SdeS: You're saying "3" and they say "8"?

C: Yeah.

SdeS: Hmm. I have a thought for you to think about while we go consult. An idea for you. What if they are right?

After the Pause

His friends' viewing him as being at 8, his viewing himself as being at 3 (meaning at least some progress), his student's seeing him as funny, his viewing himself as at his best teaching English, his doing activities in spite of his difficulties, his idea that after the miracle he would not be talking about problems to his best friend or his wife, and the idea that, after the miracle, he would start on the book—all are raw material for helping him to construct a next step toward a solution.

I used the scaling question about his willingness to do a task [units 294 through 305] because, although he is busy with many activities, these activities are not seen as part of a solution but rather as a part of the war against the problem. The question [294] is an attempt to frame any homework activity as somehow different, an activity clearly aimed at making things better.

[319] SdeS: I want to thank you for coming in today.

C: Yes. OK.

SdeS: It's been a pleasure talking with you and I'm certainly impressed with several things about what you've been saying. I get the idea, for instance, that the publishers—one example of what I'm think-ing—they see something in you that you don't see. I can't tell you how many plans for books they reject in proportion to ones they encourage.

C: Yes.

SdeS: So, they see something in you. Your friends see something in you—they say you're at 8.

C: Yeah.

[325] SdeS: Your students in the English classes, they see something. The woman who said you are funny saw something in you. So, I think there's a lot about you you don't know. There's a lot of strength and maybe even a comedian.

C: Comedian. If you think of the fact that all important comedians are really sad inside . . .

SdeS: I'm not so sure. That's just folklore. The funniest people I know aren't sad inside. [I wish I had thought of the distinction between

"comedians" and "clowns" at the time. "Clowns" are the ones who
are crying on the inside.] Anyway, I suspect that there is a lot more
about you that you don't know, that would be useful for you to
find out. This is in line with what you're friend says—you are at 8.
He may be right. I'd like you to think some more about that.

C: Yes.

SdeS: And we have an idea that you might find useful—an experiment. You might learn something about you from it. It might,
at first, sound to you like too much work. We think you can do it.
OK? What we suggest you do, as an experiment, is when you and
your wife go on this trip together for the next four days . . .

[330] C: Yes.

SdeS: You speak only in English with her these next four days and
pretend that the problems you usually talk about can't be translated into English.

C: [Laughs heartily]

SdeS: And see what difference that makes to how you feel about
things, and so on. And then let your therapist know what you
learned.

C: OK.

SdeS: OK. [Getting up out of the chair]

C: Well, thank you very much. [Shaking hands]

SdeS: It was nice meeting you and I want to wish you the best of luck.

C: Thank you again.

IN LEIPZIG

The following transcript[1] is from a consultation session done in Leipzig, Germany (November 1992) with Wolfgang Eberling (Norddeutsches Institut für Kurzzeittherapie) serving as interpreter. The client had
had one previous session with Ralf Vogt, who is a psychologist in
private practice in Leipzig. In order to bring a "new mind" or at least a

[1]Thanks to Mary Jo Robinson for her patience in developing this transcript which was—like
developing any transcript—a very frustrating activity, made more so by all three of the
participants who, now and then, accidentally switched from German to English or from
English to German. For the sake of simplicity, most of this is put into English.

different perspective to the therapy I, as is my custom in these situations, knew nothing more about the case.

Throughout the interview, after a question was translated, the client would usually wait several seconds before responding. During this pause, he moved his eyes around or gazed off as if searching for his answers. Throughout, the client spoke directly to me rather than to the interpreter, which is quite rare.

[1] Steve de Shazer: Thank you for coming today.
[2] C: [Nods and smiles]
[3] SdeS: I understand you have to leave right on time . . . to get to work.
[4] C: [In English] One hour.
[5] SdeS: OK. We will do our best to make sure it's only one hour.
[6] C: [Nods]
[7] SdeS: There's no guarantee, but—we hope this will be useful for you, but there's no guarantee.
[8] C: [Nods]
[9] SdeS: What kind of work do you do?
[10] C: [In English] I am a gardener.
SdeS: A gardener: Is that good for you?
C: [Nods] It's a good profession for me.
SdeS: Good, good. And, let's see . . . OK, shall we start?
C: [In English] OK. Please.
[15] SdeS: So, the first question starts like this.
C: [Smiles]
SdeS: [Using a clipboard to write on] Zero (0) stands for the problems you came into treatment for are gone, solved; and minus ten (−10) stands for how things were before you started therapy.
C: [Nods]
SdeS: Where would you say you are today between −10 and 0?
[20] C: Minus nine.

Things are better: the client sees some improvement since he began therapy. Whatever the improvement involves now needs to be talked about so that we know what to build on. Unless this improvement is talked about there is some danger that whatever differences there are will simply disappear.

[21] SdeS: Un huh. And, how did that happen that you went from
−10 to −9? How did that happen?

C: [Gestures with arms] Through the conversations I had with the
therapist and thinking over the situation.

SdeS: OK. Your thinking and the conversations, what difference has
that made?

C: [Gestures with hands] The therapist to me is a partner in the conversation and someone to talk to whom I can trust. And this en-
ables me to bring out and talk about my problems.

[25] SdeS: Good, good. And, as a result of that, are you doing something different?

C: It's hard to say about oneself.

SdeS: Yes.

C: [Looks at ceiling, gestures broadly. Long pause] I think about, that
I can cope better when I have the situation of being blocked psy-
chologically inside. So that I can go on faster then.

SdeS: OK.

[30] C: Cope with it better.

SdeS: OK. And what difference do you think other people would see
about you between −10 and −9?

C: [Shakes head] I think they don't notice any differences.

SdeS: −9 now, where do you think between −9 and 0 people will
begin to notice differences?

C: −7.

[35] SdeS: OK. Good, good. What do you think the first thing they'll
notice will be?

Some of the improvement is attributed to the previous therapy
session (line 24), so whatever therapist and client did together must
have been useful. The improvement he describes (lines 28 thru 32) is
simply taken at face value and more details can be developed later.
Talking about the −7 conveys the consultant's expectations that the
client will continue to make improvement and the other people will
notice these. Clients frequently say that once other important people
notice some difference, any reactions they make can become a rein-
forcement of the client's changes.

[36] C: [Long pause. Gestures with hands] So, I think what they'll
notice first is that there aren't any problem situations for me where

sometimes I hesitate or stop. To deal with those [situations] and deal with those successfully.

SdeS: OK. And, when you're doing that — successfully like that — how will other things change as a result for you?

C: Do you mean things that I'm doing or things that are around me?

SdeS: Both.

[40] C: Mmmmm. [Hand gestures] Well, I think that, for instance, I think what I do and what I can do will be of a different value for me. So, the evaluation of what I do will change. Maybe things that are important in either way, good or bad, they will be less important. They will change in the value I give to them. Also, the same thing will happen in relation to people.

SdeS: OK. And how will that change? In relation to other people?

C: I will have the courage to talk to other people.

SdeS: Un huh.

C: Have more courage.

[45] SdeS: To meet new people?

C: Yes. Another part . . . the ability to leave behind some other people. Just leave them there and go away. People who get unimportant or people who are not sympathetic to me.

SdeS: OK. OK. And . . . where would you think you would meet these new people?

C: In clubs, at the theater, for instance. Traveling.

SdeS: OK. And how often do you go to the theater and clubs now?

[50] C: Maybe twice a month.

SdeS: OK.

C: And, overall, once a year I do some traveling.

SdeS: And, at −7, how often do you think you'll be doing these things?

C: I think theater, concerts, exhibitions, movies, that will be twice as much as now.

The client's use of the future tense when talking about −7 (beginning in line 36) indicates, perhaps, that he fully expects to reach −7. (Were he to have used a conditional tense, then I could have asked him to estimate his own confidence in reaching −7. In that situation, a scaling question probably would have been useful: "With 10 standing for as much confidence as is humanly possible and 0 standing for

absolutely no confidence whatsoever, how confident are you that you
will reach −7?")

Whatever other changes are included in his −7, the cultural activities and meeting new people will increase in an observable fashion.
Thus he has some ways to measure his own progress. Now that we
know something about −10, −9, and −7, it is time to find out about
0. What, as exactly as possible, is he looking for? How will he know
therapy has been successful?

[55] SdeS: OK. And, ah, now, perhaps a difficult question . . .
C: Yeah.
SdeS: Suppose that one of these nights, when you go to sleep, while
      you're asleep, there was a miracle . . .
C: [Nods]
SdeS: And the problem that brought you to therapy, this −10 [points
      to scale], was gone [snaps fingers] and you were at 0 like that. But
      this happened while you were sleeping, so you cannot know that
      it happened. So, once you wake up this next morning, how will
      you find out there has been a miracle?
[60] C: [Shifts in chair. Long pause. Hand gestures throughout] Not in
      the first moment, but when I go out into the street and somehow I
      come together with people.
SdeS: What will you notice?
C: That I can talk in an easier way. More relaxed. And that I can
      perceive other people in a different way.
SdeS: When you're perceiving people in a different way, how do you
      think they will react to that?
C: Also in a different way.
[65] SdeS: Uh huh.
C: In a positive, but also in a negative way.
SdeS: And what else will let you know that this miracle has happened?
C: [Long pause. Shrugs] I don't know. [Smiles]
SdeS: Uh huh. How about other people? How would they know? How
      would they discover that there was this miracle? . . . You can't tell
      them about it, right? Because it happened while you were sleeping.
      So, how would they know?
[70] C: [Long pause. Gestures with hands] They'd perceive me in a
      different way and I'd start to go out and do things I didn't dare to
      do until now.

SdeS: What sort of things?

C: [Smiles broadly. Shifts position]

SdeS: Anything you can tell us about?

C: [Broad gestures with arms. Long pause] Maybe I'd go out dancing again.

[75] SdeS: You enjoy dancing?

C: Sometimes, yes.

Zero seems related to −9 and −7 in that what he describes involves a continuation of the same sorts of activities rather than something drastically different. So we have some idea of what the client wants out of therapy. The client's smiling response (line 72) led me to *guess* that his miracle picture had become too private to be talked about, particularly in this rather public context. (Some of the team later thought that the client had simply run out of material.) Therefore, I thought that, even more than usual, I needed to protect the client's privacy (line 73). The client, of course, has a perfect right to choose not to talk about anything he decides not to talk about; the "I don't want to talk about it" message, whether implicit or explicit, needs to be taken seriously.

[77] SdeS: Let's see, you were saying that it's −9 today. Have there been different times recently when it was better than that?

C: [Shakes head] Never.

SdeS: Days . . . minutes . . .

[80] C: Hmmm.

SdeS: Hours.

C: Yes, yes.

SdeS: What's the best it's been?

C: Hmmm. Minus five.

The client actually had some period of time when he was halfway to his goal! Even minutes at −5 might be useful in constructing a solution. However long this −5, this exception needs to be described as fully as possible, since the solution will probably involve the client's doing more of the same kind of things. (In a therapy situation, I would probably have opened this second session with the simple question, "What is better?" and we might have talked about this railroad journey much earlier in the session.)

[85] SdeS: OK. And, how recent was that?

C: Three, four days ago. On Saturday.

SdeS: Saturday. And what were you doing? What was going on?

C: [Leans back. Broad gestures with arms] I was traveling by railway, in an area I didn't know, one that was completely new to me.

SdeS: Where was this?

[90] C: All through the area of Köln, Aachen, Maastricht.

SdeS: And, what did you do when you were there?

C: [Gestures with hands] Looked through the old town, downtown.

SdeS: Uh huh.

C: I walked around, looking around for two hours and then went home again.

[95] SdeS: So, did you stop in Aachen?

C: One hour.

SdeS: One hour, and Köln for?

C: Two hours.

SdeS: Were you with other people or were you alone on this trip?

[100] C: [Shakes head] I started alone in the beginning but during the trip I met other people.

SdeS: These other people that you met on this trip, were these people you can and will meet again?

C: I don't know. I could see them . . .

SdeS: It's possible.

C: If I want to. I really don't know if I want to.

[105] SdeS: Uh huh.

C: It's possible.

SdeS: OK. And you had a good time, comparatively.

C: Yes.

SdeS: More or less. OK. So, what was the best part? The actual journey on the train or walking around visiting the city . . .

[110] C: [Looks up. Smiles]

SdeS: Or was it meeting the people?

C: The journey on the train and sightseeing in the city.

SdeS: What impressed you most about Köln?

C: [Nods. Gestures with hands] The cathedral. Before starting, that was the most important thing for me.

[115] SdeS: Good, good. All right, now! [Shifts in chair]

C: [Also shifts in chair]

Now that we know that -5 can be reached in the western section of Germany, which he might attribute to the "reunification" or to being on holiday, I ask about other exceptions, i.e., whether or not -5 can be reached at home.

[117] SdeS: Has there been a recent time that you can remember, when it was close to -5, when you were here in the Leipzig area?
C: [Nods] Yes, yes, in the theater.
SdeS: And when was this?
[120] C: Two weeks ago.
SdeS: And what was it about that that made it -5?
C: A very pleasant atmosphere. [Long pause] I dressed up a little bit more than usual.
SdeS: Right.
C: [Eyes moving around—appears to be searching. Broad gestures with arms] I was able to put myself in a different world while this play was going on.
[125] SdeS: Right. When you did that, when you put yourself in a different world, while the play was going on, does that continue after the play is done, for a while?
C: [Nods vigorously] Yes.
SdeS: About how long, would you say?
C: That's different.
SdeS: Uh huh.
[130] C: Sometimes hours, sometimes days.
SdeS: Sometimes days! So you, you could sometimes stay at this -5 for ... hours? Days? Do you think? Or is it just this special situation?
C: That would be nice, but it's ... that's ... I can't do it just any time.
SdeS: Right. But you do get into this special world ... and you can do that for ... hours or days, for the play?
C: [Nods]
[135] SdeS: And is that ... close to being at -5 ... after the play?
C: [Nods] Yes.
SdeS: OK. OK. Good, good. What we want to do is take some time out to think about what you've been saying and discuss it among the team here. And then we will let you know what our thinking is. So, we'll take a 10 minute pause. But before we do, I'm wonder-

ing, is there's anything that you think we should know, we need to
know, that seems important to you, that we haven't even touched
on?

C: [Shakes head] No.

SdeS: OK. Maybe then some coffee?

After the Pause

Several things seemed quite important for constructing a closing message. First of all, the two exceptional times were both in out of the
ordinary situations. His pleasure or even excitement while describing
the trip and the special world around the play gave the team the idea
that the client's rating of −5 was probably low.

If possible, a way needs to be developed for the client to be able to
transfer the behaviors and feelings of the special exceptions into his
usual day-to-day living. The fact that the exceptions happened in two
rather different contexts suggests that such a transfer might be possible for this client.

Although there was some talk about 0, the minus five, including all
of the feelings and behaviors described, seemed much more real to
the client. It is something that he has had recent experience doing
and therefore might be used as the basis for a homework task.

In spite of the shortness of the interview—or perhaps because of
this shortness—we were able to figure out what we needed to know
and what we ought to do. There was not much, if any, extraneous
material to sort through. Perhaps having an interpreter allowed us to
make maximum use of the scales which, at least in large part, bridge
the language differences.

[140] SdeS: First of all, we want to thank you for coming today . . .

C: [Nods]

SdeS: . . . and talking with us in front of all these people [sixty]. We
think that that takes some courage and, therefore, we think that
your idea that you're at −9, that rating for yourself, is too low. We
would have guessed higher than that.

C: [Nods]

SdeS: Well, we think you sometimes underestimate yourself.

[145] C: [Nods]

SdeS: For instance, we think it took a lot of courage to come here today, to take a trip to Aachen and Köln. It takes a lot of flexibility and courage to travel alone.

C: [Shifts in chair]

SdeS: And meet people, people you will leave behind and people you won't leave behind . . .

C: [Raises eyebrows quizzically]

[150] SdeS: You know, traveling to Köln and going to the theater . . . are different worlds. You have lots of different cultural interests, and that impressed us.

C: [Nods]

SdeS: And it takes a lot of flexibility to appreciate both these kinds of things.

C: [Nods]

SdeS: Now, we'd like to suggest to you an experiment . . .

[155] C: [Nods. Smiles]

SdeS: Between now and next time you talk with the psychologist,

C: [Shifts in chair, searching with eyes, and then nods]

SdeS: And that is, each day you toss a coin . . . [Demonstrates]

C: Uh huh.

[160] SdeS: And, when it come up "heads" (like this), then on that day, we'd like you to pick one hour when you are doing your normal regular routine . . . working or whatever . . . And, during that one hour, we want you to pretend that you are at least at −5 . . .

C: [Gestures with arms. Nods. Smiles] Uh huh.

SdeS: And very carefully observe what difference that makes to how things go for you.

C: [Leans forward. Appears to be listening very carefully to the interpreter] And the rest of the time?

SdeS: Both, during and after.

[165] C: [Nods] Yes, yes.

SdeS: OK? And see what happens. I think you can learn something from that. And, I hope that I find out how it goes for you.

C: [Nods]

SdeS: Thanks again for coming. Nice meeting you.

C: [In English] I thank you.

[170] SdeS: [Shaking hands] Wiedersehen.

*　　*　　*

One year later, during a second demonstration interview in Leipzig, the client reported that things had significantly improved for him. He had been on a business trip looking at Amsterdam's parks and had been going to the theater, movies, exhibitions, dancing, etc., at least once a week throughout the previous year. He had also been feeling better physically and therefore missed less work. At this time he was tired of living alone and very interested in developing a stable relationship with a woman.

Chapter Twelve

SQUEAKING INTO A FIVE

Compare knowing and saying: how many feet high Mont Blanc
is — how the word "game" is used — how a clarinet sounds — If you
are surprised that one can know something and not be able to say
it, you are perhaps thinking of a case like the first. Certainly not
one like the third.
— *Wittgenstein (1958, #78)*

IN THE FIRST SESSION the client said that she had trouble relating to
her daughter and finding her own spot in life. She then began to
describe the troubles she had had in the past and those which continued into the present. All of these troubles she attributed to "having
been raised to be a hysteric, moronic individual."

In response to the miracle question, she said that she would "feel
that I don't have to be a figment of other people's imagination" and
would therefore "feel at peace." Furthermore, she would no longer
have this "weight in my mind and this weight in my heart." When
asked about how her daughter would know that this miracle had happened she replied that her daughter would think that she is "finally
a mother." During the session, there were no behavior or pictorial
descriptions of what might happen as a result of these changes. Given
such a broad and general depiction of the day after the miracle, the
client was asked this scaling question: "With 10 standing for the day
after the miracle and 0 standing for how things were way back when
you started therapy, where would you rate yourself today?" She saw
that things were better in her life due to years of therapy, but she
could only say that things were certainly not at 0 any longer.

Regardless of the therapist's question, the client would respond with

complaints from the past, some of which were continuing in the present. The therapist would accept these responses and then ask about
how that sort of thing would be different after the miracle. The client's
response would be a firm "I don't know," followed with another complaint.

The session ended with a series of compliments about how hard
the client had worked to make her life better. Because of the client's
responses to the miracle question and the scaling question, no specific
task was suggested.

> Anything that the patient actually can do. Anything that he can
> do. Preferably something in relationship to his problem. . . . What
> do they show you that they can actually do?
> —*Milton H. Erickson (Haley, 1985, p. 152)*

SESSION TWO

[1] Insoo Kim Berg: Last time you were here was about a month ago.
[2] C: Mm hm.
[3] IKB: And, I'm just wondering what's been better with your daugh-
ter?
[4] C: Nothing.
[5] IKB: Nothing's better with your daughter?
C: No.
IKB: She's still living with you though?
C: Yeah. Mm hm.
IKB: And she must be out of school now?
[10] C: Yeah, for summer.
IKB: For summer.
C: Mm hm.
IKB: So what does she do with her life, do with her time?
C: Mmmm . . . waste it.
[15] IKB: Waste it?
C: Ah ha.
IKB: Would she say she's wasting her time?
C: I don't think so.
IKB: You don't think she would say she was wasting her time?
[20] C: No, but I don't see anything that looks like it's an accomplish-
ment.

IKB: Right.

C: I see just wasting.

IKB: Ah ha, so she's not taking any classes, she's not taking any, she's not going to . . . well I guess at 16 she doesn't want to go to camp?

C: Well she was . . .

[25] IKB: She's not working?

C: She more or less failed out this whole last half of semester.

IKB: Right.

C: And um, she had a fantastic way of forever saying, um, "I'm doing fine," or a . . .

IKB: So she thinks she's doing fine?

[30] C: She was saying while she was going . . . when she was attending this last semester

IKB: Right.

C: She was doing fine, that they were helping her, she wasn't going to fail, she was in special classes, she was getting all the special help she needed.

IKB: But she wasn't doing very well?

C: No. And then the final grade came and I was shocked.

[35] IKB: Now is this a situation with her, that she can do better, but is not doing, or she doesn't know how to do better, and therefore she needs help to do better? Which is the situation here?

C: Well, I think she has the potential.

IKB: You do?

C: Um hm.

IKB: You do believe that?

[40] C: Oh yeah, but I . . .

IKB: What tells you that?

C: Well, I think because she's very bright basically.

IKB: How do you know that?

C: Well, you know, the things she says and does.

[45] IKB: Like what?

C: I'm not stupid myself. I consider myself an intelligent person. I don't . . .

IKB: You are?

C: Yeah.

IKB: And she is too?

[50] C: I think she is too, I don't consider myself an ignorant . . .

IKB: OK.

C: At times I consider myself ignorant, when you make a mistake . . .

IKB: Everybody does, everybody makes mistakes.

C: Other than that I have to consider myself . . .

[55] IKB: So you both are very, very bright people?

C: You have to remember that I had two years of college and I have a professional degree . . .

IKB: Right.

C: You know so . . .

IKB: Right.

[60] C: I, you know, can't be ignorant.

IKB: So you think that Rebecca is also very bright? So that tells you she can do better?

C: Well, it's just, you know, observing her from the time she was born until now. Her sister, her sister is excelling in everything.

IKB: Ah.

C: Her sister is, ah, she's just somebody that you, you know, have a tendency to be a little proud of.

[65] IKB: Really?

C: You can't say too much of it . . .

IKB: How old is . . .

C: To Becky.

IKB: How old is she?

[65] C: Her sister is ah, . . . 21 now.

IKB: 21.

C: Yeah, but she . . .

IKB: She's not living with you and Rebecca?

C: No. Because ah, she'd sit in a corner, she'd rather sit in a corner . . . and she would ah, she would always read a book and she would do nothing else but read a book.

[70] IKB: Which one?

C: The older one.

IKB: The older one. But she's doing fine?

C: Apparently with schooling, she's now in Germany . . .

IKB: She's also very bright, too, then?

[75] C: I, I think, you know, they're bright in different ways. Each one is bright bookwise, um, Rebecca is bright when it comes to life, but still, I think she has the potential if she could, um, if you could anchor her somewhere, you know, to do the same thing.

IKB: So you have some idea what they need, what both children need?

C: You know, the older one, no. I guess trying to draw her out and get a balance between studies and life generally.

The client is saying that things have not improved since the previous session; the miracle and scaling questions in the first session only gave the client and therapist some very broad, nonspecific guidelines but no way to judge success (or failure). Therefore, the therapist needs to do something different in hope that that will make a difference because continuing to approach things in the same way is just more of the same of something that is not working, which is the exact definition of a problem.

What Does the Client Want?

IKB: I want to pick up from last time you were here about a month ago. I'd like to sort of review things, because I'm sure you have had some chance to think about, think about what brought you here last time.

C: Mm hm. Right.

[80] IKB: And can I sort of review that and then, what do you suppose ... what do you suppose you need to see different in your life with you and Rebecca and whatever the circumstances, so that you can say to yourself, "This is really a good idea that I started this therapy again." I think you have had lots of therapy before.[1]

C: OH ... YEAH.

IKB: So what do you suppose this time there has to be done so that you can say that I got that piece accomplished this time, by coming here?

C: I just don't have any family unity. You know. There's been no, there's no real communication, there's no family unity, there's no happiness between us ...

---

[1] In the previous session (the first) we learned that along the way the client had been given two heavy diagnosis: Borderline personality and/or schizophrenia.

IKB: So you'd like to see family unity?

[85] C: Well we, it seems as though, from the time that they were born, it was, a relationship with my husband where he just took over the girls lives . . .

The client's shift to complaints about the ex-husband (an area of complaint) is interrupted and she is brought back to the task of defining "family unity."

IKB: Let me get some ideas about this. So family unity means what? What do you mean by family unity?

C: Me, with my two daughters. I would like to have a better relationship, like I can sit here and talk about Rachel, but Rachel doesn't give two shits about me. Matter of fact she'd like to see me dead somewhere, or locked up in a nursing home somewhere. That's the bottom line. You know, but I sit here and I say things like I really admire Rachel, I'm really happy for her, but if you had her in the same room with me, she could care less. You know, she . . . she would walk in this room, she would take one look and say, "Oh mom's here," and out she'd go.

IKB: OK. You want that changed.

C: Well sure . . .

[90] IKB: What about . . .

C: There's never been an improvement . . .

IKB: Right, what about you and Rebecca?

C: Same thing, Rebecca will touch base just a little bit, it's like if you're in agreement with what she's doing in her life, you know. And the reason for it is because it's like my ex-husband took control of these two from day number one . . . and still is the controlling factor . . .

IKB: So . . . it looks like that's not going to change.

[95] C: No.

IKB: His being in the picture.

C: Right.

IKB: He's going to be in the picture . . .

C: . . . I mean like girls that haven't been promiscuous, and their attitude has been one of being real loose about everything, um, they're not, they're very loose about everything, their attitude is very open and free, and ah . . .

[100] IKB: What do you suppose . . . it sounds like you have a big problem here . . .

C: With two girls . . .

IKB: With two girls . . .

C: I think have been pretty screwed up . . .

IKB: And wanting family unity . . .

Again the client is brought back to defining her goal.

[105] C: Right.

Constructing Goals

[106] IKB: What can I do to be helpful to you so that you can say, "I'm glad I went and talked to that lady?"

C: Well I don't know, you see what's happening is, Rebecca and I still live together, we live together but we don't communicate, we don't have any kind of, she's always off, you can't keep tabs on where she is. If I say anything, her father says, "Mind your own business, she can take care of herself."

IKB: Rachel is out of the house now.

C: Yeah, Rachel is out of the house.

[110] IKB: She lives on her own?

C: Yeah, but see, Rachel and I never really got along. I've always tried to get along with her, from the time she was just little, I've been buying my way through her life.

IKB: So, where should we start? You and Rebecca? Or you and . . .

C: Me and Rebecca I guess.

IKB: You and Rebecca, you want to start there.

[115] C: Yeah.

IKB: You want to start with you and Rebecca?

C: See, I love Rachel, but Rachel hates me.

IKB: Of course mothers do love their children.

C: Yes, right. And when I show up where she works, like, "What are you doing here?"

[120] IKB: So let's start with you and Rebecca.

C: Yes.

IKB: . . . the beginning part of it anyway.

C: Right. Yeah. That's with the start.

Constructing a Small First Step

IKB: So what do you suppose you'd like to see happen between you and Rebecca that would tell you that at least we are getting started on the right track? It's not finished yet, but it's getting started on the right track?

[125] C: Well you know, if there's ever anything like um, our relationship is so limited, it's like getting past this limited level.

Constructing an Exception

[125 continued] It's a level of, like, if I want her to do something for me, like I'll say, "If you clean those dishes and straighten up I'll give you $5.00." What's that, what's to straighten up? You put your, you check the time and it's like 20 minutes and you've done it for five bucks. Isn't that right?

IKB: So she does it then?

C: It just depends. If she's real strung up and she's very full of a lot of anxiety, and I can't tell, then um, she'll snap back at me and she'll let me know that she doesn't have the time of day for me or it.

IKB: Even for five bucks?

C: That's right.

[130] IKB: Ahhh, so sometimes she might do it and sometimes she might not do it?

C: Yeah.

IKB: Cleaning up or picking up things around the house.

C: Right. Sometimes I can get past that and sometimes I can't.

IKB: What's the difference, why sometimes she does and why sometimes she doesn't?

[135] C: Because they're her feelings and it's her life and she, she's in control of my life and the house, and everything else . . .

IKB: If she was here, and if I were to ask her, "What's the difference? How come you sometimes do it for five bucks?" An easy five bucks, I would guess . . .

C: Right.

IKB: "You earn five bucks."

C: Sometimes I even give her ten, you know.

[140] IKB: You do?

C: Oh sure. I just have this . . . I feel sorry for her and it looks like she's really having a tough time, you know, and I'll offer her ten dollars . . .

IKB: So then sometimes she does it, and even for ten bucks, doesn't do it?

C: Sometimes no, right.

IKB: OK, so what do you suppose she would say was the reason, between this and this?

[145] C: Because of her life.

IKB: That's what she would say?

C: If she's going to run off with a girlfriend or a boyfriend, or maybe her dad . . . see everybody else is more important in her life than me. You know, um . . .

IKB: Now is that would you say, I notice that Rebecca is about 16.

C: Mm hm, she's about 16.

[150] IKB: Is that typical for 16, or do you think she is not so typical for most 16 year olds, about things like that?

C: But we could say that in that area you could say yes, but then you could say that in every area. You could say the fact that she never cleans her room, that's typical. You could say the fact that she, um, sleeps over by her boyfriend's house, that's typical. You could say everything is typical.

IKB: So you don't want that?

C: Well, no.

IKB: Oh, OK. I'm trying to understand this, I'm trying to figure out
. . .

[155] C: I mean everybody could say every 16 year old, whatever they seem to do . . .

IKB: Yeah.

C: Whether it's take off with their friends, whether it's come home late, whether it's not get up early, sleep in bed, that's all typical.

IKB: . . . If I were to ask Rebecca whether she thinks she is a typical 16 year old?

C: Oh, she'd agree.

[160] IKB: She would.

C: Ah ha.

IKB: So she thinks she is pretty typical.

C: Oh I'm sure.

IKB: She thinks there is nothing wrong with her.

[165] C: Oh absolutely, because I think that this is the culture, the

way the culture's going and society here. You know, it's like the sky is the limit, but if you put us probably in um, another culture, they would be watching their children.

IKB: Would she say, would she say she wants to have this family unity as you do?

C: Oh, I don't think so.

IKB: You don't think so?

C: I think if she wanted anything, it just might be for her mother to be out of her business. I'm sure, probably, you know. But if you kept talking to her and kept talking to her, she may just say that um, maybe possibly a little bit more understanding of her mother, maybe possibly.

"Family unity" is getting more and more defined in interactional terms. That is, from mother's point of view it is one thing and from daughter's it is quite something else.

[170] IKB: Understanding of, of . . .

C: Me.

IKB: You?

C: Right.

IKB: She wants to understand you more?

[175] C: I don't understand her and she doesn't understand me.

IKB: So, she would say that's what she wants, mutual understanding of each other.

C: Right. I would think so.

IKB: Ah. OK. She might say that . . .

C: Well, you know, I'm just assuming, you know.

[180] IKB: Yeah, OK. So . . .

Constructing Another Exception

C: Sometimes she can be nice to me, you know.

IKB: Yeah?

C: Sometimes. Sometimes she can be nice to me.

IKB: Say some more about that, what does she . . .

[185] C: Well sometimes she'll clean the house up.

IKB: She does?

C: Yeah.

IKB: On her own?

C: Yeah, sometimes she'll do that.

[190] IKB: On her own, without you . . .

C: Without me, right.

IKB: . . . paying five bucks?

C: Yeah, sometimes. Right.

IKB: Yeah.

[195] C: Sometimes she does that, very rarely . . .

IKB: Does she do a good job when she does it?

C: There was a time when I would say "no," but now I'm just saying she did it.

IKB: . . . True . . . be grateful for whatever they do.

C: Good. I'll even tell her "oh great."

[200] IKB: Oh.

C: And then when she's gone I'll run the vacuum cleaner all over, you know.

IKB: . . . Right, OK. So she would say, what, she wants the same kind of family unity that you want or she wants a different kind of family unity than you want?

C: Um . . . I get a comment from both of them that I'm just not your normal mother. You know, and ah,

IKB: This is not all that unusual.

[205] C: And I don't like to, you know, let's face it, um, depending upon what family or environment we've been in, everybody is different. You could put me in one family and I could work out.

IKB: True.

C: And then another family I wouldn't work out.

IKB: Of course.

C: You know, I think a lot of it has to do with their father's influence. So, I'm just not right, I'm not a right mother as far as their father is concerned.

[210] IKB: Well, I guess he is just as stuck with you as their mother as you are stuck with him as their father.

C: Well you know, being divorced from him has helped me a lot . . .

IKB: Good.

C: Because I realize that when I was married to him, he was a person who I was not really emotionally and mentally compatible with.

IKB: Right. Let's come back to this with you and Rebecca. What do you suppose she would say it would take for the two of you to at least understand and talk to each other a little bit more? What would it take?

[215] C: Everything always falls on my shoulders. It's like I should shut up.

IKB: That's what she would say?

C: I should be ah, you know, leave her to do what she wants, because her father does that. When she's in his territory, she has spent the summer there and what not . . .

IKB: Sure.

C: When she's in his territory, then what happens is he just lets her come and go. He lets her make decisions for him.

[220] IKB: So you have very different parenting ideas.

C: I don't want to have her making decisions for me because I'm saying to myself, I have many more years up on her to have a little bit more knowledge here. I don't want her telling me something . . . and he does it, he lets her make the decisions and . . .

IKB: So what would she say, if she were sitting here and I were to ask her, what would she say it would take for the two of you to at least talk to each other, at least be nice to each other, understand . . .

C: Stay out of her business.

IKB: She would say that? Stay out of her business?

[225] C: Um hm. Um hm.

IKB: Um hm. OK.

Another Exception

[227] C: The only time we ever really relate is if I'm going shopping with her.

IKB: Ah, she likes that.

C: But that's not the way it always relates.

[230] IKB: So tell me about this, when you go shopping together, she wants to come along with you for shopping?

C: Not all the time, if it fits into her plans.

IKB: Then she wants to.

C: Right.

IKB: OK.

[235] C: Right.

IKB: . . . typical, sounds like a 16 year old to me. Let me . . . what
would she say it would take for the two of you at least to . . .
C: Nothing.
IKB: She would say nothing?
C: That's right. Because as far as she's concerned, I should always butt
out. It's me who wants to find . . . I'm looking around for an answer. I'm trying to find something.

Over and over the client mentions that she thinks that her daughter
wants her to butt out, to shut up and to leave her alone. However,
these exceptions suggest that it is at least not quite so black-and-white.

[240] IKB: To?
C: To get along with her.
IKB: Get along with her.
C: Sometimes she gets me so upset that I'd just as soon say, you
know . . .
IKB: So tell me about the times the two of you get along reasonably
well, not ideal, not perfect, but just reasonably . . . well, we can live
with this. It's not ideal but we can live with this.
[245] C: Well, then I found her being real nice. You know, like we'll
be in the department store and then, she'll even, if she comes over
she'll say, um, "Oh, this would look nice on you." She'll even find
something for me.
IKB: No kidding?
C: But I have my own taste and she tells me I'm very . . . that I have
terrible taste . . .
IKB: Sure.
C: Ah . . . you know.
[250] IKB: Sure, after all there's a difference . . .
C: . . . what you're supposed to look like.
IKB: . . . look like a 16 year old.
C: Right, yeah, smoke pot and look like a hippie.
IKB: No. So sometimes she is trying to be nice to you that way. I
guess she's making an effort that way?
[255] C: Sometimes. Sometimes.
IKB: Hm. What else does she do to try to get along with you?
C: Well sometimes she doesn't, sometimes she's purposeful. If she's
real mad at me she'll tell me that she's going over by her dad to

stay with her dad, you know. She'll let me know that they're going out together, or she'll tell me about something that she's buying for her, so I, you know, she's playing parents.

IKB: Well . . .

C: She's doing her thing.

[260] IKB: People do that.

C: Right.

IKB: To see what they could get out of both, right?

C: I suppose. Obviously.

IKB: Right. Now, so what do you want to do about this, how do you want things to be different between you and Rebecca?

[265] C: Well, I've always wanted to try and work it into some kind of a relationship, but it just doesn't seem, you know, just doesn't seem to be working at all.

IKB: Hm. So you would like the social relationship to be worked on between you and Rebecca?

C: Mm hm. She'll run to all her friends and she'll take her dog first, before me. And her sister was the same way with her little dog. It was like they'd come home from school and I could have had the house just impeccably neat and clean, and maybe I'd made a dress or blouse for one of them or the other, and made what they like, it's like, "Oh, hi, Harold" — the dog was like always first. So I used to always say, "Harold, you are going one day, you are going!" And he did.

IKB: He did, really.

C: I sent him on his merry way.

[270] IKB: You did.

C: I did.

IKB: Ah. Did it work out?

C: Oh yeah, he's happier with this older, retired couple.

IKB: Ah.

[275] C: Good for Harold.

IKB: Good.

C: Yeah, I'm glad I didn't have to see him any more, but then it didn't take very long and her sister bought her a little dog.

IKB: Oh.

C: So Rachel went off with her dog, and I sent it with an older couple 'cause she couldn't keep it where she was at with her dad, he couldn't have animals in the house, so then she goes and gives her sister a little—oh, I can't believe this—and it's like this dog goes with her everywhere.

Back on Track

[280] IKB: OK. I'm still wondering about this . . . what can I do to be helpful to you? I'm somewhat lost about this. What can I do to be helpful so that you and Rebecca can have a family unit?

C: I don't know, can you figure it out? You know. I can't. I've been trying.

IKB: Figure out what? What can I help you to figure out?

C: How to get along with Rebecca and ah,

IKB: OK. OK. Let me get some ideas there. Suppose somehow you figure out how to get along with her. I don't know what . . .

[285] C: I resent her. I resent her tremendously.

IKB: You do?

C: As a matter of fact, sometimes I can't stand her. I actually hate her.

IKB: Ah ha.

C: But her sister I like, even though her sister is nasty at times, but this one, I just, this one is so irritating. So, she's very annoying, she's irritating, she's deliberate. She came home one day, she had a tattoo on her ankle and she very tactfully said, "Well, what do you think of tattoos," and I said I really don't like them. I don't think people should put them on their bodies and she said um, "Well, my girlfriend" (I forget what her name was) "gave me one when I was up in Fond du Lac." And I said oh. See it's like she's purposeful. She's deliberate. She's antagonistic. She's aggravating. She's . . . and . . .

Given how the client sees her daughter and her firm commitment to causal thinking it is little wonder that she has a hard time imagining how things could be different. But the "exceptions" indicate or at least suggest that at times things do go better between mother and daughter.

[290] IKB: So . . .

C: So then I saw it was on her ankle.

IKB: Now, do you have to, do you want to get along with her, even
though you . . .

C: I do, yes.

IKB: . . . resent her and you hate her sometimes?

[295] C: Right. Um hm.

IKB: You don't want . . . you still want to get along with her.

C: That's not right for me to feel that way. I mean she, she may be
that way because of, I think, a lot of her father's influence. And
the fact that I didn't plan on having her. I was going to divorce her
father, and he was the one who tricked me into, you know going
to bed with him, and I ended up getting pregnant with her and it
hung me in that marriage a little longer. It was very disgusting and
very upsetting. Very depressing. I cried all the time every day. I
made up my mind I was divorcing him no matter what, kid or no
kid.

IKB: I'm still lost about this. How can I help you? What can I do to be
helpful?

C: It's a birth that wasn't really wanted.

[300] IKB: I understand. I understand.

C: And then . . .

IKB: . . . What can I do to be helpful to you?

C: You know it's like, find my way into her life and have a relationship.
There's been a lot of resentment, a lot of unhappiness.

A New Track

IKB: I guess . . . we are just . . . what a terrible life you have, what a
terrible problem you have.

[305] C: Mm hm. See, you . . .

IKB: Nothing has gone very well for you . . .

C: Let me just tell you something, OK?

IKB: Just a minute.

C: OK.

[310] IKB: Now, it seems like your life is not going very well.

C: Definitely not.

IKB: Many, many ways.

C: All the time . . .

IKB: Right. And so, you know, I mean, it seems like your marriage

was bad, your childhood was awful, and your children are not be-
having.

[315] C: That's right. You got it.

IKB: Right. So.

C: It's hell all the time.

IKB: Right.

C: You know.

[320] IKB: Right. Right. And in spite of that you want to have this
sort of, ah, normal family unit?

C: Well, who wouldn't? You know, after a while you get all these years
of this crap.

IKB: Sure . . . deserve it.

C: I think I'm a nice person. You know.

IKB: Right.

[325] C: And it's like I'm constantly getting my nerve endings sandpa-
pered down.

IKB: Right. Now do you think that somehow . . . what would it take
to rise above all this, do you think? Above this miserable life you
have had? What would it take, do you think?

C: I don't know. You think I'm . . . I'm still searching. I'm still trying
to find the answer.

IKB: About?

C: What would it take to make things work or to get above this?

[330] IKB: OK.

C: You know.

IKB: Now, you have been searching a lot . . .

C: Oh yes, you bet.

IKB: Yeah.

[335] C: All the time.

IKB: All the time.

C: All my life.

IKB: You've been in therapy a long time searching for that.

C: I've come a long way.

[340] IKB: Right.

C: There was this time when I couldn't even converse or even think
this way.

IKB: Right.

C: I had to make my mind work.

IKB: Right.

[345] C: I used to say to myself, how can I think like these other people? I used to wonder, how can they think things out and reason things out and get questions and be able to . . .

IKB: OK.

C: I used to think that way.

IKB: OK.

C: And finally it took me a *looooong* time.

[350] IKB: But you did it.

C: I came this far.

IKB: But you did . . . it's great.

C: Absolutely. Absolutely.

IKB: So what you want to do with your daughter, is this a continuation of hard work you had been putting in trying to have sort of like a normal life?

[355] C: I think I'm, I think I'm fighting my ex-husband's, his environment, I think I'm fighting his influence, I think I'm fighting . . .

IKB: Are you still fighting, or are you done with that?

C: Because that input has been put into her and her sister.

IKB: I see. Even through your children.

C: Oh yeah, because he's like, now here's an example . . .

[360] IKB: Wait . . . wait a minute, now let me ask you . . . it occurs to me you certainly deserve a better life.

C: I hope so.

IKB: Than what you have been dealt with. Right?

C: Yeah.

IKB: You know, I mean it seems like you've had one after another bad . . .

[365] C: Mess . . . right.

IKB: Bad luck, I mean nothing but bad luck.

C: Mm hm. I can't understand why.

IKB: Of course not. I mean, who can explain this? There is no way of knowing that. So, knowing that, knowing that you have really come a long way . . .

C: Right.

[370] IKB: You've really come a long way.

C: Oh yeah. I was a vegetable basket.

IKB: Really. Really. It also seems like you have a long way to go.

C: Yeah, yeah.

IKB: Since knowing that, how badly do you want to try something different, do some experimenting? Do something different with Rebecca so that you can have a normal . . . something close to normal mother-daughter, mother and 16-year-old daughter relationship?

[375] C: I have to live with her so . . .

IKB: I know.

C: Yeah, I don't want her to fail, she didn't even go to summer school. I don't want her to fail through the next semester, or even flunk out of high school.

IKB: So you want her to do better.

C: Well sure. Even though I don't . . . even though she irritates the living daylights out of me . . .

[380] IKB: Yeah.

C: With everything she does. I mean you know.

IKB: So let me ask you then.

C: Can I just tell you this real quick? She even let some boy take her virginity away from her when she was 14 and wrote it up in her diary.

IKB: Mm hm.

[385] C: You know, and I found this.

IKB: Mm hm.

C: And when I was 13½, I was raped and didn't want my virginity taken from me.

IKB: Right. Right.

C: I'm reading this and I'm just totally freaked out.

[390] IKB: Of course.

C: I can't believe this kid, it's like every time I turn around . . .

IKB: Let me ask you then, let's say, do you think we could draw a line . . .

C: Or maybe I'm not normal. Maybe that's normal for this life and these people to just "the sky's the limit" or "do whatever you want" and anything's OK.

IKB: For Rebecca.

[395] C: Maybe that's what this life is all about and I'm just . . . maybe I have a set of standards or wrong ideas or something about life.

IKB: There certainly is . . . why it's called the generation gap. Right. We have different . . . we grew up in a different way, we have a different set of standards.

C: Well, I was beaten all the time.

Inventing a Doing Scale

IKB: . . . Yes . . . OK. Let me ask you then, I still need to know this. Let's say, if you could draw a line here [on a clipboard], top here stands for 10, and bottom here stands for 0. So, 0 to 10.

C: Mm hm. Mm hm.

[400] IKB: And 10 stands for, up here . . . [pointing to scale drawn on clipboard] stands for, you will do just about anything humanly possible to . . .

C: Try . . .

IKB: Try to make things better between you and Rebecca, so you at least get a long a little bit better.

C: Yeah.

IKB: OK. That is just for now. Zero stands for . . . everything is going to hell, why bother?

[405] C: Almost.

IKB: Where would you say you were at, between 0 and 10 right now?

C: Probably 2.

IKB: Two.

C: Mm hm.

[410] IKB: Wow.

C: Yeah, right. Yeah, I'm getting there.

IKB: Wow. That's great. I mean that's great. Two.

C: That's pretty good.

IKB: That's pretty good considering . . .

[415] C: Yes.

IKB: how serious the problem is.

C: Oh, right.

IKB: Yes. Considering. That's great.

Although at first glance a response of "2" seems comparatively low and this response might be read as the client's not be willing to do very much, with this client in this context the "2" represents significant improvement and accomplishment. A 2 response is, after all, quite different from a 0 response or an "I don't know."

Inventing a Confidence Scale

[418 continued] Now let me ask you another one, OK?

C: OK.

[420] IKB: This time the 10 stands for you have every reasonable hope that this, what you want, can happen.

C: Oh my god.

IKB: Knowing what you and Rebecca have been through. Because I don't even know Rebecca. OK. I haven't even met her, but knowing what you and Rebecca have been through.

C: She's a shock. She's a shock.

IKB: Knowing what she's like, knowing what kind of child she is: Ten stands for you are very confident that what you want, this family unity you want, can happen. Very confident. It can happen. Zero stands for "might as well as fold up the tent and go home." Where would you say you were at between 0 and 10? Right now.

[425] C: Confident?

IKB: Yeah.

C: I'm squeaking into a 5.

IKB: Yeah.

C: I'm trying to work up into a 5. All right.

[430] IKB: That's great. That's great. What . . . sounds like you've come up a little bit . . .

C: Well, yeah.

IKB: Ah ha.

C: Because um, I'm just trying with her.

IKB: Right.

[435] C: Unless I, well actually it's 4, but I'm squeaking into 5, I said.

IKB: Squeaking into 5.

Again, considering the context and how the client has depicted her story, a 4 that is squeaking into 5 is rather impressive. Switching to this new track seems to be paying off. Certainly "a 4 squeaking into 5" can be read as incorporating the idea that change can happen.

[436 continued] OK. Suppose you got to 5, comfortable 5?

C: Comfortable 5?

IKB: Not squeaking but sort of, you know, comfortable 5.

C: Well, then everything would be . . .

[440] IKB: What would be different between you and Rebecca?

C: Well, I'm sure that then there'd be a way of really balancing or seeing more clearly, you know, how to relate.

IKB: To her.

C: Yeah.

IKB: So suppose you did that. You got to 5.

[445] C: Mm hm.

IKB: I don't know how you're going to get there, but let's suppose you
get to 5.

C: OK. Yeah.

IKB: Got to the halfway point. What would be going on between you
and Rebecca that is not going on right now?

C: Well you know, that I'm sure that ah, it's like, when we wake up
and when we cross paths, that um, there's a feeling of ah, you
know some peace there, a little harmony.

   And not that she's resentfully doing her own thing, and I'm just
in her way and she'll even say to me sometimes, ah, you know,
"When are you leaving? I'm going to have my friends come over
and I don't need you here."

[450] IKB: Mm hm.

C: So I would like to be able to have some harmony where I wouldn't
like to have a kid shouting out at me, what am I reading or . . .

IKB: So that would be 5?

C: Or she's running the house.

IKB: So that would be 5 when you can do that, when she can do that?

[455] C: Well don't you think so? If you're at that halfway point it's
like you have some kind of, doesn't have to be 100%, but like
there's kind of a feeling of a little that you can somewhat get a
long, you know. It's not like you're completely getting along.

IKB: . . . Right. Right.

C: You know, or try to.

IKB: OK. Sounds reasonable to me. OK. Suppose you got to 5.

C: Yeah.

[460] IKB: OK.

C: Mm hm.

IKB: What do you suppose Rebecca would say how you are different?
If she were sitting here and I would ask her, "How is it now that
you are at 5, you and mother are 5. How is your mother different?"

C: Well, she'd be seeing me more like um, ah, her parent and someone
that she can come to and talk to.

IKB: So she would say I feel comfortable to go and talk to my mom.

[465] C: Yeah, that I can, possibly express how I feel and I could know
that she, you know, understands me.

IKB: Makes sense to me. OK. So what would she say, what kind of a clue would she get from you that would tell her that it is OK to come and talk to mom and you, you know, you and your mom can reasonably talk to each other about . . . things can get pretty hot sometimes with 16 year olds. What would she say?

C: And the fact, and this is why I think it is very difficult for me to, you know, to relate, I can't get through, I can only go so far, I can slide in so far. I mean like, for instance, if I call his house [her father's] and I say like, "Gee, where's Rachel, she's got mail here." He'll say, "What the hell's it to you?" "Well, she's got this mail." "Well, mind your own business." "Well, why do you think I'm get- ting these letters, they're for her and I'd like to give them to her." "Well, did she tell you where she was?" And I said "No." Then he says, "Then I'm not telling you." So you know, I mean it's like I get this kind of thing, and if I'm asking, "Where's Rebecca, Rebecca hasn't been home, she wasn't home last night, is she over by you? Tell me what's going on." So it's like I'm trying to figure out a way to get into her life and he's in the background, I think he's basically controlling everything, even though she lives with me, and it's hard for me to work into something, and I don't want to see her failing in school, because then he blames me.

IKB: So to get to 5 . . .

C: Yeah.

[470] IKB: We have to change you and Rebecca, or we have to change you and your ex-husband?

C: I, I think there is, you know, if we could put him out of the picture . . . completely.

IKB: I can't do that.

C: Not shoot him?

IKB: I'm sure you feel like poisoning him sometimes.

[475] C: Oh yeah . . .

IKB: Right.

C: Lighting a match to his . . .

IKB: Right. Right. Well that's not going to happen.

C: No. Can't do it.

[480] IKB: So. What's the likelihood of him changing?

C: . . . Never. The only time he's nice is if he's just practically right at death's door. When he had his stroke, then he quickly, my number was in his mind and then he called me. Then when I got over there.

IKB: So what do you suppose he would say, what it would take for you, his ex-wife, for him and you to get along on behalf of the children?

C: I'm real nice to him. I'm always very nice.

IKB: Well, what would he say?

[485] C: He is very rotten to me. You know, I'm always very nice and he . . .

IKB: Well, would he say it would take . . .

C: He wouldn't want it. He wants me out of the picture. Um. You know. I'm sure if I. . . . His first ex-wife died two years ago and it was like "Too bad it wasn't you." You know so, um I . . .

IKB: But would he say he wants to get along with you?

C: Oh no, definitely not.

[490] IKB: He would say no.

C: No . . .

IKB: Even though this is good for the children.

C: Absolutely. He wouldn't want to, even though it was good for the kids, he would say "no way." He wants to be controlling these two and . . .

IKB: And it's not going to stop, it sounds like.

[495] C: I don't think so.

IKB: He's not going to give up on that.

C: No.

IKB: Controlling the kids.

C: No.

Constructing What the Client Can Actually Do

[500] IKB: Ah ha. So what are you going to do about this?

C: That's what I'm trying to figure out, you know. I don't know. I'm trying to get up to the 5.

IKB: I know. I know. I know. So can you get up to 5 with the father in the background, or are you thinking as long as the father is in the background, you cannot get to 5?

C: You know, maybe that's true, because I have had thoughts lately, a lot of times, about him somehow or another disappearing. Maybe then I'd get to 5, and 6, and 7.

IKB: Six and 7. But that's not likely to happen.

[505] C: No.

IKB: That's short of murder . . . I mean that . . .

C: . . . antagonize him to the point where he has another stroke, you know, I guess a person could do that, but then you'd start feeling guilty because then you created it.

IKB: Yeah. Right. You don't want that either. So which is it? As long as the father is in the background, nothing can get better between you and Rebecca?

C: It doesn't seem that way. She went and spent last night with him again.

[510] IKB: Yeah.

C: It just is very difficult. Doesn't seem that way.

IKB: Is that right?

C: Yeah.

IKB: So what is your solution to, what do you want to do? About all these situations? Sounds like he's not going to go away.

Reinventing the Wheel:
The Client Invents Her Own Homework Task

[515] C: Well, maybe I could just try figuring out a way of being tactfully conversive. You know.

IKB: Sure.

C: Maybe, to Rebecca.

IKB: OK. Say some more about it. What kind of, what exactly . . .

C: Maybe trying to start to reason with her that, um, you know, I would just like to say to her, do you have, actually what I should do is, oh, but every time I get in the car then she says to me, "You're always talking about something," or she turns the radio on or she brings her little Walkman and puts her earphones on, so I think possibly, probably if we're, if I go over to Taco Bell and get something for both of us, and we're eating together and then I tactfully say something like, "You know . . . "

[520] IKB: Hm.

C: "I've been seriously thinking, I know I'm not the mother that you say you wanted me to be."

The similarity between the idea which the client is beginning to talk about here and John H. Weakland's homework task in the case discussed in Chapter Seven is rather striking.

[521 continued] "I don't know what type of mother you're looking for. I wish you could draw a picture for me, or you know, tell me in some way what's missing and um, what you feel that I could do to, you know, make something work between us."

IKB: Hm.

C: You know, because even though.

IKB: What would you guess she would say, if you were to do this?

[525] C: It just depends. You know I'll have to watch when she's in a good mood or bad mood.

IKB: Right. Right.

C: You know, if she's in a, if she's in a lousy mood, we can't even discuss it that day. But if she's in a halfway decent mood, actually maybe what I should do is find out what mood she's in.

IKB: Yeah, good idea.

C: You know, you start talking and you start saying it and you get bashed . . . to smithereens literally . . . and that's the end of it.

[530] IKB: Yeah. Now, so you think that if you somehow tactfully find . . .

C: Find out how she is . . .

IKB: . . . and then you start to talk to her about this . . .

C: Right.

IKB: . . . will she respond to you, will she tell you?

[535] C: I don't know.

IKB: Oh.

C: You know, this is, this is what I have to find out.

IKB: . . . worth trying, sounds like, right? I mean . . .

C: Yeah, right.

[540] IKB: Because she's important to you.

C: Yeah, because she is my daughter, I'd . . .

IKB: Of course.

C: . . . hate to have her lost in never-never land.

IKB: Oh no.

[545] C: . . . for the rest of her life, a drop out. . . . It's like, oh no, let's not do that.

IKB: Right.

C: Let's get with our own peer group.

IKB: OK.

C: Let's, you know, try to . . .

Details, Details

[550] IKB: So suppose you have some idea about when and how you will figure out whether she is in a halfway decent mood and then you will suggest you go to Taco Bell and talk to her . . .

C: Oh no, I go to Taco Bell.

IKB: You will bring the food.

C: Right.

IKB: At home?

[555] C: Because when we're sitting in the car, I have a tendency to talk and then she tunes me out.

IKB: Right.

C: So rather than do that, I would just go get it and bring it back.

IKB: Right.

C: And then check for mood.

[560] IKB: And then you would, OK.

C: You know, and then maybe talk to her and ask her, you know . . .

IKB: OK.

C: If she's having a good day or what's been going on.

IKB: Sounds like . . .

[565] C: And then possibly say something like, if she says that she's been having a good day and everything's been relatively all right, then well, the reason why I ask this is because I just wanted to spend about 15 minutes, you know, limiting it, so . . .

IKB: Right.

C: . . . she doesn't think this is going to go into . . .

IKB: Right.

C: She doesn't want to talk to me for hours on end.

[570] IKB: Course not. Course not. Not many 16 year olds do. So how did you figure this out?

C: Talking to you.

IKB: Oh?

C: I just guess I figured it out. 'Cause, you know, you've been asking me these questions.

IKB: OK.

[575] C: Somehow or another.

IKB: So in thinking about it, you were able to come up with some ideas about what to do.

C: That's right. That's right.

IKB: Good. Good. OK. Great. OK. Well, I sort of ran out of questions. I'd like to go talk to my team and I'll come back with some
ideas.

C: OK.

After the Pause

[580] IKB: We are struck by how, it's almost like you have been, gone,
I mean been to hell and back, and your life has just been weird.

C: Well, I haven't been back, I'm still there.

IKB: You're still there?

C: I'm still burning in the fires.

IKB: Well, it looks like you're coming back though. It seems like. But
you really have had some very unfortunate things happen to you,
and in spite of that, you're still very, very committed about your
daughter. That you want to make this a family unit. You want to
improve things between you and her and somehow, it sounds like
you've been thinking about a lot of how Rachel, Rebecca and you
could be family unit, in spite of the serious interference from their
father.

[585] C: Um hm.

IKB: You're still hanging on to that.

C: Um hm.

IKB: And you know it has come up to almost 5, that's amazing. That's
just absolutely amazing. Just absolutely amazing. We like your idea,
your ability to think things through.

C: Oh . . . well, I had to learn how to do that.

[590] IKB: OK. But you are doing it. We just saw an example of that.

C: Right.

IKB: To think things through, and we really like this idea of you
having this tactful conversation with Rebecca and we suggest your
idea about sort of figuring out, you know, what kind of mood she's
in, coming back with food from Taco Bell . . .

C: OK.

IKB: And sitting down, having this real tactful conversation.

C: Mm hm.

[595] IKB: Now, we have a suggestion about that.

This suggestion about limiting this conversation even further comes from Weakland's example (Chapter Seven) and over 20 years of experience with this particular task and other similar ones.

[596] C: OK.
IKB: That is, that no matter what kind of mood she is in . . .
C: Mm hm.
IKB: OK, you can sit down and start talking to her, as you start to say, say you have been, like you were saying, that "I have been a bad, rotten mother for you," and just stop right there. Don't go any further.
[600] C: OK.
IKB: Don't say anymore, that's it.
C: Um hm.
IKB: If you feel like you want to say something more, don't say it, keep eating or if you can't help yourself . . .
C: Shove food down my face . . .
[605] IKB: Stop and walk out. Walk away.
C: Mm hm.
IKB: Stop right there. OK.
C: Mm hm.
IKB: Because I think that that would give you some chance of maybe squeaking up to 5.
[610] C: Ah ha. To see what she is going to say.
IKB: So see what she is going to say, and I would sort of suggest to you, act like you're not interested.
C: Mm hm. OK.
IKB: You're not interested in finding out what she is going to say about that.
C: But I should be listening.
[615] IKB: Of course. You should be watching what kind of mood she's in, when she is going to come approach you to talk about this, or she's not going to. We don't know how she's going to react.
C: Mm hm.
IKB: It's really difficult to know.
C: Right.
IKB: But that's as far as you should go.
[620] C: OK.

IKB: Don't go any further than that. So this is a first step. First small
step. There are going to be lots of other steps.
C: OK.
IKB: OK. All right. OK.

In the following session the client reported that things were better.
However, she was unable to describe any way or ways in which things
were better. She was also unable to describe what criteria she used to
make that judgment. She was still just squeaking into 5 but she was
closer than she had been before.

Through the scales both therapist and client are able to have some
way to judge whether or not their work is paying off. Clearly, what
exactly 5 might mean will probably remain a mystery. Five, or even
getting closer to 5, is better than 4 and that is all that really matters.

Chapter Thirteen

SURFACES:
IN QUEST OF A SOLUTION

We have arranged for ourselves a world in which we can live—by
positing bodies, lines, planes, causes and effects, motion and rest,
form and content; without these articles of faith nobody now
could endure life. But that does not prove them. Life is no argument. The conditions of life might include error.
—*Friedrich Nietzsche (1974, p. 177)*

IN EVERY WORKSHOP, seminar, training session, questions come up
about how to handle things when the person is sent by someone else
rather than coming more or less exclusively on his or her own volition.
Sometimes a husband is sent or brought along by his wife, sometimes
a wife is sent or brought along by her husband, sometimes a child is
sent or brought along by his parent(s), and sometimes a person is sent
or brought along by a case manager, parole officer, probation officer,
etc.

From my perspective, these cases are more similar to other cases
than they are different. In all situations, the therapist needs to find
out what the persons want to get out of coming to see a therapist. It
may be to change their own life or to change someone else's. In either
case, how will they know they got what they came after? With some
people who are brought in or sent in, all they want is to get the sender
to stop sending them. Of course, the sender has his or her own ideas
about what should happen in the therapist's office.

In some ways, both the person sent (or brought) and the sender are
clients, simultaneously. If the person sent gets what he or she wants

but the sender does not, can we rightly consider our work successful? If the sender gets what he or she wants but not the person sent, can that be considered a success? In both cases, my answer is "No." As much as possible, both need to get what they want for the work to be considered successful.

Of course there are exceptions to this, particularly when the sender believes there is a specific problem and a related specific solution and the person sent *disagrees*. Or, to put it differently, when the sender wants the therapist to join him or her in attempts to convince the person sent that he or she has a problem, even though the person sent does not consider it to be a problem! Then, perhaps, the best that can be hoped for is to help the person sent get the sender off his or her back. This might, of course, mean that we fail in the eyes of the sender.

WHO IS THE CLIENT?

[1] Steve de Shazer: Well, we work as a team, and I guess there'll be some of our team back there, watching and listening and hopefully using their brains to help us. And after about a half-hour or so, I will go talk with them about what you've been saying that's useful and then come back and let you know what our thinking is. So that's the way we work. So, in your own words, what brings you here today?

[2] Client: Her. [Laughing, pointing to the case manager]

Clear and simple. However, the question remains: Does this "client" want something for herself?

[3] SdeS: Yeah? How come?

[4] C: She feels I have a prob . . . uhh problem eating, well, I know it's a problem with eating but I don't see anything wrong with it.

[5] SdeS: Um hmm. She does. So she's the one who needs therapy? [Laughing]

[6] C: Yeah . . . [Laughing]

[7] SdeS: From your point of view.

[8] C: Yeah.

[9] SdeS: OK, so how will we know, you and me, that she . . .

[10] C: That she's right, right?

SdeS: No, no, no, no, no. How will you and I know when she's convinced that you don't need to come here?

C: When I can eat on my own.

SdeS: Um hmm.

C: And not have to be forced. And keep it down.

[15] SdeS: Um hmm. I see. OK. So that will convince her that you don't need to come here?

C: Will that? [Asking the case manager]

SdeS: Uh no, no, no, no, no, no.

C: Oh, from my point of view?

SdeS: Yeah, from your point of view.

[20] C: Yeah.

SdeS: Yeah?

C: Yeah.

SdeS: Once? If you did that once that'll convince her?

C: No.

[25] SdeS: OK.

C: Once will only make her see I'm pushing.

SdeS: Um hmm. So eating and keeping it down . . .

C: Yeah.

SdeS: And what else? Or does it have to be for some period of time or what? It's gonna . . .

[30] C: For the rest of my life.

SdeS: . . . take to convince her? Oh geez, then she's never gonna get convinced. [Laughs]

C: Umm. [Laughs]

SdeS: You're gonna be dragged in here all the time for the rest of your life?

C: No. I guess about a week.

[35] SdeS: About a week? Do you think a week might . . . ?

C: I don't know. I'm just saying.

SdeS: You're guessing at that.

C: Yeah.

SdeS: OK. OK, well, maybe we'll ask her in a minute, but is there anything else that might convince her?

[40] C: [Pause] If I can take three meals a day, that's basically what she wants.

SdeS: How many days before she's convinced?

C: How many days before she's convinced?

SdeS: Yeah, if you take three meals a day.

C: Umm.

[45] SdeS: How many days would it . . .

C: Would it take to convince her?

SdeS: Yeah.

C: That I'm gonna keep it up.

[50] SdeS: Convince her that you don't, she doesn't need to drag you
in here. How many days in a row would that take . . . of three meals
a day to convince her she doesn't need to drag . . .

C: I don't know.

SdeS: . . . you in here. Guess.

C: Uhhh . . . hmmm . . . ummm as long as I'm in treatment with her I
guess, I don't know.

SdeS: Umm.

[55] C: I don't know, I don't know.

SdeS: OK.

C: I just . . . huhh . . . Let's ask her, it's easier. I don't know.

SdeS: Now, OK, is this not eating three meals a day or eating and not
keeping it down — do you see that as a problem too?

C: Mm hm.

At this point it is still not entirely clear that the "client" sees this
eating business as anything more than a problem for the case manager.
Is getting the case manager off her back all the "client" wants?

[60] SdeS: OK. [To the case manager] So is that right? Is that, would
that convince you? Either one of those, both of those, or what
would convince you?

Case manager (CM): That she can tolerate food.

SdeS: Mm hm.

CM: She says she has an . . . to food and she starved herself when she
was pregnant.

SdeS: Mm hm.

[65] CM: And we're very concerned about her.

SdeS: Mm hm. So how would you know that that's solved? When she
can tolerate food? How would you know that?

CM: When she can keep food down.

SdeS: Mm hm. How much and how long?

CM: And start feeling better.

[70] SdeS: Well, to start feeling better, that's another thing entirely.

C: [Laughs]

SdeS: . . . to keeping food down. How much and how long before you're convinced that she . . .?

CM: Several months.

C: Several months.

[75] CM: Mm hm.

SdeS: Mm hm.

C: That's the rest of my life.

SdeS: That's not quite the rest of your life, we hope.

CM: No, I'll say six weeks.

[80] SdeS: Six weeks. OK. OK. That's a little bit shorter than the rest of your life. A little bit longer than one week. OK. And you said also feeling better.

CM: Mm hm.

SdeS: What do you mean by that? How would you know she's feeling better? Let's put it that way.

CM: She'd have more energy. Uhh . . .

SdeS: How would she show that to you? How would you find out?

[85] CM: She wouldn't, she'd be able to sit up and when I call her she wouldn't be just coming up out of a deep sleep or in bed all day.

SdeS: Mm hm.

CM: She'd be more active.

SdeS: Mm hm. What sort of things might she be doing?

CM: Coming to treatment four days a week.

[90] SdeS: Mm hm.

CM: Umm . . . participating and being more alert.

C: Three days a week.

SdeS: Um hm. OK. Three days, four days . . . OK.

C: Seven days . . . here we go. [Laughs]

[95] CM: [Laughs]

SdeS: [Laughing] OK, so she'd be more active and . . .

CM: More alert.

SdeS: More alert, and how would you know she's more alert? What would give you that signal?

CM: She wouldn't come in all slumped over. She wouldn't sit at a table and lay on it, she wouldn't lay on my couch.

[100] SdeS: Mm hm.

CM: And she'd just act like she has more energy.

Constructing Exceptions

SdeS: Mm hm. Mm hm. Have you ever seen her like that?

CM: Like she has more energy?

SdeS: Mm hm.

[105] CM: Uh, two times.

SdeS: When were those?

CM: The day she had her baby.

SdeS: Mm hm.

CM: . . . in the hospital.

[110] SdeS: And when was that, how long ago?

CM: About a month ago.

SdeS: OK, Mm hm.

CM: And I commented that it's the first time I've seen her smile, look
    peppy.

C: [Laughs]

[115] CM: After she ate.

SdeS: Mm hm.

CM: She finally got some food in her and, uh, I went to see her
    psychiatrist with her and she was more alert and talking.

SdeS: Mm hm. When was that?

CM: Two, three weeks ago.

Two exceptions have been identified so we now know that what the
case manager is looking for is something the client knows how to do.

[120] SdeS: Mm hm. Well, psychiatrist. OK. So we have a psychiatrist,
    and you [points to CM], and now you're coming here. How come?
    Why not go talk to the psychiatrist about this?

CM: We did. ·

SdeS: Mm hm.

CM: And we got the referral here through him . . .

C: That's how we got here.

[125] SdeS: Mm hm.

C: Mm hm.

SdeS: So why are you seeing a psychiatrist?

C: Is he talking about Dr. X?

CM: Mm hm.

[130] SdeS: I don't know who I'm talking about. Whoever you were seeing . . . three weeks ago.

C: That's what . . .

SdeS: How come?

C: [Laughs] 'Cause I'm screwed up. No, umm . . .

SdeS: Who says, you or them [pointing at CM] . . . or somebody else?

[135] C: A lot of people but that was . . . something had to calm me down. But I'm seeing him because he's my medicine doctor. He gives me my medicine.

SdeS: Ahhh.

C: . . . to keep me controllable.

SdeS: You need meds to keep you controllable?

C: Mm hm.

[140] SdeS: How come?

C: Manic depressive.

SdeS: Mm hm.

C: So I have to take drugs to control myself basically.

SdeS: How long have you been doing that?

[145] C: Since March 20th of '92.

SdeS: Mm hm. Does it work for you?

C: Mm hm.

SdeS: She's saying you don't seem to have enough energy. Is it too much? Does it . . .

C: I don't eat with it.

[150] SdeS: . . . calm you down too much?

C: I don't eat, I just take the medicine, when I take the medicine. I don't take it every day.

SdeS: Mm hm.

C: Well I do now [laughs] but I wasn't like I was supposed to.

SdeS: Mm hm. Mm hm. So when did you start taking it like you're supposed to?

[155] C: About two weeks ago.

SdeS: About two weeks ago. Have you noticed any difference?

CM: Mm hm.

SdeS: Yeah?

CM: Mm hm.

[160] SdeS: But not more energy though? Is that what you're saying, you haven't seen more energy in the last two weeks?

CM: Uhh, not a whole lot, but she's got anemia, too, so and a new baby and all the stresses that go with that but . . .

SdeS: Mm hm.

CM: . . . she's trying real hard now.

SdeS: Mm hm.

[165] CM: And so . . .

SdeS: Mm hm. Mm hm. OK, well, so, how'd you get involved in this?

CM: She was a client at our outpatient clinic and they brought her down to our program which is a day treatment program for cocaine . . .

SdeS: Mm hm.

CM: . . . addicted young women and poly-addicted and she just wasn't eating, wasn't getting better, still, well she'd cut back on the drinking quite a bit.

[170] SdeS: Mm hm.

CM: But we were real concerned because she was starving herself and her baby and . . .

SdeS: Mm hm.

CM: So her treatment plan was to eat.

SdeS: Mm hm.

[175] CM: Eat foods she chose and . . .

SdeS: Mm hm.

CM: . . . when she could do it but she had to eat every day. Something.

SdeS: Mm hm.

CM: One thing every day.

[180] SdeS: Mm hm.

CM: And she worked hard on that.

SdeS: Mm hm. OK.

CM: But then she says she throws up, so I didn't know that.

SdeS: OK, so . . .

[185] CM: And what brought it to head was she just relapsed recently with 24 beers, and I said, "How could you possibly get 24 beers down?" and she said "I throw them up."

SdeS: Mm hm.

CM: So I said, well, we gotta look at this.

SdeS: Mm hm. OK.

CM: She wants me here for support.

[190] C: I want her here because I'm afraid.

SdeS: Of what?

C: Being here by myself.
SdeS: Why?
CM: [Laughs]
[195] C: I am.
SdeS: Ahh you're well . . . afraid of what?
C: Being here by myself. Why am I afraid to be here by myself?
SdeS: Yeah.
C: I don't know.
[200] SdeS: What are you afraid of?
C: I don't know.
SdeS: Doesn't make any sense.
C: I know. [Laughs] That sounds strange, that I'm afraid to be by myself, I don't know what I'm afraid of, I'm just afraid to be here by myself. I don't know, I'm afraid of what you guys might say, I don't know. The results or something.
SdeS: Hmm.
[205] C: I don't know. I think that's it.
SdeS: Well, OK. So uhh . . .
CM: Once you admit you're afraid you always keep your appointments.
C: I noticed that. Maybe it's something new, that's why I'm afraid.
SdeS: Well . . .
[210] C: Because I've never been here before.
SdeS: Yeah, OK, that makes some sense anyway. Yuh. And uhh, let's see. [Pause] Well, I have a strange question for you.

Up until this point in the session the client was becoming more and more restless minute by minute, culminating in using her lap as a drum played by both hands. Simultaneously with my saying "a strange question," all of the client's restless behavior ceased.

[212] C: OK.
SdeS: OK?
C: Mm hm.

Constructing the Day after the Miracle

Up until this point, the client, the case manager, and I have been involved in a goal-focused language-game built around the case manager's ideas about what the problem is and her goals for the client, which are related to that problem. We now have some idea of what the case manager wants, but only what the client wants in relation to what the case manager sees as a problem.

At unit 211 I begin a shift toward a solution-focused language-game, trying to help the client figure out what it is she wants from this therapy. It turns out that she wants more than meeting the goals the case manager has for her.

At least for this session, the distinction between goals and solution is clear. Goals are what the client wants from therapy in *relation* to the problem, while solutions are what the client wants from therapy *independent* of the probem.

[215] SdeS: Yeah, actually it's for both of you but you go first. Suppose that one of these nights, maybe tonight, but one of these nights, you go to sleep, and while you're sleeping a miracle happens. OK?

C: Mm hm.

SdeS: And the problems that brought her . . . that got her to bring you here are gone. [Snaps fingers] Just like that. OK?

C: Mm hm.

SdeS: But you can't know that because it happened while you were sleeping.

[220] C: OK.

SdeS: Once you wake up the next morning, in the course of that day, how will you discover there's been a miracle?

C: 'Cause I would get up and I would fix breakfast . . .

SdeS: Mm hm.

C: . . . and eat . . .

[225] SdeS: Mm hm.

C: . . . with my children and keep it down.

SdeS: Mm hm. What would you eat?

C: What would I eat?

SdeS: Mm hm.

[230] C: Boiled . . . two hard boiled eggs, bacon, and probably toast.

SdeS: Mm hm.

C: And a glass of juice.

SdeS: Mm hm. And you'd keep it down.

C: Yeah.

The more details about her eating normally the better, because these details can become rather "fact-like."

[235] SdeS: Mm hm. OK. And after that, what . . . what else would be different? What other signs would you have?

C: I'd be in my own house. I wouldn't be staying with my mom.

SdeS: Mm hm.

C: I'd have a beautiful turquoise car.

SdeS: OK. Mm hm.

[240] C: I mean I would just be a happier person.

SdeS: Mm hm. How would that show? What would you do that you're not doing now?

C: I would be on my way to work.

SdeS: Mm hm.

C: Umm.

[245] SdeS: Any kind of work in particular?

C: A secretary, word-processor at the present time, moving up to bigger and better.

SdeS: Mm hm.

C: Umm. I would just be all around a happy . . . a different person.

SdeS: Mm hm. How . . .

[250] C: I wouldn't have a problem with eating. I wouldn't be weight conscious.

SdeS: Mm hm.

C: We'd be one happy family. Me and my children . . .

SdeS: Mm hm.

C: . . . and my boyfriend.

[255] SdeS: Mm hm. How, if your children could tell us, how would they discover that this miracle had happened?

C: 'Cause I'd wake up smiley instead of yelling.

SdeS: Mm hm. OK. What else might they notice?

C: Hhhhmm. That I eat, I don't just push it off.

SdeS: OK.

[260] C: Mmm. And I would take more time to play with them instead of just helping my oldest study.

SdeS: Mm hm.

C: It would give him time for himself, too.

SdeS: Mm hm. OK . . . what else?

C: I think that's it.

[265] SdeS: OK. And how would your boyfriend discover this miracle had happened?

C: He'd see me eating and wouldn't drink.

SdeS: Mm hm.

C: I wouldn't even smoke cigarettes.

SdeS: Mm hm.

[270] C: God! [Laughs]

Did she surprise herself with that part of the miracle picture?

[271] CM: [Laughs]

C: I wouldn't, umm, smoke marijuana.

SdeS: Mm hm.

C: I'd have my license.

[275] SdeS: Your license?

C: That'd be a surprise to him. Yeah.

SdeS: What . . .?

C: My driver's license.

SdeS: Your driver's license. OK.

[280] C: That'd be a big surprise to him.

SdeS: Mm hm.

C: Umm, I could tell him NO and not feel guilty. [Laughs] Not feel bad about saying no to him.

SdeS: Mm hm. OK. And anything in particular that you're referring to?

C: No. Just say no.

[285] SdeS: Mm hm.

C: I don't like to say no to him. Actually, I don't like saying no to the boys either, but I have to sometimes.

SdeS: Mm hm. You're better at it with the children than with him?

C: Yeah, 'cause they can't look at me straight and make me feel bad.

SdeS: Mm hm. OK, so you'd be saying no to him sometimes. What would . . . what else would he notice?

[290] C: I'd be happier.

SdeS: Mm hm.

C: I'd smile more.

SdeS: Smile more.

C: I wouldn't get depressed so easily. I wouldn't let people get to me as easily as I do now either.

[295] SdeS: What do you mean? What would you do instead?

C: Laugh along with 'em.

SdeS: Mm hm.

C: Even though I'd probably hate . . . oh, this is the miracle, no I wouldn't hate it, I would laugh along with 'em.

SdeS: Mm hm. Well you might still hate it?

[300] C: No.

SdeS: No?

C: I'm not even gonna hate it. This is a miracle.

SdeS: Mm hm.

C: I have to make it seem like one.

[305] SdeS: OK.

C: Uhh. But he would really know I was happy if I was able to do everything that I wanted to do . . .

SdeS: Mm hm.

C: . . . with my life. Freely without worrying about financial problems. Umm food, clothes, I mean be able to get things if I needed it.

SdeS: Mm hm.

[310] C: And if I did need I wouldn't . . . he would also notice I wouldn't have a problem asking.

SdeS: OK. That'd be different?

C: Oh yeah, he'll know something's wrong then, or something's different.

SdeS: Something's different anyway. Yeah. Uh huh. OK.

C: And that's it.

[315] SdeS: OK.

C: Oop, one more thing. No, No.

SdeS: Yes? Go ahead.

C: No, no, no, no.

CM: No?

[320] SdeS: No? OK. All right.

C: You know.

SdeS: Too private and too personal. OK. Gotcha. How would your mother know?

C: How would my mom know?

SdeS: Mm hm.

[325] C: She and I would talk.

SdeS: Mm hm.

C: We would get along.

SdeS: What would be the first sign to her that this miracle had happened? The first thing she'd notice?

C: I would say something to her and she wouldn't criticize it, she would actually try to listen.

[330] SdeS: Mm hm.

C: And then I wouldn't feel so bad after she is done, then I wouldn't cry. We would actually talk. We wouldn't just throw mixed signals to one another.

SdeS: Mm hm. OK. OK. Huh well, how would she [pointing toward CM] know?

C: How would she know?

SdeS: Mm hm. Without your telling her. How would you . . . how would [CM] know?

[335] SdeS: She'd just know. [Laughs] She always just knows. Umm.

SdeS: What signals would she be reading in you? How would she know about it?

C: From everything that happened. Everything with my mom, Mike, and the kids. She'd know.

SdeS: Mm hm.

C: I'd have a goal to meet.

[340] SdeS: Mm hm.

C: Wouldn't depress. I'd be completely off drugs and alcohol and cigarettes.

CM: Mmm.

C: I'd probably . . . [laughs] umm, no, I wouldn't cook every day.

CM: [Laughs]

[345] SdeS: Not every day.

C: That's not a miracle.

CM: [Laughs]

C: That's more than a miracle.

SdeS: [Laughing] OK. How many days would you cook?

[350] C: OK, OK, OK, five.

SdeS: Five. Mm hm.

C: No, not on Fridays and Saturdays, and not Wednesday nights, so I'd cook four days.

SdeS: Mm hm. OK. So you'd be cooking four days. That would be a real strong signal.

C: I'd be able to handle my money better.

[355] SdeS: Mm hm.

C: Umm . . . I'd make all my meetings on time like I did before.
SdeS: Mm hm.
C: And I'd be able to finish up school and get a job. And I'd be han-
    dling my treatment, children, eating, and just balancing a number
    of things into one day.
SdeS: Mm hm.
[360] C: And able to cope with it.
SdeS: Mm hm. Mm hm. OK.
C: And I'll be off the drugs. I'll control myself.
CM: You mean the medications?
SdeS: The meds?
[365] C: Yes. Mm hm. Yes.
SdeS: Oh, OK.
C: I'd be off the meds.
SdeS: OK. Anything else?
C: No.
[370] SdeS: OK.
C: I can't think of anything else.
SdeS: Well, if you do, let me know.

The "client's" response to the miracle question and her descriptions
of how she and the other people around her would be affected is quite
rich and detailed, particularly in a context where she has been brought
by the case manager. Prior to line 236 the conversation is entirely
focused on the problem(s) that the case manager sees and thus the
goals are her goals and not the client's. The client's picture of the day
after the miracle includes much more than just eating normally. At
this point, it is becoming clearer and clearer to me that the client
wants something for herself (a solution) and she is not in my office
just to get the case manager off her back (a goal).

[372 continued] What about you? How would you discover this, would
    you think?
CM: I wouldn't have to ask the routine: "Did you take your medi-
    cine?"
C: "Did you eat?"
[375] CM: "Did you eat? What did you eat?"
SdeS: How come? What would . . . how would you discover it? That
    you didn't need to ask that?

CM: I'd probably notice a change in how she behaves.

SdeS: Mm hm.

CM: Come in and maybe like everyone else go into the kitchen and fix something to eat and we wouldn't applaud [clapping], it would just be a normal kind of thing. It wouldn't stand out.

[380] SdeS: Mm hm.

CM: She might even say she likes food and this is what she fixed.

SdeS: Mm hm.

CM: She gets excited about cooking.

SdeS: Mm hm. Is there anything that she would do that she's not doing now that would be a very clear signal if you would just happen to meet her on the street, let's say? In some other context?

[385] CM: I'd love to see her at a restaurant! [Laughs]

SdeS: OK.

CM: And I'd go, huh, it wouldn't have to be the big WOW, you know.

SdeS: OK. So if you ran into her by chance in a restaurant that would certainly signal it for you.

CM: Mm hm. And looking like she's enjoying herself there, not playing with her food but . . .

[390] SdeS: Mm hm.

CM: And maybe she'd be there with her mother . . . having lunch.

SdeS: OK. OK.

C: That's a miracle!

CM: [Laughs]

[395] SdeS: That would be a miracle?

CM: That would be a miracle.

SdeS: Uh huh. OK. OK. And uh, what about your friends? How would they notice? How would they discover there had been a miracle?

C: Friends? Hmmmm. How would my friends know there has been a miracle? I wouldn't gag when they mentioned food.

SdeS: Mm hm.

[400] C: Umm. When everybody's giving suggestions for lunch I'd give some.

SdeS: Mm hm. OK.

C: And I'd eat. I'd eat along.

SdeS: And uh . . .

C: I'll tell I walked away from sex. And they'll know it's a miracle. [Laughing]

[405] SdeS: Ahh. OK.

C: Oh God.

SdeS: OK.

C: Oh God.

CM: [Laughing]

[410] SdeS: So if you were to tell that to somebody, your friends, then they'd know something had happened to you?

C: Yeah.

SdeS: Mm hm. OK.

C: Well, two or three would.

SdeS: Mm hm.

[415] C: The rest of 'em would probably tell me I'm lying. [Laughing]

Inventing a "Progress Scale"

SdeS: OK. Well, let's see, OK. I'm gonna do it this way I guess. Just to give me some sort of picture. Uhh, a scale, hmm, from zero to 10.

C: Mm hm.

SdeS: With 10 standing for this whole package. How things are for you the day after the miracle. That's what 10 stands for.

C: Wait a minute. Say that again please.

[420] SdeS: 10 stands for this whole package of things you were talking about.

C: The miracle day?

SdeS: The day after the miracle. Right.

C: OK.

SdeS: And zero stands for, oh, I don't know, things were at their worst?

[425] C: OK.

SdeS: Where would you say you are today? [Turning toward CM] Where would you say she is? Don't change your mind. Where would you say you were today between zero and 10?

C: 10 is the day after the miracle?

SdeS: Mm hm.

C: Zero's at your worst?

[430] SdeS: Mm hm.

C: Umm, today I'd say I'm about a 3.

SdeS: About a 3.

C: I guess.

SdeS: OK. How's that fit?
[435] CM: 5.

So, there has been some improvement since things were at their worst. Interestingly, puzzlingly, the case manager sees more improvement than the client does. And yet she is the one who brought the client!

[436] SdeS: You give it a 5. OK. OK. So what do you think about that . . . she says 5 . . .
C: Mm hm.
SdeS: . . . and you say 3. What do you think she sees that you don't see? How come she says 5?
C: Sarcasm, I don't know.
[440] CM: [Laughs]
C: What do you see? Show it to me.
SdeS: Yeah, what does she see?
C: Umm. Maybe because I feel better about it, being here now.
SdeS: Mm hm.
[445] C: I'm not so nervous.
SdeS: Mm hm.
C: Umm, I don't know, what do you see?
SdeS: But did that surprise you that she said two points higher than you?
C: No.
[450] SdeS: No?
C: She always sees me different than I see myself.
SdeS: Oh, OK.
C: That's nothing different or nothing unusual about that.
SdeS: Mm hm. OK. I guess it sort of surprised . . .
[455] C: I guess because I'm smiling, too.
SdeS: Mm hm. Mm hm. It sort of surprised me.
C: Considering my day's been pretty shitty, or my week's been pretty shitty in certain spots. I guess, yeah.
SdeS: So, what would it, how would things have to be different for you to have said 5?
C: If the doctor wouldn't have told me I need to sit down more.
[460] SdeS: Mm hm. OK.
C: And others wouldn't try to enforce it.

SdeS: Mm hm.

C: 'Cause I'm not goin' to be able to do it in the first place 'cause it's hard as hell.

SdeS: Yeah. Uh huh. So how would you know you were at 5?

[465] C: I wouldn't be bleeding and clottin' all over the fuckin' place.

SdeS: OK.

C: That's one thing that's gonna be fuckin' yucky.

CM: Mm hm.

C: I'm sick of this.

[470] SdeS: OK. What else?

C: That, that would do it.

SdeS: OK.

C: That alone would do it.

SdeS: Mm hm. And what has to happen for that to happen?

[475] C: I have to do what my doctor said.

SdeS: Mm hm.

C: Take it easy.

SdeS: Mm hm. And that's not easy for you. To take it easy.

C: No.

[480] SdeS: It's hard for you to take it easy.

C: Yeah.

SdeS: Mm hm.

C: It's hard for me just to sit and do nothin'.

SdeS: Mm hm.

[485] C: Or sleep all fuckin' day.

SdeS: Mm hm.

C: I mean I'm not the most active person in the world, but there's still things that I'd rather do than ask others to do for me. That's basically it.

SdeS: Mm hm. Mm hm. So if you were to follow your doctor's orders . . .

C: Yeah.

[490] SdeS: . . . how long would it take to solve that problem?

C: Probably not long.

SdeS: Not long?

C: Probably not.

SdeS: Mm hm.

[495] C: Doin' it my way it seems it's gonna take forever.

SdeS: Mm hm. Well . . . so what do you need to do?

C: Follow what he said.

SdeS: How do you, what do you need to do to get yourself to do that?

C: Hide my shoes? I don't know.

[500] CM: Hmmm . . .

C: I, I, I don't, that's not a real solution 'cause I will go in socks, believe me.

CM: Oh geez.

SdeS: Oh, then she'll have to hide shoes and socks.

C: I'll go barefoot, that's no problem. Lock me in somewhere I guess. That's basically my point. And make sure the windows bolted 'cause I just might climb out.

[505] SdeS: Mm hm.

C: That's basically it. I mean there's no real way that I'm just gonna sit.

SdeS: Unless you were to decide . . .

C: Or, or make . . .

SdeS: . . . to do it yourself.

[510] C: Make everything around me neat enough to my satisfaction.

SdeS: Mm hm.

C: Then I be able to kind of sit and relax.

SdeS: OK, what would it take for you to make yourself do that?

C: Well, my kids would have to be sleeping, clothes would have to be ironed, washed.

[515] SdeS: Mm hm.

C: The bedrooms have to be clean, my bedroom has to be clean, kitchen has to be clean. I mean the house in general, everything just has to be clean.

SdeS: Mm hm.

C: It's got to be satisfactory to my eyes.

SdeS: Mm hm.

[520] C: To my expectations and then I might just walk away from a dirty glass. I don't know.

SdeS: Mm hm.

C: I doubt it but, let's say I would.

SdeS: Mm hm.

C: Right now let's just say I would.

[525] SdeS: Mm hm. But you are very sure you wouldn't do that.

C: I know I wouldn't.

SdeS: That's what I sort of figured, yeah.

C: It's just hard for me.

SdeS: So what're you gonna do?

[530] C: I . . . I don't know? I, maybe I'll play a game with my son tonight. I don't know.

SdeS: Mm hm.

C: Yeah, that's what I'll do, I'll help . . .

SdeS: Mm hm.

C: . . . spell out his name to me.

[535] SdeS: Mm hm.

C: All the way.

SdeS: Hm hm. But what're you gonna do about this bleeding problem?

C: I can't, [laughing] I can't change that. I just have to deal with it.

SdeS: How?

[540] C: So if I, if I relax like he said, then that should resolve itself.

SdeS: Mm hm. But you gotta get yourself to do that.

C: I wanna study with my son on writin' his name tonight. I'm helping him learn to write his name.

SdeS: Mm hm.

C: But that's what he's learnin' this month at school so . . .

[545] SdeS: Right.

C: I guess we could do a little bit more of that. And listen to more cartoon tapes.

SdeS: Mm hm.

C: And read stories.

SdeS: Mm hm.

[550] C: And then after they eat dinner, we'll play a game, but I'm, I'm not, I'm gonna try to, I'm not gonna say I'm definitely gonna relax tonight, I'm gonna try.

Inventing a "Success at Relaxing Scale"

SdeS: OK. On a scale from zero to 10, with 10 being you'd bet on you being able to succeed at relaxing tonight and zero being you wouldn't, there's not a snowball's chance in hell.

C: Uhh . . . 2.

SdeS: 2.

C: 2. It's, I, I'm gonna, I'm gonna really really try.

[555] SdeS: Mm hm.

C: I mean I'm gonna try real hard. It's hard. Just thinking it is hard.

SdeS: Mm hm, mm hm, mm hm.

C: God.

SdeS: OK. I've got two other questions before I go talk to my team. Umm, when was the most recent time that you ate three meals and kept them down? Three meals in a day?

[560] C: 1989.

SdeS: Mm hm. Mm hm. OK.

C: That was the last time I ate decently.

SdeS: Three meals, yeah, OK. Now when was the most recent time you ate one decent meal, and kept it down, in a day?

C: Today.

[565] SdeS: Today?

CM: Hmm.

SdeS: How'd you do that?

C: Because I didn't want to throw it away.

SdeS: Mm hm.

[570] C: 'Cause my boyfriend was there.

SdeS: Mm hm.

C: No, I didn't puke it up 'cause he was there, I didn't throw it away because of the person who bought it for me.

SdeS: Mm hm. How did you manage to do that?

C: He doesn't let me go to the bathroom after I eat. So it was a forceful thing.

[575] SdeS: Mm hm. Mm hm. And so how, what'd you eat?

C: A sandwich.

SdeS: What kind?

C: Ham and cheese.

SdeS: Mm hm. Mm hm. OK. So is this, is this boyfriend always this, ahh, influential?

[580] C: Since he came to my therapy session [with CM] this week, yeah.

SdeS: Mm hm.

C: Yeah.

SdeS: Mm hm. Mm hm.

C: Oh, gosh.

[585] CM: [Laughs]

C: He's been like this since Tuesday. [To CM] You've created a monster.

SdeS: Where would he say you are? You said 3, she said 5. Where would he say you are?

C: On there? He'd probably agree with her.

SdeS: He'd agree with her. OK. So, after you ate this sandwich . . .

[590] C: I felt shitty.

SdeS: . . . and then you, so what, and he wouldn't let you, or you didn't because he was there, whichever way it went.

C: He wouldn't let me go to the bathroom.

SdeS: Ahh . . . and you said you were feeling kind of bad about it, did you say? You didn't like the sandwich?

C: I didn't like it being inside of me, no.

[595] SdeS: OK. And how long did it take you to get over that feeling?

C: Until I guess it was completely digested.

SdeS: About how long?

C: I don't know.

SdeS: So when did you . . . how?

[600] C: I laid down. I couldn't go get rid of it, so I laid down and went to sleep.

SdeS: Mm hm. Mm hm. OK. OK. And how long were you, did you sleep do you think?

C: About two hours.

Inventing a "Doing Scale"

SdeS: About two hours. OK. Well, I guess we have another one of these same, another one of these zero to 10, OK?

C: Mm hm.

[605] SdeS: And then I'll take some time out. Ahh, 10 stands for . . . you'll do God damn near anything that we might suggest to help you get closer to 10. And zero stands for, well, the opposite of that?

C: [Laughing] OK.

SdeS: Where would you say you are, between zero and 10?

C: Right now?

SdeS: Mm hm. Today. Right now.

[610] C: [Pause] About a 10, 'cause I wanna resolve what she thinks is a problem.

SdeS: You wanna get her off your back then.

CM: [Laughs]

C: Basically, yeah.

SdeS: OK. I'll be back in oh, five to ten minutes.

After the Pause

Does the client's 10 mean she will do anything to get to her own 10, to get what she wants? Or does it mean she'll do anything to get the case manager off her back? Are these the same or different? Prior to unit 603–614, the client listed 38 ways that she, her kids, mother, friends, and boyfriend would discover that the miracle had happened. However, unit 603–614 suggested that getting the case manager off her back remained her primary focus. The question remained: Who is the client?

The client rates herself at 3 on her way toward 10 (which stands for the day after the miracle). And she will know she is at 5 when she is more relaxed since she has followed doctor's orders and the bleeding has stopped. I deliberately did not ask about the client's 4 because her 5 was too narrowly defined and the advantage of the scale is lost when a number is defined too narrowly.

[615] SdeS: OK. Ready?

C: Ready.

SdeS: OK. The team and I are impressed with how well you described your picture of this day after the miracle and what you said in that tells us that you have your own mind, your own values, and you know where you want to go. It's clear.

C: Yeah.

SdeS: And, getting there may take at least some hard work. Maybe even a lot.

[620] C: I know.

SdeS: And, we're not sure how you're gonna go about gettin' there. But we think that it's worthwhile trying to get there and working on gettin' there. And so, what we suggest you do, between now and next time we meet, is to observe whatever you do and whatever happens, that begins to move you up to 4, and gets you up to 4. OK? But, keep this secret to yourself. Maybe make notes or something like that, and particularly from [CM]. OK? Let's see if she can figure out when you moved up that one step. OK. And the team and I are glad that you wanted [CM] here today because her view is slightly different from yours, and her view might prove useful. So the team and I want to invite you [the client] back, and invite you to bring her [CM] back when you come back, and what we would like to do is this: [To client] As soon as you reach 4, you call and set up another appointment. As soon as you [CM] think she has moved up one step on the scale, you call and set up the appointment. Whichever one's first.

CM: Mmm.

SdeS: We'll see which one is first.

C: OK. [Laughing] [To CM] So you have to read me.

Now it is not a question of whether or not the client will move up one step on the scale, but only a question of who will notice *first* that she has done so. That is, the client has to move up on the scale before either of them can call to set up an appointment and clearly I am telling them that I fully expect her to move up one step and I fully expect one or the other to notice the improvement *first*. Obviously, noticing it first does not mean that the other person did not notice, just that she noticed it second. In this way we can come close to having both women be clients simultaneously, since both seem to be interested in getting what they want from coming to therapy.

Of course my preference would be that the client notice first and call first. It would be better for her self-esteem to have to prove her improvement to me and the case manager rather than having the case manager again seeing the client as better than the client sees herself.

Although we invited the "client" to return and said that if she wanted to bring the case manager along that was OK we decided to leave the next appointment unscheduled in order to respect the "client's" right to decide for herself. All in all, it is not totally clear whether or not the client wants therapy or just wants to get the case manager off her back. From line 235 up until line 610 I had become more and more convinced that she wanted something for herself and was not there just to please the case manager.

The case manager reported some weeks later that things had improved quite a bit, that the client had moved up at least one point on the scale. The case manager thought that the session had given some direction to her work with the client and that neither she nor the client thought that further sessions were required.

Chapter Fourteen

WAIT A MINUTE, THAT WOULD BE A MIRACLE!

You can never plan the future by the past.
— *Edmund Burke*

PRIOR TO THE MID 1980S, my colleagues and I usually thought of alcohol and drug abuse as somehow, in some way(s), different from other human problems. In part, this was probably due to the relative rarity of clients who came to brief therapists specifically about alcohol and/or drug "abuse" problems. Reasonably enough, the widely accepted "disease model" (Fingarette, 1988; Peele, 1989) of abuse leads abusers to seek more specialized help, such as that thought to be provided by drug and alcohol counselors, rather than seeking help from a generalist who specializes in brief therapy.

The strongest reason behind our acceptance of this point of view was the privilege given to the disease concept of alcoholism and to Alcoholics Anonymous by Gregory Bateson (1972).[1] Bateson, whose thinking about systems and systems theory influenced the development and growth of both family therapy and brief therapy, described the AA view as a systemically "correct" one (Bateson, 1972, p. 337). According to Bateson, once an alcoholic hits bottom, there is no escape. All his efforts have shown him that he cannot *not* drink, but once at bottom he knows that if he continues to drink he will go mad

---

[1]Alcoholism is the only "disease" Bateson singled out for study in his many years of work in the area of psychiatry. See Chapter Five.

241

or die. Thus the alcoholic at bottom necessarily must choose between two "wrong" alternatives. The alcoholic's position at bottom is an example of the kind of situation Bateson and his colleagues (Bateson, Jackson, Haley, & Weakland, 1956) called a "double bind." According to Bateson (1972), the only escape from this double bind is what AA calls "surrender."

From this perspective, a referral to AA was the only sensible thing for a therapist to do because, as Bateson put it, "Alcoholics Anonymous . . . has the only outstanding record of success in dealing with alcoholics" (Bateson, 1972, p. 310). (Bateson's belief in this so-called success was entirely "based on data from the publications of Alcoholics Anonymous" [Bateson, 1972, p. 310].)

Bateson's point of view was, of course, entirely dependent upon the presence of a disease called alcoholism as defined by AA and his reading of the AA literature. Once alcoholism is defined in any way different from the way AA defines it, Bateson's entire argument becomes at least questionable.

A SHIFT IN PERSPECTIVE

Occasionally over the years, for a variety of reasons, some clients with alcohol and/or drug abuse problems nonetheless did seek out brief therapists to help them deal with this problem (for some examples, see de Shazer, 1982, pp. 50–64, 133–134). When this happened, we dealt with these cases "as usual" and the success rate for the "abuse" cases turned out to be no different from that for other cases. We saw the success of these cases as "flukes" (not anomalies vis-à-vis alcoholism). Therefore, success was attributed to either (a) the client's being an unusual person who was able to overcome the disease in an unusual fashion or (b) a mis-diagnosis, i.e., the original diagnosis of "alcohol abuse" was wrong. Subsequently, however, our view has shifted to the possibility that treating alcohol abuse problems is no different from treating other kinds of problems that are brought to brief therapists. While these cases might traditionally be seen as anomalies (within the alcoholism model), within brief therapy they have come to be seen as "business-as-usual" (for some examples, see Berg and Miller, 1993; de Shazer, 1988, pp. 132–138, 145–150, 152–159).

This shift in our point of view is parallel to and concomitant with a shift in perspective toward the whole concept of alcoholism in a wider context that has been developing for years. Perhaps surprisingly, the change in perspective originated within research into the treatment of alcohol abuse and it primarily affects the widely held belief that alcoholics are always "one drink away from a drunk" and thus alcohol abuse involves a loss of control.

> Almost everything that the American public believes to be the
> scientific truth about alcoholism is false.
> —*Herbert Fingarette, (1988, p. 1)*

Davies (1962) sounded the death knell for the concept of alcoholism with his paper "Normal drinking in recovered alcohol addicts." Prior to his paper, alcoholism was seen as a disease, involving a more or less simple and unified concept. It was thought, and still is thought by many, that total abstinence was the only alternative open to alcoholics because, during the addictive phase, "an overpowering need to continue drinking and to obtain drink by all means, as well as a dependence upon drink" (Davies, 1962, p. 94) develops. However, with Davies' (1962) invention of "normal drinking in recovered alcohol addicts," the concept of alcoholism was forever tainted and undermined: We have to doubt the validity of the folkloric idea that "once an alcoholic, always an alcoholic."

In all likelihood, even prior to 1962, some clinicians already knew that sometimes, some alcoholics began to drink again without any of the problems associated with or part of alcoholism. However, prior to Davies, these exceptions were dismissed as flukes and/or chance events and/or the patients were deemed to have not been real alcoholics, i.e., they were misdiagnosed. As flukes, chance events, or examples of misdiagnosis, these cases were dismissed as trivial, as not relevant to "alcoholism" as such. Davies, too, could have suppressed his discovery of these cases. However, he decided to write about them and, at least in this sense, he invented "normal drinking" in recovered alcoholics.

Since alcoholism had long been seen, and still is seen by many, as a disease, it involved a totalizing concept which means that all other (non-standard) views of alcoholism were marginalized, trivialized, and seen as supplemental; therefore they could be ignored. But the work of Davies (1962) and Davies, Scott, and Malherbe (1969) was a dangerous addendum to the concept, a marginal note that seriously qualified and questioned the text.

Logically, if some "recovered" alcoholics *could* begin or resume normal drinking, then this had to be included as one of the possibilities within any concept of alcoholism. Even if it were to be a matter of chance, if normal drinking were *possible* for even a small minority of clients, then this chance outcome became a necessary possibility. Thus, alcoholism needed to be redefined to include the possibility that, in any particular case, the client might be able to begin or resume normal drinking.

Heather and Robertson (1981) followed this and subsequent research through to this conclusion:

> Whether or not alcoholic behaviour is "primarily influenced by neurophysiological mechanisms or internal drives," and there is no convincing reason to suppose that it is, this is irrelevant to the demonstrated fact that alcoholic drinking is subject to the same kind of environmental contingencies and modifiable according to the same kind of principles as all drinking behaviour. One does not have to be a radical behaviourist [sic], and to believe that reference to internal states has no place in scientific discourse, to realize the profound significance of this. If alcoholic drinking is modifiable in the same essential way as normal drinking then there is no sense in describing a specific disease of alcoholism and no sense in searching for the roots of a general and irreversible loss of control in the alcoholic. In consequence, the main theoretical foundation of the abstinence requirement in treatment is radically undermined. (pp. 126–127)

It is important to note also that, logically and empirically, if there is a disease, then there must be a cause. However, "research . . . has shown that no one causal formula explains why [some] people become heavy drinkers. Indeed, the attempt to find a single catchall 'cause' of a single 'disease' has repeatedly led researchers astray" (Fingarette, 1988, p. 65).

The lack of a unified definition and the weakening of the disease concept of alcoholism completely undermines Bateson's notion of surrender as the only possible escape from alcoholism. At the very least there are many alcoholisms or, perhaps more radically, there are none at all. In either case, a multiplicity of treatments, each tailor-made for a specific case, seems the most appropriate alternative. Clearly a one-treatment-for-all approach means that that treatment will not fit for many, many clients.

CONTEXT

> Context is, of course, the key. The fact that the meaning of an utterance is always determined by a context that is partly non-verbal is the reason why semantics is the most difficult area of linguistic research. Meaning in actual speech can never be analysed in purely linguistic terms, because the relations between addresser, addressee and topic are not contained within the linguistic data.
> —*David Lodge (1990, p. 78)*

The situations in which events occur influence how the participants describe the events to themselves and other people. Of course, event and context are not discrete and cannot be differentiated exactly. The context influences the event while the event affects the context. However, at least in part, the context surrounding an event helps to give meaning to the event itself. Since the context or situation in which events occur is described using language and the context helps us understand and describe what it is that is going on, the context is subject to the same ambiguities that influence the event itself.

Context can limit possibilities and even constrain options to the point of making certain behaviors impossible. For example, eating with your professor while sitting on the floor is normal, expectable behavior in Korea or Japan but would be almost unthinkable in Germany. In the U.S., eating with your professor while sitting on the floor is a possibility with certain professors in certain places dependent upon certain circumstances. That is, sitting on the floor while eating with your professor is either OK or not-OK depending upon the context in which it happens. In and of itself, the behavior—without reference to context—is *neither* OK *nor* not-OK and/or *both* OK and *not* OK: it is an undecidable question.

Similarly, alcohol abuse does not occur in a vacuum. Like any other human behavior, there is a context that surrounds the abuse. In fact, context helps to define abuse as "abuse" and thus the context is in fact a significant part of the behavior known as "abuse." That is, in one particular context (say, as an absurd example, an AA meeting), drinking one beer might be seen as "abuse," while in another context (a pub) drinking three pints of beer might be seen as "normal."

Obviously, the various people involved in a situation are part of the context for each individual's behavior. Abusive drinking might be considered "normal" when an individual is with a group of abusive drinkers, while one beer might be seen as abusive when an individual is having dinner with a Mormon family. In fact, having just one beer with a group of abusive drinkers might be considered "abnormal" if they happen to notice this behavior.

From a treatment point of view, context is rather important, since a change in behavior or attitude does not happen in isolation. Any change in context might lead to or promote non-abuse or non-drinking and/or a change in context might serve to reinforce non-abusive drinking or non-drinking.

$250,000 IS ENOUGH

[1] Steve de Shazer: Well, I don't have any of that information. So, uh, tell me something about you. What do you . . .

[2] Client: Well, I'm here because I'm . . .

[3] SdeS: No, no, not about that. . . . Tell me something about you, who you are.

[4] C: My name is Frank Jones. Thirty-two years old, um, . . .

[5] SdeS: What do you enjoy doing?

[6] C: I like basketball.

[7] SdeS: Basketball?

[8] C: Mm hm.

[9] SdeS: What else?

[10] C: Bowling.

SdeS: Um hm.

C: I do a lot of drinking and listening to music and stuff.

SdeS: What kind of music?

C: Basically, all kinds.

[15] SdeS: Yeah?

C: Mm hm.

SdeS: No particular favorites?

C: No particular. . . .

SdeS: OK. And how do you pay your bills?

[20] C: Well, I really, with my wife and I . . . we pay 'em together.

SdeS: Mm hm. OK.

C: As far as me working, you know, I'm not working one of the best jobs in the world, but I'm surviving.

SdeS: Mm hm.

C: Scrapin'.

[25] SdeS: What kind of thing do you do?

C: I've been working lot of various jobs.

SdeS: Yeah.

C: In the last few months.

SdeS: So, OK, what, what brings you in?

[30] C: Well, right now I'm dealing with a drinking problem.

SdeS: Mm hm. OK. And uh . . .

C: Sometimes I drink . . .

SdeS: You say, right now . . .

C: Well, I've been dealing with it . . .

[35] SdeS: Mm hm.

C: But right now I just feel this is the time in my life to really . . . get into it, do something about it. 'Cause I have been in treatment in the past.

SdeS: OK.

C: I don't know how serious I took 'em but I know what it's about.

SdeS: Mm hm.

[40] C: And I'm, I'm aware of my addiction, I know what it'll do to you. I guess I'm being hardheaded 'cause I know better.

SdeS: OK. And, uh, so . . . there are times when you are controlling it OK?

C: Yeah, many times.

SdeS: Mm hm. Mm hm. OK, and ah . . .

C: I guess that's just the addiction part . . . when there's time when it's good to you and sometime it ain't as good as you think. And you . . .

[45] SdeS: Well, what about in the last few weeks? Some days have been better than others?

C: Some days yes, it has . . . it has been better.

SdeS: Mm hm. OK. And when was the most recent good day? Without . . .

C: Without problems . . .

SdeS: Mm hm.

[50] C: Just about every day.

SdeS: Mm hm.

C: It's just the physical part, really, that, that makes things uncomfortable for me when I drink. Although, you know, I might have problems in my life just like anybody else.

SdeS: Oh, of course, yeah, sure.

C: But, right now it's the physical part that is starting to make me sick
a lot.

[55] SdeS: Mm hm. Mm hm.

C: [Unintelligible] . . . is out of control, my eating habits.

SdeS: Mm hm. OK.

C: My eating habits and all that kind of stuff.

SdeS: OK.

[60] C: And um . . .

SdeS: But some days you . . . don't do any, you don't drink at all?

C: I haven't went a day without drinking in a while.

SdeS: No?

C: Several months.

[65] SdeS: OK.

C: But every day I drink beer all day long. Drink beer until I go to
sleep.

SdeS: Mm hm. I see. OK. Well . . . let's uh . . . and then you say you've
been in treatment before?

C: Yes, I . . .

SdeS: And what about that treatment that's worked for you?

[70] C: What's that?

SdeS: What about the treatment that was good for you? What did you
find helpful?

C: You know the treatments, OK, one treatment that I was in the
longest you might be familiar with – [a well known program]?

SdeS: Mm hm.

C: OK, I was in there for three months.

[75] SdeS: Right.

C: I liked it.

SdeS: Yeah.

C: I did. I really liked it.

SdeS: Mm hm.

[80] C: 'Cause it . . . like peaceful, quiet, it was away from the things
that, you know, if you want to call 'em a problem.

SdeS: Whatever.

C: Isolated away from . . .

SdeS: Right.

C: . . . the other atmosphere and you know, you can get a hold of yourself, you can get your body back in shape and you can get a pattern going.

[85] SdeS: Right.

C: I like that.

SdeS: Mm hm.

C: What it is on the street . . . you can't do it because you're constantly caught up in their chain, you know.

SdeS: So, after the . . .

[90] C: treatment center . . .

SdeS: . . . 90 days in there, how long were you able to maintain it?

C: About a month and a half.

SdeS: Mm hm.

C: About a month and a half.

[95] SdeS: OK.

C: And the best time I could say when I was dry was dating back to my younger years when I first started drinking.

SdeS: Uh huh.

C: When I was on Antabuse . . .

SdeS: Mm hm, OK.

[100] C: I like that . . .

SdeS: Mm hm.

C: Because you know, as long as I kept myself busy and filled that empty space, I was OK.

SdeS: Mm hm. OK. But you could do it without the Antabuse too.

C: I have did it . . .

[105] SdeS: Yeah.

C: A few months ago, for like four days.

SdeS: Mm hm.

C: But I didn't take the right decision. I didn't go to no AA meeting.

SdeS: Mm hm.

If Antabuse and going to AA are helpful to him, if they are useful for him, then part of the resolution *to the drinking problem* may involve AA and Antabuse. However, we do not yet know if his solution is that narrowly defined.

[110] C: You know, I needed the support. I didn't go to that.

SdeS: Mm hm.

C: I just caught myself just going to stay home and just quit cold turkey, but I ended up in the same

SdeS: Mm hm.

C: I guess I can break the spell.

[115] SdeS: Mm hm. You can. So, I have a somewhat strange question, but, uh, suppose that ah . . . when you go home tonight and you go to bed and you go to sleep, a miracle happens. OK? And the problem that brings you in here is solved.

C: Mm hm.

SdeS: But you can't know it.

C: Mm hm.

SdeS: 'Cause it happens while you're sleeping.

[120] C: OK.

SdeS: OK?

C: All right.

SdeS: So, when you wake up tomorrow morning, what will you notice, what will give you the clues that maybe a miracle has happened?

Constructing the Morning after the Miracle

C: I probably wouldn't have a headache.

[125] SdeS: OK. Yeah.

C: I probably wouldn't feel like I'm leaving something behind.

SdeS: Mm hm.

C: Because, you know, in your dreams sometimes you never have a chance to complete it, so you therefore you feel like you left something.

SdeS: OK.

[130] C: Way it is with all the other crap that kinda linger on me, if it was gone,

SdeS: Mm hm.

C: I probably feel like I'm high . . .

SdeS: OK, yeah.

C: . . . a natural high.

[135] SdeS: OK. And what would that feel like? Can you tell me some more about that?

C: What would it feel like?

SdeS: Yeah, this natural high.

C: The good feeling of joy. The first time I felt, the first time I realized what Santa Claus and a big Christmas was . . .

SdeS: Mm hm.

[140] C: With the snow and the presents . . .

SdeS: Mm hm. OK.

C: That feeling. When you wake up early in the morning you got your presents and Santa Claus there. That kind of feeling.

SdeS: OK. OK. And as a result of that, you wake up feeling this way, this natural high, joy and all that. And, um, what difference will that make to what you do . . . that day? Or starting that day, what difference will it make?

C: It make a whole lot of difference.

[145] SdeS: Mm hm.

C: I have those days . . .

SdeS: Mm hm.

C: And I get up in a good mood singing to myself and just do something I hardly ever do, just get up and clean the whole house and mop the floors . . .

SdeS: OK.

[150] C: I guess you can say that it would make me very energetic . . .

SdeS: OK. And um . . .

C: . . . powerful and willful to do everything good, just, you know, where is . . . I know how to do things some days I don't even try.

SdeS: All right. OK.

C: I have good moods, it's just that I don't put 'em to use.

[155] SdeS: Mm hm.

C: I guess my self-esteem is so low right now too. I really don't feel like it's worth trying, only thing important to me is search around for a can of beer tomorrow . . .

SdeS: Mm hm.

C: And going to sleep . . .

SdeS: OK. And after this miracle, what would be different about that, do you think? If that's not there, searching around for the beer, what would you do instead?

[160] C: Besides the everyday, average . . .

SdeS: Yeah.

C: Working.

SdeS: Well, even that too, yeah, sure, whatever, but what would tell you that this time there has been a miracle and something's really different, you know. Yeah, besides work, so . . . OK, you'd be doing to work, what else would you do that would signal to you that it's a miracle?

C: Because I know I would be, even people that I might, you know, dislike or wouldn't care too much about being around.

[165] SdeS: Mm hm.

C: I probably would get along with them.

SdeS: OK.

C: I probably would just walk up and shake their hand. You know . . .

SdeS: Mm hm.

[170] C: Not that I do it or not that I won't do it, I might just pull up to park my car and help a old lady across the street.

SdeS: Mm hm.

C: Where sometime, you know, I just, you know how you just pause a minute, just let them go ahead and get past you 'fore you pull up.

SdeS: Oh.

C: This particular day, I might park the car and get out and help her cross the street.

[175] SdeS: OK. OK. So . . .

C: Them kind of things will let me know, in fact, that a miracle has happened, 'cause if the miracle didn't happen I would be too mean and too grouchy,

SdeS: Mm hm.

C: Not that I would just, just, just pick on people or just, you know, just, just look at people in the wrong way, just that I be, would be the grouchy type.

SdeS: Right.

[180] C: That way, is if I'm in a store, if you step on my feet, you know, I look at you like, you know, even though I know it's a mistake I give you a look.

SdeS: Right. Right.

C: Sometime I do that now, somebody step on my feet like they in a goofy hurry or something,

SdeS: Mm hm.

C: I might look at 'em crazy, like slow down.

[185] SdeS: Mm hm.

C: Sometime I might say OK, excuse me, I understand. It go both ways.

SdeS: OK. And what's the difference?

C: There's a good feeling; there's a bad feeling.

SdeS: Right, but is there something different about the day that will tell you . . .

[190] C: I don't know, I don't know that, I really don't know.

SdeS: OK.

C: You know, this is one of those — how do you say — one of those bad days.

SdeS: Yeah. Yeah. Sometimes bad days and good days, sometimes there are other things that, uh . . .

C: Trigger.

[195] SdeS: . . . trigger it, or don't trigger it, you know, whatever.

C: . . . too, I believe if I, if I was to wake up and have a miracle happen like that . . . I feel like my fight with alcohol would be over.

SdeS: Mm hm.

C: You know.

SdeS: Right.

[200] C: The problems that led to alcohol would be over.

SdeS: Mm hm.

C: You know, that's like I don't have to worry about that kind of crap no more, I got a fresh start, everybody's just, just going about their life and let me go about mine.

SdeS: Mm hm.

C: If I make mistakes, let me see 'em, just don't try to rule my life, you know.

[205] SdeS: Right, right. OK, so . . .

C: . . . be more sociable, you know, a lot like now, there's a lot of people, relatives and friends,

SdeS: Mm hm.

C: that I wouldn't too much care about being around because I know that if I have a good day going or whatever, they're gonna trigger it by saying something stupid. Or something out of the way

SdeS: Uh ha.

[210] C: that really . . . to you and makes you mad.

SdeS: Mm hm. Mm hm.

C: And so that just because you really ain't too fond of being around each other . . .

SdeS: Right.

C: But whereas, if that miracle happened, I could be around, around them . . . wouldn't even bother. And when they say I look at them you know, I laugh it off.

His picture of the day after the miracle is not narrowly focused on his "drinking problem." He wants something more from therapy.

Constructing Exceptions

[215] SdeS: Mm hm. There's some good days and some bad ones, you know, good moods and bad moods and all that, but are there some days that are sort of more like this miracle than other days? You've had days where you've had pieces of this miracle? Things like it?

C: Yeah.

SdeS: When's the most recent one? That's sort of like the miracle?

C: Good or bad?

SdeS: Good ones. Good ones. Sure, good ones.

I had no idea what a "bad one" would mean so I decided to put that aside at least for a while.

[220] C: When I woke up the day after I got married.

SdeS: Mm hm.

C: That was in June. [Five months earlier]

SdeS: Mm hm.

C: I never thought I would.

[225] SdeS: Mm hm.

C: Never. I always was against it. I didn't look at the next man for doing what he wanted to, I just say it was something that I would never do.

SdeS: Mm hm.

C: Not at that . . . you know, my young age.

SdeS: Right.

[230] C: And I woke up and I thought about it and as it hit me I said, "I'm married."

SdeS: Mm hm, OK.

C: I don't know if it was a good feeling or bad, it's just something that really made me stop and think.

SdeS: Mm hm. Mm hm.

C: And I look back on, you know, how wild I used to be and . . . [long pause] I don't know.

[235] SdeS: Yeah.

C: And here it is now I'm married. . . . You know, you, just like the . . . you never can say, well, I'm going to be dead at 25.

SdeS: Right.

C: You can't say I'm going to be married at 25. You can wish to be married by that age, but you never know.

SdeS: That's right. You never know.

[240] C: When it's going to happen. Like me, I said I would want to be married in my early thirties.

SdeS: Mm hm.

C: And when I'm 32.

SdeS: Mm hm.

C: And when I woke up that day it hit me. I really thought about it. It hits me now sometimes.

[245] SdeS: So, you surprised yourself?

C: I think so.

SdeS: Yeah.

C: I think so and . . . I can accept the fact that I'm married true enough. . . .

SdeS: Yeah.

[250] C: I accept the responsibility but what really got me was the commitment.

SdeS: Mm hm.

C: You know.

SdeS: Mm hm.

C: . . . something inside of me made that commitment I didn't even know about.

[255] SdeS: Right.

C: You know, it was ready, but I wasn't. My mind . . .

SdeS: I see. I see what you're saying.

C: My heart was ready, but my mind was kind of confused about it.

SdeS: Mm hm.

[260] C: And you know your heart leads the way, you know.

His "heart leading the mind" and his surprising himself might turn
out to be useful metaphors for helping him develop a solution.

Broadening the Scope of the Day after the Miracle

[261] SdeS: Yeah, so, on the day after the miracle, . . . since you didn't
know it happened, you can't tell her, but how would your wife
discover this? What would signal her?

C: Right now, my wife really don't think I'm that happy.

SdeS: Right.

C: Because I was going through this change with her family.

[265] SdeS: Mm hm.

C: Day to day in the pulls of our marriage.

SdeS: Mm hm.

C: They didn't show no support whatsoever.

SdeS: Right.

[270] C: But they showed some support for her other sister that got
married a month before us.

SdeS: Uh huh.

C: See, and I know that's kind of depressing my wife, too, but she's
being strong because every woman dream of her marriage day.

SdeS: Mm hm.

C: And now they have another sister gonna get married in June and
they . . . get ready for this and pay a lot of money, and you know,
put a lot of support [pause] behind . . .

[275] SdeS: Uh huh.

C: And do it for her.

SdeS: Mm hm.

C: They didn't even show up.

SdeS: Mm hm.

[280] C: So right now, I'm still in kind of you know, mixed about it,
and I know my wife is too. She says she don't, but she is.

SdeS: Yeah, probably.

C: So right now, she's probably thinking that I'm not too comfortable
with her because her family didn't show us support, even though
the fact that I married her,

SdeS: Right.

C: Not them. But I know she, she's feeling it.

[285] SdeS: Sure.

C: And I kinda felt it, too, 'cause I felt like regardless what they might of disliked about me, whatever, I'm still their daughter's choice.

SdeS: Mm hm.

C: As long as I'm making their daughter happy or their sister happy, that should've been enough for them.

SdeS: Yeah.

[290] C: So . . . I think that kinda got a cloud over me . . .

SdeS: OK. After this miracle, how would she have discovered there had been this miracle?

C: How would she discover it?

SdeS: Yeah. That you had this miracle happen to you, overnight. How would she discover that?

C: I think [pause] I think she would notice the glow.

[295] SdeS: Mm hm. How? What would, what would you do that would show her? What would give, how, what would be different that she'd notice?

C: Well, its just something that I haven't done . . . when she gets up to go to work the next morning I'd walk her to the car and give her a kiss.

SdeS: OK. That'd be different, that would tell her something is changed about you?

C: Yeah, 'cause I don't do it.

SdeS: Mm hm.

[300] C: I be laying in bed [pause] and sometimes she'll come in and kiss me . . . and she she going.

SdeS: Mm hm.

C: And I'll just lay there 'cause you know, I'll still be like in a sleep. I hear her, though.

SdeS: Right.

C: But she wouldn't be used to me getting up, walking her to the door and kissing her instead.

[305] SdeS: OK.

C: Or getting up and fixing breakfast.

SdeS: OK.

C: Those kind of things.

SdeS: OK.

[310] C: When she kind of like watching her weight anyway, so it, breakfast really don't matter to her.

SdeS: Mm hm.

C: But that would be something different.

SdeS: Right.

C: She would notice that I'm in a good mood.

[315] SdeS: OK. And, um . . .

C: You know she came to me and said, "You want a beer?" And if I
say "no" in an energetic way

SdeS: Mm hm.

C: She would know, she would think something then.

SdeS: OK, you said "no" and meant it.

[320] C: Right.

SdeS: Mm hm.

C: You know, like, "No, thank you," and not depressed about it, not
saying "no," you know, 'cause you really want it but you're sick and
you're scared to drink 'cause you don't want to start.

SdeS: Mm hm.

C: But say "no" and say "no" with a smile on my face. She would know
then.

[325] SdeS: OK. OK. Um, that would be a good clue for her. What
else do you think might give that clue as the day goes by? What
other things might.

C: She wouldn't see, she wouldn't see me sitting around like I do
sometimes in a day, wondering

SdeS: Mm hm.

C: You know, the TV could be on but I could be sitting there like
this, she thinks I'm looking at the TV but I'm really thinking.

SdeS: Mm hm, mm hm.

[330] C: You know. Fantasizing or whatever you want to call it,
but . . .

SdeS: OK.

C: It's a little more than fantasizing 'cause it be [pause] you know, you
be thinking about days that you dealing with it.

SdeS: Mm hm.

C: But I try to hide it.

[335] SdeS: OK.

C: If she wouldn't see me do that too often.

SdeS: OK. What would you do instead, do you think?

C: Probably read a book.

SdeS: OK. Hm hm. So if she saw you doing that then.

[340] C: If she saw me in a book more often, then if she saw me in a

book more often and more of a smile on my face, she would know something's changed.

SdeS: Mm hm.

C: Like I say right now she feeling that I'm kind of more or less depressed.

SdeS: Mm hm.

C: You know, and me and her discussed this that I told her that I was fixin' to come here . . .

[345] SdeS: OK.

C: As far as she, she kind of feeling it, too.

SdeS: Mm hm. Was she surprised when you told her you were going to do this?

C: No, but she was surprised when I went because I have made appointments before and didn't go through with it.

SdeS: Uh huh.

[350] C: I was going to come yesterday, but . . .

SdeS: Right.

C: She ended up going somewhere with her daughter and I didn't have no way to get here 'cause my car is not running right now.

SdeS: Hmm.

C: And I live a pretty good ways from here. I s'pose I could've walked.

[355] SdeS: Mm hm.

C: But I guess I was lazy.

SdeS: So you, so you're, you're making it here today, that's going to surprise her.

C: It surprised her.

SdeS: Mm hm.

[360] C: And um . . .

SdeS: Did it surprise you?

C: In a way.

SdeS: Mm hm.

C: Because I know it's something that I could use and I never really got off my butt and did it.

As is the case with many people, his miracle picture broadens out considerably once it becomes interactional. And we have something that surprises him and his wife.

[365] SdeS: Right.

C: And now it's like I, I push myself to go ahead and get what's gonna do something good for me.

SdeS: And how come this time, do you think?

C: I think I'm getting older.

SdeS: OK.

[370] C: And I'm realizing life and I think I'm starting to take life as more of a value.

SdeS: Mm hm.

C: Than I did in the younger years by a not care attitude.

SdeS: OK. Yeah.

C: You know how you sometimes can be hardheaded in life. You know, I never went to jail or prison or anything, it's just that a lot of things came my way I really didn't take advantage of.

[375] SdeS: Mm hm.

C: Nice jobs, had jobs, jobs, jobs. Little ones, you know . . .

SdeS: Yeah.

C: My mother always did look out for me.

SdeS: Mm hm.

[380] C: You know, I never really, she, she didn't like me drinking.

SdeS: Right.

C: I would go behind her back and drink. You know, I just feel like I let a lot of people down . . .

SdeS: Mm hm.

C: . . . that had confidence in me.

[385] SdeS: And yourself.

C: Right, that's most important, so I feel like by me, you know, seeking professional help that I can use, I feel like I couldn't go wrong.

Inventing a "Success Scale"

SdeS: Well, OK, I got some other kinds of questions I want to get to. Um, . . . number questions. OK, let's say that zero stands for . . . how things will be after this miracle. OK?

C: Mm hm.

SdeS: And minus 10 stands for your drinking problem at its worst.

[390] C: Mm hm.

SdeS: OK. Where would you say you are right now, between minus 10 and zero?

C: Be honest with you?

SdeS: Mm hm.

C: Probably about 3.

[395] SdeS: About 3. Minus 3, you mean?

C: Minus 3.

SdeS: OK, so it's a lot better than at its worst?

C: No.

SdeS: No.

[400] C: It's a lot worse than better.

SdeS: OK.

C: That's minus 3.

SdeS: Yeah . . . well . . . let's try and do something like this. [Using the blackboard] That's zero. After the miracle. Minus 10, going that direction.

C: OK. I'm up . . .

[405] SdeS: This is the worst [pointing to − 10].

C: Oh, OK, how about a 8?

SdeS: Here [pointing to −8]?

C: Right, 'bout 7 to 8. 7-1/2 to 8.

SdeS: Minus 7, minus 8. OK. Now we got that straight. OK. And how did, what's the difference, how do you get from minus 10 to minus 7?

A mistake. I should have used our standard 0 to +10 scale. After having talked so much about the day after the miracle, the − 10 to 0 version of the scale seemed to confuse him.

[410] C: A number of things.

SdeS: Mm hm.

C: Um. Compared to what I feel now . . . than if I would feel during the miracle. That's about that, 'cause I have a few things to be happy about.

SdeS: Mm hm.

C: But I also have a few things that's bothering me.

[415] SdeS: Right.

C: So, and, and, the alcohol is 5 of the 7 points up that way.

SdeS: Mm hm.

C: You know.

SdeS: OK, OK.

[420] C: So, that's, that's alcohol is a big percentage of it.

SdeS: Mm hm.

C: But I can take the other 2-1/2, the other 3, and it could be a variety of things. You know, I could blame it, my car not running right now.

SdeS: Yeah, yeah.

C: You know, I got to drive the wife's car and I got to hear her mouth.

[425] SdeS: Right.

C: Um, my financial is messed up right now. You know, I'm not exactly set, I mean.

SdeS: Yeah.

C: Any other . . .

SdeS: Of course . . .

[430] C: I have done better.

SdeS: OK. Good. Good. Right.

C: You know [pause] and those are major things right now.

SdeS: Mm hm.

C: 'Cause I don't have my car to really get me around and do what I want to do and, you know, go for jobs and stuff because she work a certain hour. And I take her car everyday, I drop her off at work . . . and I go do my . . . jobs, I try to find full time work but what's gonna happen if I get hired at a job paying me $9 or $10 an hour and I have to go to Menomonee Falls every morning at 7 o'clock?

[435] SdeS: Right.

C: And she starts at 7:30 on the southside.

SdeS: Right.

C: You see, that's what bothering me.

SdeS: Sure. Of course.

[440] C: That's the kind of stuff that's on my mind now and I never, it's been since the first time I drove. Well, this is not the longest, this might be the second time in a ten-year period that I've been without a car.

SdeS: Mm hm.

C: But I usually get one regardless of how much it costs, you know, I usually get one right away.

SdeS: Right, right.

C: But right now, I don't have the money to get one, I guess it will be a miracle for me to get the money to get one.

[445] SdeS: Mm hm. Mm hm.

C: You know, then I got to help pay these bills. And you know, a few more of the things that was kind of like depressing me, but it don't bother me no more, you know, what I was telling you earlier.

SdeS: Right.

C: That doesn't, that doesn't matter. It used to. Really had a toll on me and probably just now wearing off.

SdeS: Mm hm.

[450] C: But at one time it got me real down and out but I thought about it and say, hey, I'm away from it now, you know. It's out in the open. I know how they feel about me, they know how I feel about them, so just leave it at that, you know.

SdeS: Right, right.

C: That kind of stuff that was bothering me.

SdeS: Mm hm.

C: Other than that, I got a few things to be happy for. I got a nice house.

[455] SdeS: Mm hm.

C: I have a nice wife.

SdeS: Mm hm. Good, good.

C: You know.

SdeS: It's going OK for you two right . . . since you got married?

[460] C: Yeah, we have our ups and downs.

SdeS: Of course.

C: Everybody else does, and we hanging in there. She's sticking by my side.

SdeS: Mm hm. Good.

C: I'm not gonna wear that to the ground, 'cause anybody's patience can wear out on you.

[465] SdeS: That's for sure.

C: Yeah, that's for sure. And, but she understand what most of the pressure is coming from.

SdeS: Mm hm

C: You know, she understand the, um, the things that I have to deal with right now.

SdeS: Mm hm.

[470] C: You know, but I don't use it as a crutch, something to blame anything else on. Only thing I can say is well, this is something that happened in my life, OK, I can't take it away, I can't change, the best thing I can do is try to forget about it and let it be.

SdeS: Right.

C: It'll blow over, I can't stop right there. If I stop right there, I never should have came this far.

SdeS: Mm hm. OK.

C: But, other than that, I just feel like if I really get a hold to the right thing to cling to, I think I could be a very happy young man. Really.

[475] SdeS: OK. Well . . .

C: 'Cause I been depressed for too long.

SdeS: Yes, yeah.

C: And they tell me depression is the worst sickness there is. So, people have come over it, right?

SdeS: Oh, yeah.

[480] C: Yeah.

SdeS: Now, let's see, how do I want to . . . do, do this a little differently, but, you know, the numbers. . . . This time we'll make 10 be the top, going up from zero.

C: OK.

(Accidentally) Constructing a Surprise for the Therapist

SdeS: OK. So 10 stands for oh, . . . you want this . . . the miracle that we've been talking about, as badly as anybody can want anything, OK? And zero is the opposite of that, which is, if it happens, it happens, if it doesn't, it doesn't. Where would you say you are?

C: Zero.

[485] SdeS: Yeah, yeah? Mm hm.

C: Because . . . I, you know, I wouldn't want to build myself up too high, to fall down too hard.

This is the first time in the years of using this question that I had ever received a "0," but his reasoning behind the answer is quite sound. A sound principle is involved here: One never really knows what the question was until you've heard the answer. (If I were to allow myself to have an ideal answer to this question it would be his with his explanation. However, the answer one gets is the answer one gets and that is all there is to be gotten. The client's answer, whatever it might be, is the one that needs to be accepted and taken seriously.)

[487] SdeS: Mm hm.

C: You know, I mean . . .

SdeS: OK.

[490] C: There's a lot of things I want out there.

SdeS: Mm hm.

C: If I can't have it, I want a, I want a new car. I'm not gonna go rob no bank for it. Because I feel like if it's gonna come to me,

SdeS: OK.

C: I couldn't stop it from coming, I couldn't stop it from going.

[495] SdeS: Mm hm.

C: So, either it come to me I can deal with it.

SdeS: OK.

C: Well, I wouldn't want to win no 30 million dollar lottery, though.

SdeS: No?

[500] C: No.

SdeS: How come?

C: [Pause] I would lose my mind. Really.

SdeS: Yeah?

C: I would go from $30 in my pocket and take a dollar and play a number, ten hours later, I got 30 million. No. That be too much for me. I couldn't handle it.

[505] SdeS: Mm hm.

C: Because I feel like if you too poor and can't handle it, you hurt yourself. And if you too rich and can't handle it, you hurt yourself.

SdeS: I see. That makes sense.

C: I can go for a $250,000 Super Cash, that would set me for life, for all I want in life, that would set me.

SdeS: Uh huh.

[510] C: . . . homes, nice little, invest in a nice little business. Just sit back and run my business and maintain my property.

SdeS: Mm hm.

C: Have me a little money aside, that's all I want. I'm not greedy.

Inventing a "Wanting to Stop Drinking Scale"

SdeS: OK. Well, let's go . . . another one then. Ten stands for you want to stop drinking, or, yeah, OK. Yeah, to stop drinking. And you want that very badly, as badly as you can want that. And zero is, well, if I drink, I drink, if I don't, I don't.

C: Well, see, I look at that differently.

[515] SdeS: Why?

C: 'Cause I can't just say if I drink, I drink, if I don't, I don't, because sooner or later my . . .

SdeS: But that's why I said that's what zero means.

C: Right. OK. Because I can't say that the way I can say my money . . .

SdeS: Right.

[520] C: I can't put them in the same category.

SdeS: Right.

C: 'Cause sooner or later my health is gonna step in and stop me somewhere.

SdeS: Right.

C: So I got to think about my health. Do I want to get to the point where I have cirrhosis of the liver and it might be too late to stop? Or do I want to stop now? That's different.

[525] SdeS: Right.

C: So they can take the money and go somewhere else with it. I ain't gonna have no life, anyway.

SdeS: Right. OK, so,

C: I could say I staying at 10 . . .

SdeS: You're, you're saying you're at 10 . . . OK.

[530] C: Right. 'Cause I really, truly want to stop. No doubt about that.

SdeS: OK. And, now, let's see. Well, ready for another one like that?

C: Oh, yeah.

Inventing a "Confidence Scale"

SdeS: OK. This time 10 stands for, I don't know the details about this, but 10 stands for you are as confident as you as a human being can be that you can do that. That you can stop. And zero stands for "Oh shit, I ain't got a snowball's chance in hell." Where would you put yourself on there?

C: About 5.

[535] SdeS: About 5.

C: Yeah.

SdeS: OK.

C: 'Cause I would never take it all away, just take it away from me like that, just give up and say I can't. I would at least give it a 50% of a chance to try it.

SdeS: OK.

[540] C: And I have to deal with whatever happens after that.

SdeS: OK. So, that's ... that sounds pretty reasonable. Um, sounds pretty reasonable, especially since it's important to you.

C: Yeah, it's important to me. Very important.

SdeS: Mm hm.

C: If I stop drinking I would be a happy man. That's what's depressing me.

[545] SdeS: Yeah? I guess you were saying before, too, that uh, the difficulty is: What are you going to do instead of drink?

C: That's the problem I always had.

SdeS: Right.

C: Yeah, now if I can take that ...

SdeS: It's different from that 90 days in the hospital.

[550] C: Right.

SdeS: As it is out on the street.

C: On the street. If I can take all that energy and time and the brain cells I waste for being depressed, and the muscles I waste for being sore the next day, if I can put all that to something positive besides putting that to alcohol, I would be, things would start coming my way, I, I couldn't handle it.

SdeS: Mm hm.

C: You know, you'd be like. . . . Wait a minute, then . . . that would be that miracle!

His recognition of the full implication of the miracle provided me with the title for this chapter. I introduced the miracle concept in unit 115 and following that point he repeatedly used and developed it. Much of what he described as part of the miracle and many of the things that have happened to him and that he can do fit with the picture developed by Heather and Robertson's research (1981) into the wide-ranging contextual and situational changes associated with shifting to "normal" drinking patterns. However, whether these sorts of things are grounds for predicting a favorable outcome in this particular case or any case is questionable. In fact, we have to question whether prediction is possible in any case. Regardless, these sort of things will naturally and normally lead us to be more optimistic.

In various studies, Heather and Robertson (1981) report that the shift to normal drinking is frequently associated with improvements in employment, improvements in family and social adjustments, moves to different locations, and other major changes in life situations. Interestingly, they report that "nothing had been done to bring about these far-reaching personality changes" (p. 26). That is, these major changes are seen as "spontaneous," as not brought about by treatment. Furthermore, these changes are seen as (1) neither causing the return to normal drinking nor as (2) "caused by" the newly developed change in drinking behavior but just as (3) changes in life situations accidentally associated with the change in drinking behavior.

These changes in life situation and in drinking pattern do not need to be seen as causally related in either direction. Even the details of the sequence of events is not terribly important, since these changes can equally well be seen as a mutually reinforcing set. Again, it is enough logically to say that these changes happen with some frequency in some cases. Study after study (see: Fingarette, 1988; Heather & Robertson, 1981; Peele, 1989) shows that situational or contextual factors influence drinking as much as they influence any other human behavior.[2]

[555] SdeS: That's what we're talking about.
C: OK. Now it hit home, huh?
SdeS: Mm hm.
C: That's the miracle.
SdeS: Mm hm.
[560] C: Yeah. OK. If I can do that, if I can take all the energy that I have, maybe turning to some type of helper for a church or something
SdeS: Or something.
C: Or for young kids, or . . .
SdeS: Yeah, something.
C: Go work around a library, part time, or just stay confident, yeah, I'd be happy.

The client is creating the conditions for change which might also serve as the signs of the day after the miracle.

---

[2]Even when the subjects of the study have unlimited access to alcohol, the situation seems to influence the subjects' drinking decisions more than anything else (Fingarette, 1988).

[565] SdeS: That's, that's where it's at.

C: Yeah.

SdeS: It's uh, you get out there and there's all these temptations.

C: When you quit and you get out there, there's temptations.

SdeS: Right. So you gotta do something to overcome the temptations. You gotta do something instead of drink. Drinking takes up time, doesn't it?

[570] C: A lot more time that it take up for . . . for you to drink one can of beer feels like it took three hours away from you.

SdeS: Mm hm.

C: 'Cause you be moving so fast and time just be ticking.

SdeS: Right. So, that's the big question. What are you going to do instead?

C: I think that's something very important for me to think about.

[575] SdeS: That's right.

C: Because regardless of if I stop drinking or not, if I don't have a goal set for me to do something . . .

SdeS: Yeah.

C: . . . it ain't gonna do me no good to stop.

SdeS: Right. Mm hm.

[580] C: OK.

SdeS: OK. What I'd like to do right now is take about 5, 10 minutes, go talk to my partner back there. And, you can sit here and wait and I'll be back in about 5, 10 minutes and let you know what our thinking is about things.

C: OK.

As an experiment, take a 10- or 15-minute break here before you continue reading. What should I be sure not to do? What pieces of what he said can be combined in what ways to develop a useful closing message?

After the Pause

[583] SdeS: Well, we uh, certainly are impressed with what you're talking about this, the morning after you got married.

C: Mm hm.

[585] SdeS: With your discovering that sometimes your heart wants something, like getting married and making that commitment. Uh, even though your head didn't . . .

C: It was clogged.

SdeS: . . . know it, yet.

C: Couldn't really make a decision . . .

SdeS: Yeah. But you . . .

[590] C: My heart had already made the decision.

SdeS: Yeah, and um, and we're thinking that maybe that's what's going on here again. And here you are today.

C: Oh, OK. OK.

SdeS: And uh, we have an experiment that we'd like to suggest for you. Ah, I think we think you'll learn something from this experiment.

C: You think so?

[595] SdeS: Yeah. OK?

C: Mm hm.

SdeS: And, we want you—this is secret, OK? And what we want you to do between now and next time we get together is to pick two days and ah, on those two days, secretly, pretend that this miracle has happened.

C: Mm hm.

SdeS: And observe on those days, 'cause I think we think you're right about this, observe what you do when you overcome the urge to drink. And observe how your wife responds on these days. And keep it a secret from her. Don't tell her either before or after. Keep this whole thing a secret for yourself. And next time when you come, we'll talk about what you learned.

[600] C: OK.

SdeS: OK?

C: When will that be?

SdeS: Well, we'll go out there and figure that out. Sometime in the next few weeks.

C: Other than that, how was the interview?

[605] SdeS: OK. How 'bout for you?

C: OK, I enjoyed it.

SdeS: Good. That's the way it should be. Always think we should have some fun doing this.

This is the first time in thousands upon thousands of sessions that the client has asked me about how the interview went for me. And it is also the first time that a client has spontaneously remarked at the end of a session that he enjoyed it! Sometimes clients will make these remarks at follow-up or long after therapy is over.

Chapter Fifteen

EPILOGUE

A ... problem has the form: "I don't know my way about."
— *Ludwig Wittgenstein (1958, #123)*

FREQUENTLY BY THE END of a session clients are beginning to know their way about or at least are starting to have some confidence that they can find their way about. Thus there is no need for a therapist to overwhelm clients by making lots of suggestions or by inventing "novel tasks ... in the Erickson style" (Efran & Schenker, 1992, p. 72); rather, the therapist simply needs to support clients' going in their own chosen direction with the confidence that once they get where they want to go they will then know their way about.

Having spent most of the '70s and part of the '80s designing "novel tasks in the Erickson style," I still find it difficult at times to restrain myself from proposing such interventions to clients. However, these fancy tasks are very difficult to design; furthermore, teaching therapists to design such clever tasks is not an easy job. In the great majority of cases these clever tasks seem to be no more, perhaps even less, effective than simpler ones based principally on what the clients have already said they know how to do.

*   *   *

Contrary to what Steven Friedman thinks (1993, p. 72), "the miracle question" and "other solution-focused methods" do not "always [or ever] create miracles" (pp. 71–72). Nor can they naively be expected to create miracles: Doing therapy is not that easy. In fact, no matter what the method, therapy never creates anything whatsoever. The miracles clients describe do not ever happen (Efron & Veenendaal, 1993) and they cannot be expected to happen. The miracle question was not designed to create or prompt miracles. All the miracle question is designed to do is to allow clients to describe what it is they want out of therapy without having to concern themselves with the problem and the traditional assumption that the solution is somehow connected with understanding and eliminating the problem.

The details and specifics of where the clients want to go and what they wish for frequently change in the course of therapy, much to the surprise of both clients and therapist. That is, even though we depend on the clients' answers to the miracle question to give us some sense of direction, actually, whether clients can know what they wish before their wish is fulfilled cannot be known. "And the fact that some event stops my wishing does not mean that it fulfills it. Perhaps I should not have been satisfied if my wish had been satisfied" (Wittgenstein, 1958, #441). For therapists to expect clients to know at the beginning of therapy exactly where they want to go is unrealistic; if they did, they probably would not need therapy. For this reason we do not find it necessary to contract with clients (a) for a specific number of sessions or (b) for specific goals or (c) to measure progress on specific goals. To do so would again constrain and limit the possibilities for change and limit the possibilities for the clients to invent or discover something that satisfies them as much as or more than what they imagined or wished for when they described their ideas about the morning after the miracle.

* * *

I hope that you come away from reading this book with at least some satisfaction, although you might not have gotten exactly what you wished for at the start. It is not exactly the book I wished it to be before I started writing and it is not the book I thought it was going to be even when I was halfway through. More than previous books, once I started on this one it took on its own sense of direction and I just simply followed along; but I am satisfied. The book represents my practice as it has evolved and it represents my current thinking about the results of what my clients and I do together when we are doing brief therapy — the pragmatics or behavioral effects of communication (Watzlawick, Beavin, & Jackson, 1967, p. 22) as measured by the practical results of our joint endeavor.

Gustav Mahler once said that each of his symphonies was a separate and distinct world. Each one had its own language, mores, etc. The same could be said of each book. Each book also has its own language, its own organization, its own gestalt, its own particular character. At least in this particular case, part of this character depends a lot on the authors cited that help to make my solo voice into sort of a chorus. A lot of voices living, dead, and fictional have had their say along with mine. I hope that my use has in no circumstance been abuse. When they had something to say that I thought they said well, I let them speak for themselves. Perhaps sometimes they spoke too long or too often, but I find paraphrase too difficult.

Similarly with the clients. I wanted them to have their say and therefore the transcripts of whole sessions. In this way it is as much their world as possible. As when I do therapy, I wanted to keep my part to a minimum; therefore there is little paraphrase and very little editing. Reading the transcripts gives you, the reader, everything you would have heard listening to an audiotape.

Certainly I did not intend to develop nor have I developed a Theory or a Grand Design; rather than developing a Theory that attempts to explain everything or can be used as if it were designed to explain everything, the more theoretical parts of this book should only be seen as descriptions of my tools. Nothing more. The extent to which I have successfully described my tools is one of my main ways to measure whether or not I have done what I set out to do. Your view and mine might be different on this.

I also had a lot of fun writing, putting together, and assembling this book. I can only assume that if you got this far you did not find it too boring, but it is perhaps too much for me to expect you to have had as much fun reading it as I had writing it. However, I do hope that you got at least a modicum of pleasure out of your reading.

REFERENCES

Ackerman, N. (1966). *Treating the troubled family.* New York: Basic.

Bakhtin, M. (1981). *The dialogic imagination* (C. Emerson & M. Holquist, Trans.; M. Holquist, Ed.). Austin: University of Texas Press.

Bandler, R., & Grinder, J. (1975a). *The structure of magic.* Palo Alto: Science and Behavior Books.

Bandler, R., & Grinder, J. (1975b). *Patterns of the hypnotic techniques of Milton H. Erickson, M.D.* Cupertino: Meta Publications.

Barnard, C. (1993). O'Ireland! *Modern Maturity,* Feb/Mar issue.

Bass, A. (1988). The double game: An introduction. In J. H. Smith & W. Kerrigan (Eds.), *Taking chances: Derrida, psychoanalysis, and literature* (pp. 66–85). Baltimore: Johns Hopkins University Press.

Bateson, G. (1972). The cybernetics of self: A theory of alcoholism. In G. Bateson, *Steps to an ecology of mind.* New York: Ballantine.

Bateson, G. (1979). *Mind and nature: A necessary unity.* New York: Dutton.

Bateson, G., Jackson, D.D., Haley, J., & Weakland, J.H. (1956). Toward a theory of schizophrenia. *Behavioral Science, 1,* 251–264.

Berg, I. K., & Miller, S. (1993). *Working with the problem drinker.* New York: Norton.

Bidley, D. (1962). *The psychology and ethics of Spinoza.* New York: Russell & Russell.

Capra, F. (1977). *The tao of physics.* New York: Bantam.

Chomsky, N. (1968). *Language and mind.* New York: Harcourt, Brace, Jovanovich.

Chomsky, N. (1980). *Rules and representations*. New York: Columbia University Press.

Clifford, J. (1988). *The predicament of culture: Twentieth century ethnography, literature and art*. Cambridge, MA: Harvard University Press.

Condillac, E. (1947). *Oeuvres philosophiques de Condillac* (Georges Le Roy, Ed.). Corpus Général des Philosophes Francais. Paris: Presses Universitaires de France. Cited in J. Derrida (1980). *The archeology of the frivolous* (J. P. Leavey, Trans.). Lincoln: University of Nebraska Press.

Coward, H. (1990). *Derrida and Indian philosophy*. Albany: State University of New York Press.

Culler, J. (1976). *Saussure*. London: Fontana Press.

Davies, D. L. (1962). Normal drinking in recovered alcohol addicts. *Quarterly Journal of Studies of Alcohol, 23*, 94–104.

Davies, D. L., Scott, D. F., & Malherbe, M. E. (1969). Resumed normal drinking in recovered psychotic alcoholics. *International Journal of the Addictions, 4(2)*, 187–194.

Dell, P. (1985). Understanding Bateson and Maturana: Toward a biological foundation for the social sciences. *Journal of Marital and Family Therapy, 11*, 1–20.

de Man, P. (1983). *Blindness and insight: Essays in the rhetoric of contemporary criticism*. Minneapolis: University of Minnesota Press.

de Man, P. (1986). *The resistance to theory*. Minneapolis: University of Minnesota Press.

Derrida, J. (1973). *Speech and phenomena: And other essays on Husserl's theory of signs* (David Allison, Trans.). Evanston, IL: Northwestern University Press.

Derrida, J. (1976). *Of grammatology* (G. C. Spivak, Trans.). Baltimore: Johns Hopkins University Press.

Derrida, J. (1978). *Writing and difference* (A. Bass, Trans.). Chicago: University of Chicago Press.

Derrida, J. (1982). Signature event context. In J. Derrida, *Margins of philosophy* (Alan Bass, Trans.). Chicago: University of Chicago Press.

Derrida, J. (1988). My chances/mes chances: A rendezvous with some epicurean stereophonies. In J. H. Smith & W. Kerrigan (Eds.), *Taking chances: Derrida, psychoanalysis, and literature* (pp. 1–32). Baltimore: John Hopkins University Press.

De Saussure, F. (1966). *Course in general linguistics* (W. Baskin, Trans.). New York: McGraw-Hill. (Originally published as *Cours de linguistique générale*. Paris: Payot, 1922.)

de Shazer, S. (1982). *Patterns of brief family therapy*. New York: Guilford.

de Shazer, S. (1985). *Keys to solution in brief therapy*. New York: Norton.

de Shazer, S. (1986). Ein Requiem der Macht. *Zeitschrift für Systemische Therapie, 4*, 208–212. (Reprinted as A requiem for power. (1988). *Contemporary Family Therapy, 10*, 69–76.)

de Shazer, S. (1988). *Clues: Investigating solutions in brief therapy*. New York: Norton.

de Shazer, S. (1989). Therapy is nothing but a bunch of talk. Paper presented at *Social Work Symposium*, Poughkeepsie, New York.

de Shazer, S. (1991). *Putting difference to work*. New York: Norton.

de Shazer, S. (1992). Essential, non-essential: Vivé la difference. Paper presented at the *5th International Congress on Ericksonian Approaches to Hypnosis and Psychotherapy*.

de Shazer, S., & Berg, I. K. (1992). Doing therapy: A post-structural re-vision. *Journal of Marital and Family Therapy, 18*, 71–81.

Deutsch, F., & Murphy, W. (1955). *The clinical interview. Volume two: Therapy.* New York: International Universities Press.

Eco, U. (1992). *Interpretation and overinterpretation.* Cambridge, England: Cambridge University Press.

Efran, J., & Schenker, M. (1993). A potpourri of solutions. *Family Therapy Networker.* May/June, 71–74.

Efron, D., & Veenendaal, K. (1993) Suppose a miracle doesn't happen: The non-miracle option. *Journal of Systemic Therapies, 12(1),* 11–18.

Emerson, R. (1962). Power-dependence relations. *American Sociological Review, 27,* 31–41.

Emerson, R. (1964). Power-dependency relations: Two experiments. *Sociometry, 14,* 282–298.

Erickson, M. H. (1975). *Foreword.* In R. Bandler & J. Grinder (1975b). *Patterns of the hypnotic techniques of Milton H. Erickson, M.D.* Cupertino: Meta Publications.

Ferguson, C., & Moravisk, E. (Eds.). (1978). *Universals of human language.* Stanford: Stanford University Press.

Fingarette, H. (1988). *Heavy drinking.* Berkeley: University of California Press.

Foucault, M. (1978). *The history of sexuality: An introduction.* New York: Pantheon.

Foucault, M. (1980). *Power/knowledge.* New York: Pantheon.

Freud, S. (1912). A note on the unconscious in psycho-analysis. In J. Stachey (Ed. & Trans.) *The standard edition of the complete psychological works of Sigmund Freud* (Vol. 12, pp. 255–266). New York: Norton.

Freud, S. (1915–17) *The complete introductory lectures on psychoanalysis* (J. Stachey (Ed. & Trans.). *The standard edition of the complete psychological works of Sigmund Freud* (Vols. 15 & 16). New York: Norton.

Freud, S. (1938). Some elementary lessons in psycho-analysis. In J. Stachey (Ed. & Trans.) *The standard edition of the complete psychological works of Sigmund Freud* (Vol. 23, pp. 279–286). New York: Norton.

Freud, S. (1974). Letter to C. G. Jung. In W. McGuire (Ed.), *The Freud/Jung letters.* London: Routledge.

Friedman, S. (1993) Does the "miracle question" always create miracles? *Journal of Systemic Therapies, 12(1),* 71–72.

Gaita, R. (1991). Language and conversation. In A. P. Griffiths (Ed.), *Wittgenstein centenary essays.* Cambridge, England: Cambridge University Press.

Gasché, R. (1986). *The tain of the mirror: Derrida and the philosophy of reflection.* Cambridge, MA: Harvard University Press.

Geuss, R. (1981) *The idea of a critical theory: Habermas & the Frankfurt school.* Cambridge: Cambridge University Press.

Gilligan, S., & Price, R. (Eds.). (1993). *Therapeutic conversations.* New York: Norton.

Grosz, E. (1990). *Jacques Lacan: A feminist introduction.* London: Routledge.

Gustafson, J. P. (1986). *The complex secret of brief psychotherapy.* New York: Norton.

Harland, R. (1987). *Superstructuralism: The philosophy of structuralism and post-structuralism.* London: Methuen.

Haley, J. (Ed.). (1967). *Advanced techniques of hypnosis and therapy: Selected papers of Milton H. Erickson.* New York: Grune & Stratton.

Haley, J. (Ed.).(1985). *Conversations with Milton H. Erickson, M.D.*, Vol. 1. Rockville, MD: Triangle Press.

Heather, N., & Robertson, I. (1981). *Controlled drinking.* London: Methuen.

Hoyt, M. (1994). On the importance of keeping it simple and taking the patient seriously: A conversation with Steve de Shazer and John H. Weakland. *Constructive therapies.* New York: Guilford.

Irigaray, L. (1985). *Speculum of the other woman* (G. Gill, Trans.). Ithaca: Cornell University Press.

Jabès, E. (1959). *Je bâtis ma demeure: Poèmes, 1943–1957.* Paris: Galimard. Translation cited in Derrida, J. (1978). *Writing and difference* (A. Bass, Trans.). Chicago: University of Chicago Press.

Jackson, D. D. (1967). Aspects of conjoint family therapy. In G. Zuk & I. Boszormenyi-Nagy (Eds.), *Family therapy and disturbed families.* Palo Alto: Science and Behavior Books.

Janik, A., & Toulmin, S. (1973). *Wittgenstein's Vienna.* New York: Simon & Schuster.

Jastrow, J. (1948). *Freud: His dream and sex theories.* New York: Pocket Books.

Lacan, J. (1981). *Speech and language in psychoanalysis* (A. Wilden, Trans.). Baltimore: John Hopkins University Press.

Lacan, J. (1993). *The seminar of Jacques Lacan: Book III: The psychoses, 1955–1956* (J.-A. Miller, Ed.; R. Grigg, Trans.). New York: Norton.

Lodge, D. (1990). *After Bahktin: Essays on fiction and criticism.* London: Routledge.

Madigan, S. P. (1993). Questions about questions: Situating the therapist's curiosity in front of the family. In S. Gilligan & R. Price (Eds.), *Therapeutic conversations* (pp. 219–230). New York: Norton.

Mead, G. H. (1934). *Mind, self and society.* Chicago: University of Chicago Press.

Miller, G. (1993). Personal communication.

Miller, J.-A. (1991). Language: Much ado about what? In E. Ragland-Sullivan & M. Bracher (Eds.), *Lacan and the subject of language.* London: Routledge.

Nagel, E., & Newman, J. (1958). *Gödel's proof.* New York: New York University Press.

Nietzsche, F. (1968). *The will to power* (W. Kauffmann & J.R. Hollingdale, Trans.). New York: Vintage.

Nietzsche, F. (1974). *The gay science* (W. Kauffmann, Trans.). New York: Random House.

Norris, C. (1982). *Deconstruction: Theory and practice.* London: Routledge.

Norris, C. (1983). *The deconstructive turn: Essays in the rhetoric of philosophy.* London: Metheun.

Norris, C. (1989). *Deconstruction and the interests of theory.* Norman: University of Oklahoma Press.

Norris, C. (1992). *Uncritical theory: Postmodernism, intellectuals, and the Gulf War.* Amherst: University of Massachusetts Press.

Nye, A. (1988). *Feminist theory and the philosophies of man.* London: Routledge.

Peele, S. (1989). *Diseasing America.* Lexington: Lexington Books.

Ragland-Sullivan, E. (1991a). The sexual masquerade: A Lacanian theory of sexual difference. In E. Ragland-Sullivan & M. Bracher (Eds.), *Lacan and the subject of language.* London: Routledge.

Ragland-Sullivan, E. (1991b). Introduction. In E. Ragland-Sullivan & M. Bracher (Eds.), *Lacan and the subject of language.* London: Routledge.

Rhees, R. (1970). *Discussions of Wittgenstein.* London: Routledge.

Spencer-Brown, G. (1969). *Laws of form.* London: Allen and Unwin.

Spivak, G. C. (1976). Translator's preface. In J. Derrida, *Of grammatology*. Baltimore: Johns Hopkins University Press.

Staten, H. (1984). *Wittgenstein and Derrida*. Lincoln: University of Nebraska Press.

Sullivan, H. (1991). Homo sapiens or homo desiderans: The role of desire in human evolution. In E. Ragland-Sullivan & M. Bracher (Eds.), *Lacan and the subject of language*. London: Routledge.

Szasz, T. (1970). *Ideology and insanity*. Garden City, NY: Anchor.

Thomas, D. (1971). *The poems of Dylan Thomas* (D. Jones, Ed.). New York: New Directions.

Todorov, T. (1984). *Mikhail Bakhtin: The ideological principle* (W. Godzich, Trans.). Minneapolis: University of Minnesota Press.

Tomm, K. (1987). Interventive interviewing: Part II. Reflexive questioning as a means to enable self-healing. *Family Process, 26*(2), 167–183.

Tomm, K. (1988). Interventive interviewing: Part III. Intending to ask lineal, circular, strategic, or reflexive questions? *Family Process, 27*(1), 1–15.

Voloshinov, V. N./Bakhtin, M. (1986). *Marxism and the philosophy of language* (L. Matejka & I. R. Titunik, Trans.). Cambridge, MA: Harvard University Press.

Watzlawick, P., Beavin, J., & Jackson, D. D. (1967). *Pragmatics of human communication*. New York: Norton.

Weakland, J. H. (1993a). Conversation—but what kind? In S. Gilligan & R. Price (Eds.), *Therapeutic conversations* (pp. 136–145). New York: Norton.

Weakland, J. H. (1993b). Personal communication.

Weedon, C. (1987). *Feminist practice and poststructural theory*. Oxford: Basil Blackwell.

Wilden, A. (1981). Lacan and the discourse of the other. In J. Lacan (1981) *Speech and language in psychoanalysis* (A. Wilden, Trans. & Ed.). Baltimore: Johns Hopkins University Press.

Wittgenstein, L. (1958). *Philosophical investigations* (3rd Ed.). (G.E.M. Anscombe, Trans.). New York: Macmillan.

Wittgenstein, L. (1965). *The blue and brown books: Preliminary studies for the "philosophical investigations."* New York: Harper.

Wittgenstein, L. (1972). *Lectures and conversations on aesthetics, psychology, and religious belief* (Clifford Barrett, Ed.). Berkeley: University of California Press.

Wittgenstein, L. (1974). *Philosophical grammar* (A. Kenny, Trans.). Oxford: Oxford University Press.

Wittgenstein, L. (1980). *Remarks on the philosophy of psychology* (G. Anscombe & G. von Wright, Eds.). Oxford: Blackwell.

INDEX

281